# Red Capitalists in China

It has become a truism that continued economic reform in China will contribute to political change. Policy makers and many scholars expect that formation of a private sector will lead, directly or indirectly through the emergence of a civil society, to political change and ultimately democratization. The rapidly growing numbers of private entrepreneurs, the formation of business associations, and the cooperative relationships between entrepreneurs and local officials are seen as initial indicators of a transition from China's still nominally communist political system.

This book focuses on two related issues: whether the Chinese Communist Party (CCP) is willing and able to adapt to the economic environment its reforms are bringing about and whether China's "red capitalists," private entrepreneurs who also belong to the communist party, are likely to be agents of political change.

Comparisons with other countries, primarily in East Asia and Eastern Europe, historical comparisons with pre-1949 China, primary materials on contemporary China, and most importantly original survey data are used to help clarify the relationship between entrepreneurs and the CCP, the often intense debate over whether entrepreneurs should be allowed into the CCP, and the political implications of the growing numbers of red capitalists in China.

Bruce J. Dickson is Associate Professor of Political Science and International Affairs at The George Washington University. He is the author of *Democratization in China and Taiwan: The Adaptability of Leninist Parties* (1997) and articles in several journals and edited volumes, coeditor of *Remaking the Chinese State: Strategies, Society, and Security* (2001) and *Assessing the Lee Teng-hui Legacy: Democratic Consolidation and External Relations* (2002), and associate editor of the journal *Problems of Post-Communism*.

D1279674

# Cambridge Modern China Series

Edited by William Kirby, Harvard University

# Red Capitalists in China

## The Party, Private Entrepreneurs, and Prospects for Political Change

BRUCE J. DICKSON

*The George Washington University*

CAMBRIDGE
UNIVERSITY PRESS

PUBLISHED BY THE PRESS SYNDICATE OF THE UNIVERSITY OF CAMBRIDGE
The Pitt Building, Trumpington Street, Cambridge, United Kingdom

CAMBRIDGE UNIVERSITY PRESS
The Edinburgh Building, Cambridge CB2 2RU, UK
40 West 20th Street, New York, NY 10011-4211, USA
477 Williamstown Road, Port Melbourne, VIC 3207, Australia
Ruiz de Alarcón 13, 28014 Madrid, Spain
Dock House, The Waterfront, Cape Town 8001, South Africa

http://www.cambridge.org

© Bruce J. Dickson 2003

This book is in copyright. Subject to statutory exception
and to the provisions of relevant collective licensing agreements,
no reproduction of any part may take place without
the written permission of Cambridge University Press.

First published 2003

Printed in the United States of America

*Typeface* Times New Roman 10/13 pt.    *System* LATEX 2$_\varepsilon$   [TB]

*A catalog record for this book is available from the British Library.*

*Library of Congress Cataloging in Publication Data*

Dickson, Bruce J.
Red capitalists in China : the party, private entrepreneurs, and prospects for political
change / Bruce J. Dickson.
    p.   cm. – (Cambridge modern China series)
Includes bibliographical references and index.
ISBN 0-521-81817-6 – ISBN 0-521-52143-2 (pbk.)
1. Zhongguo gong chan dang.   2. China – Politics and government – 1976–
3. China – Economic policy – 1976–2000.   4. Businessmen – China – Political activity.
5. Entrepreneurship – Political aspects – China.   I. Title.   II. Series.
JQ1519.A5 D53   2003
324.251'075 – dc21       2002067069

ISBN 0 521 81817 6 hardback
ISBN 0 521 52143 2 paperback

# Contents

# List of Tables

# Acknowledgments

A S IS USUALLY THE CASE for scholarly studies, this book is the result of a collective effort for which I bear responsibility for the final product. At different stages of the project, many people read parts of the manuscript, provided moral support of various kinds, and offered useful suggestions. I would like to thank Merle Goldman, Leslyn Hall, Kent Jennings, Scott Kennedy, Jason Kindopp, Pierre Landry, Cheng Li, Melanie Manion, Kevin O'Brien, Mike Oksenberg, Kristen Parris, Margaret Pearson, Minxin Pei, Liz Perry, Maria Rost-Rublee, Shen Mingming, Yumin Sheng, Lee Sigelman, Dorie Solinger, Traci Swanson, Kellee Tsai, Alan Wachman, Andy Walder, Marty Whyte, Yang Ming, Yang Zhong, and several anonymous reviewers. For research assistance, I would like to thank Eddy Chun-yi Lee, In-joo Sohn, and Yuelin Zhu. For technical help with the dataset, I would like to thank Mark Kugler and Yuelin Zhu. All of them tried their best to save me from mistakes of style and substance, but they should not be blamed for whatever errors remain.

For financial support, I would like to thank the Smith Richardson Foundation, the United States Institute of Peace, and George Washington University's University Facilitating Fund. Without their generous grants, this project would have been impossible. The Luce Foundation provided a conference grant that allowed me to host a conference on "Surveying China" in June 2000, which brought together more than twenty social scientists who have conducted survey research on political and social issues in China.

I would like also to acknowledge the invaluable assistance of the Research Center for Contemporary China (RCCC) of Peking University. Center director Shen Mingming and his staff provided help on a variety of fronts, from finding housing for me and my family to theoretical and logistic support in the research itself. During three summers, the RCCC served as my generous host and I am grateful for all its help.

## Acknowledgments

Throughout the book, I draw upon previously published works. I would like to thank the Academy of Political Science for permission to reprint portions of my article "Co-optation and Corporatism in China: The Logic of Party Adaptation," *Political Science Quarterly*, vol. 115, no. 4 (Winter 2000–2001), pp. 417–450. I would also like to thank Harvard University Press for permission to reprint portions of my chapter "Do Good Businessmen Make Good Citizens? An Emerging Collective Identity Among China's Private Entrepreneurs," in Merle Goldman and Elizabeth J. Perry, eds., *Changing Meanings of Citizenship in Modern China*.

At Cambridge University Press, I would like to thank Mary Child and Bill Kirby for their enthusiastic support for the book; Cathy Felgar, Alia Winters, and Adriane Gelpi for shepherding the book through the production process; and Herbert Gilbert for copyediting. Thanks go to Nancy Hearst for a careful reading of the page proofs.

Finally, I would like to thank my family for both their support and their distractions over the years that this book took shape. My son Andrew enjoyed his two visits to China while I was doing research and developed a fascination with all things Chinese. Our house is filled with souvenirs from those trips, especially story books, kites, and music. My daughter Caitlin arrived in the midst of this project. Because playing is more fun than working, she made me become more disciplined with the time I spent researching and writing so I would have more time to play with her and Andrew. My wife Benita has been a useful sounding board for ideas, a reader and editor of various drafts, and above all my best friend for more than twenty years. Although she may have enjoyed the limited opportunities she had to go dining, sightseeing, or shopping in Beijing and Shanghai while I took a break from my research, they only partially compensated for the time she spent in fairly cramped rooms with a jet-lagged preschooler. Her ability to balance the demands of family, teaching, and writing is an inspiration to me. This book is lovingly dedicated to the three of them.

# 1

# *Introduction*

ON July 1, 2001, the eightieth anniversary of the Chinese Communist Party (CCP), party leader Jiang Zemin made a stunning proposal. He recommended that private entrepreneurs be allowed to join the CCP, ending a ban imposed in August 1989 immediately after the suppression of the Tiananmen demonstrations. He claimed they were a new social stratum making significant contributions to the country's development and modernization, and therefore deserved a place in the ruling party. Since the key task of the party for more than two decades had been promoting economic growth, this seemed like an eminently logical proposal. The rapidly expanding private sector of the economy was the source of most new jobs and economic growth and absolutely necessary to the achievement of the party's goals. From the perspective of the party's orthodox leaders, however, there was nothing logical about Jiang's proposal at all. What could be more incongruous than having millionaires in a party created to represent the interests of workers and peasants? While Jiang's proposal made front-page news in the United States, where it was described as heralding yet another step away from communist rule, it also triggered a firestorm of acrimony by more orthodox party leaders. They accused Jiang, who was leader of the CCP, president of China, and the "core of the third generation of leaders," of violating party discipline for making the recommendation without first gaining the approval of the party's decision-making bodies, especially the Politburo and its Standing Committee. They claimed the proposal itself violated both the party constitution and its traditional principles. They called on the CCP to retract the proposal and rebuke Jiang's reckless behavior. Otherwise, they warned, his proposal would spell the end of the CCP.

Why was so much attention, for and against, given to this proposal? Most observers expect that continued economic reform will ultimately lead to political change in China. Advocates of change, in China and abroad, promote economic reforms as a way of indirectly achieving other goals. They hope that

1

by expanding the role of market forces, increasing the scope of privatization, and integrating China into the international community, pressures for democratization will become irresistible. For the same reasons, those who fear the loss of CCP leadership in China and the uncertainty that democratization would create want to limit the scope of the private economy and the presence of private entrepreneurs in the party. Both sides in this debate are in general agreement about the political implications of economic and social change in China arising from the reform and opening policies. They disagree, however, on whether those implications represent their best hopes and dreams or their worst nightmare.

THE PARTY, PRIVATE ENTREPRENEURS, AND PROSPECTS
FOR POLITICAL CHANGE

Why has the Chinese Communist Party survived, when most of the other ruling communist parties have not? This basic question has been a puzzle to scholars, policy makers, and perhaps even to the CCP itself. Given the central role the CCP plays in China's political system, the prospects for political change are very much related to the CCP's own leaders and policy preferences. Whether China will embark on significant democratization or not will depend in large part on whether the CCP decides to initiate or even tolerate such change. The evidence so far is quite clear: the CCP has repressed every popular movement calling for democratization and political reform. While it has undertaken a variety of steps to open the policy process and increase accountability, these have been limited steps that fall far short of the kind of democratization its critics are calling for.[1] In recent years, the political reform process has been slow and halting, at best. For instance, party leaders seem to support the importance of accountability by institutionalizing village level elections but have so far been reluctant to sanction higher level elections. Public approval ratings for party cadres, although now part of the equation in at least some areas, seem even less important.[2]

This question of the CCP's survivability is given added significance by the desire to maintain political stability in China. The priority given to political stability is one of the strongest and most enduring features of Chinese political

---

[1] Bruce J. Dickson, *Democratization in China and Taiwan: The Adaptability of Leninist Parties* (Oxford and New York: Oxford University Press, 1997); Minxin Pei, "Is China Democratizing?" *Foreign Affairs*, vol. 77, no. 1 (1998), pp. 68–82.

[2] Tyrene White, "Village Elections: Democracy from the Bottom Up?" *Current History*, vol. 97, no. 1 (September 1998), pp. 263–267; Lianjiang Li, "The Two-Ballot System in Shanxi Province: Subjecting Village Party Secretaries to a Popular Vote," *China Journal*, no. 42 (July 1999), pp. 103–118.

culture, and seems to be shared by both state leaders and members of society. The CCP has become part of the normal order of things in China. The vast majority of Chinese know no other political system through their own experience. There is a concern that if the CCP itself were to become weak or divided, and consequently unable to govern effectively, the country itself might devolve into chaos. This concern, whether misplaced or not, is a major obstacle to those who would like to garner more public support for political change and mobilize collective action to achieve it.

Not only do many Chinese seem to believe that the CCP is essential for maintaining political stability in China, many scholars also take for granted that political change will be initiated and managed by the CCP. An alternative scenario – a tumultuous process pushed from below, with the state unable to cope with demands for change – is almost unthinkable. Not because it is unlikely, but because the consequences of this type of change would be a period of prolonged instability and disunity in China that would have severe impacts on the economy and society, and would also likely spill over into neighboring countries, thereby disrupting the prospects for peace and prosperity throughout east and southeast Asia. This may seem like a worst case scenario, but it is also the one that China's leaders offer as the rationale for the continuation of their one-party state. They assert, and many in China agree, that the state has to maintain a strong hand over the political system and postpone, at least for now, more extensive political liberalization.

This project focuses on two fundamental issues: the adaptability of Leninist regimes; and the relationship between economic change and political change, particularly whether economic privatization leads to democratization. More specifically, it concerns the CCP's willingness and ability to adapt to the needs of economic development, the growing relationship between the party and the entrepreneurs, and the political impact of the emerging class of private entrepreneurs in China.

### Party Adaptability

The political implications of China's economic reforms center on the adaptability of the Chinese Communist Party. Can it successfully adapt to the new economic and social environment its reforms are creating? Or is its ability to cope being undermined by these changes? In the midst of rapid economic change, scholars have identified trends that may be evidence of potential political transformation. On the one hand, entrepreneurs and skilled expertise are being recruited into the party. Co-optation facilitates adaptation by bringing into the party new elites who may invigorate it with new ideas and new goals.

In addition, local party and government officials are developing institutional ties with a variety of civic and professional associations in order to both pro-mote economic change and integrate the state with key groups in society. These trends give hope to some that economic reform will eventually lead to gradual political change, allowing China's transition from communism to be more like Hungary or Poland (or even Taiwan) and thereby avoid the turmoil that accompanied political change in the rest of Eastern Europe and the former Soviet Union.

Along with these promising signs of transformation are contrary signs of disintegration. Large numbers of party members are abandoning their party responsibilities to pursue economic opportunities. Party and government offi-cials are leaving their posts to go into the lucrative world of private business. Rank-and-file party members in the countryside are joining the "floating popu-lation," migrating to cities in search of high-paying jobs. The non-state sector of the economy is growing so fast that most enterprises do not have party or-ganizations within them and few new members are being recruited from their workforce. In some rural areas, party organizations are paralyzed, recruitment of new members is declining, and lineage-based clans are competing with the party for influence. These are warning signs of disintegration, of a party unable to manage its members, to have sufficient links with the most dynamic sectors of the economy, or to control the society it governs.

As later chapters will demonstrate the CCP is actively trying to adjust its organization and personnel to the rapidly changing economic and social envi-ronment its reforms are bringing about. These efforts have prompted debates within the party about whether these attempted adaptations can be reconciled with the party's traditions. At the same time, they have not fully satisfied the doubts of others about whether the adaptations attempted so far have gone far enough to remove political constraints on the economy, or even if the CCP is prepared to do so. At bottom, the debate inside and outside the party concerns the compatibility of a Leninist ruling party alongside a market economy.

### *Impact of Private Entrepreneurs*

The second key theme of this book concerns China's "red capitalists," en-trepreneurs with close personal and political ties to the CCP. Many of the most wealthy entrepreneurs formerly held high-level party and government posts, and some are even the offspring of China's leaders. A far larger number of private entrepreneurs are former mid-level officials, or simply rank-and-file party members who did not hold formal posts but left their previous jobs to go into business. This growing trend of leaving jobs in the party, government, or state-owned enterprises to go into the private sector is popularly known in China as *xiahai*, literally to plunge into the sea. This group will be referred to as *xiahai* entrepreneurs throughout this book to distinguish them from another group of red capitalists: those who were co-opted into the party after demonstrating their entrepreneurial skills and business success. In many ways, this is the more interesting group in terms of its impact on the CCP. It is also the group that has been the source of discomfort for the party's orthodox leaders, as noted above.

The emergence of private entrepreneurs in China over the past decade or so has been one of the most striking and intriguing features of the reform era. Originally limited to very small scale operations by state policy and met with suspicion by society, the private sector in China now encompasses individually owned and operated enterprises at one end and large scale industrial and commercial enterprises with hundreds of workers and scope of operations that cover the whole country and even the international market at the other. Not only are they responsible for most economic growth and job creation, and therefore essential to the local economy and the careers of local officials, they are increasingly well organized and politically active. Entrepreneurs are also beginning to convert their economic influence into political power, for instance, by competing in village elections. These trends have generated a great deal of interest among observers, in light of the important role entrepreneurs have played in fomenting political change in other countries.

### Assessing the Prospects for Political Change

Most studies on state–business relations and their implications for political change in China are based on either very broad trends or intensive work in one location, and sometimes in one economic sector. Both approaches have their virtues, but also their limitations. The macro approach allows us to identify general trends and dynamics that a more detailed look at individual cases may overlook. At the same time, it may miss important developments at the micro level that can lead to more general consequences. It also tends to have a centrist focus, paying special attention to the views among party and government leaders – the elite of the state – and less to the more diffuse economic and social elites. Local case studies, in contrast, can offer rich details about particular settings, but can also lose sight of the forest for the trees. More importantly, case studies cannot easily determine what is unique or peculiar and what is common to the system as a whole.

This study of China's red capitalists attempts to bridge this gap to better understand the political implications of economic reform. It begins with a look at how the shift from the Maoist policies of class struggle to the economic reforms championed by Deng Xiaoping had major consequences for the party. This shift affected the party's recruitment policies, its network of party organizations, and its ability to monitor and control trends in society. The analysis then concentrates on the party's strategy of linking itself to the emerging private sector. One part of this strategy was to create a variety of business associations to which most businessmen would belong. Are these business associations used to maintain party control over the private sector or can they represent the views of their members and influence the state's policies? If so, that would be a good indicator that a civil society is emerging, with potential implications for further political change. In addition to these institutional links, the party is also linked to the private sector through individual red capitalists, both *xiahai* entrepreneurs and co-opted entrepreneurs. Are the political beliefs and policy preferences of China's red capitalists significantly different from those of party and government officials? If so, they could become agents of change.

To get the data necessary to answer these fundamental questions, I used the party's own journals, books on political and economic trends published in China, and devised a survey project targeting private entrepreneurs and local communist party and government officials in China. The survey was successfully implemented in eight counties in 1997 and 1999. The counties were chosen to represent different levels of economic development and privatization. (See the Appendix to Chapter 3 for more details on the design of the survey.) These various sources of data will be used to investigate both the personal and institutional relationships that are developing between these two key groups in the course of reform. Of most importance are the survey data, the first of their kind to compare the political beliefs and behaviors of private entrepreneurs, including both red capitalists and non-party members, and the local party and government officials with whom they interact. By conducting the survey in eight different counties with varying levels of development, the data can show the impact of variations in the local context and other socioeconomic factors. They also allow me to test hypotheses suggested by previous case studies on the role of business associations and the political beliefs and policy preferences of private entrepreneurs. In short, this study will examine macro trends affecting the CCP, the specific relationship of the party and the private entrepreneurs, and the variations in individual beliefs and behaviors. By combining these different levels of analysis, this study will clarify whether the CCP is willing and able to adapt to the economic environment its reforms are bringing about, how the relationship between entrepreneurs and the CCP is changing the CCP itself and China's political system as a whole, and whether China's entrepreneurs can be agents of political change.

6

Before beginning the evaluation of the CCP's adaptability and the political impact of China's red capitalists, this Introduction will first discuss the transformation of communist systems. It will review the different views on the possible political consequences of economic reforms and the role of civil society in the democratization of Leninist regimes and other authoritarian systems. This will create the backdrop against which the relationship between the CCP and the red capitalists will be examined.

## THE DYNAMICS OF LENINIST REGIMES

Although we cannot predict the ultimate fate of the CCP, comparing the experiences of other Leninist parties can at least clarify the kinds of questions we need to be asking. The challenges faced by the CCP – how to liberalize its economy without destabilizing the political system, how to change its organization and attract new members in order to carry out new tasks, how to balance the need to adapt with the need to uphold party traditions – are not unique. Nor are the strategies it has adopted to meet these challenges. Whether it will be successful, however, will depend largely on the peculiarities of the Chinese context: the legacies of the Maoist era, past decisions by party leaders regarding the scope and pace of economic and political reform, the continued influence of orthodox voices at the apex of the political system, and the evolving relationship between state and society.

Most ruling communist parties have wrestled with the competing goals of pursuing political and social policies that are consistent with Marxist-Leninist goals and the more immediate and pragmatic task of economic production. Although both goals may be important to the party, they require rather different sets of policies that in practice may be counter-productive. Richard Lowenthal noted this dichotomy in party goals and the policies for achieving them, labeling the trade-off between utopia and development.[3] When the party emphasizes utopian goals, it relies on ideology and propaganda to mobilize society to fulfill the party's agenda. It restricts the use of markets to distribute basic goods and services, relying instead on central planning. It also emphasizes the struggle against class enemies, using terror and other revolutionary tactics to demonstrate the party's resolve to eliminate real or potential opposition. Capitalists, landlords, and officials from the old regime and even their descendants are seen as politically suspect and persecuted, imprisoned, and sometimes killed for their assumed or actual opposition to communist goals. In contrast, during

---

[3] Richard Lowenthal, "Development versus Utopia in Communist Policy," in Chalmers Johnson, ed., *Change in Communist Systems* (Stanford: Stanford University Press, 1970).

periods when development is the key goal, the party uses material incentives (e.g., higher wages, bonuses, access to consumer goods) to encourage greater productivity from workers and downplays ideological appeals. It allows wider use of markets, at least to supplement the planned economy. In its relations with society, it promotes reconciliation instead of the continuation of the class struggle, although it continues to punish "counter-revolutionaries."

The fluctuation between utopian and development-oriented policies also has implications for the party's recruitment policies. When the party emphasizes utopian policies, it needs people with good ideological awareness, mass mobilization skills, and loyalty to the party in general and the primary leader in particular. When the emphasis is on economic development, the party needs people with technical skills and managerial expertise. In China, these trade-offs in the party's goals led to the policy debates and abrupt changes in party policy that characterized the Maoist era. They also contributed to the debates in the party's recruitment and personnel policies that were prominent in the Maoist years and still resonate today, although with less intensity.[4] As will be shown in later chapters, the debate over party goals and the proper recruitment and personnel policies attenuated in the post-Mao era were not entirely eliminated, even after the party abandoned class struggle and announced that economic modernization would be the key task in the party's work.

In addition to these alternating policy cycles, Leninist parties are also concerned with establishing and maintaining their political authority. Ken Jowitt describes three stages of development common to Leninist regimes, reminiscent of the stages Huntington proposed for authoritarian regimes more generally: *transformation*, in which the elites and norms of the old regime are castigated and replaced; *consolidation*, in which the new regime solidifies the loyalty of its cadres and its domination over society, in part by drawing a clear line between state and society; and *inclusion* (what Huntington refers to as *adaptation*), in which the party attempts to integrate itself with the new social strata emerging as a result of the party's development-oriented policies. Inclusion "refers above all to an attempt to expand membership in the regime in a way that allows politically coopted social elites or activists to maintain their social-occupational identity, and the party apparatus to maintain its institutionalized charismatic

---

[4] For the policy cycles in the Maoist era, see G. William Skinner and Edwin A. Winckler, "Compliance Succession in Rural China: A Cyclical Theory," in Amitai Etzioni, ed., *A Sociological Reader on Complex Organizations* (New York: Holt, Rinehart, and Winston, 1969). The cyclical nature of party policy continued into the post-Mao period, but with less intensity and less personal danger; for a description of the cycles of opening and tightening (*fang* and *shou*), see Richard Baum, *Burying Mao: Chinese Politics in the Age of Deng Xiaoping* (Princeton: Princeton University Press, 1994).

*transformom̃ . Crowell*

status."[5] In other words, the party co-opts new groups to prevent them from being threats to the party's authority and allows them to maintain a collective identity apart from party membership. At the same time, the party continues to exclude dissidents and those it deems to be "counter-revolutionaries" from legitimate participation in the political system. In China, these policies of inclusion are clearly seen in the co-optation of private entrepreneurs and technical elites and creation of a host of civic associations, including business associations, to link state and society.

Key turning points for Leninist parties, therefore, are the abandonment of utopian policies for the sake of development and the transition from an exclusive to an inclusive orientation. As the party more closely approximates an "open system," it is increasingly influenced by trends in its environment.[6] To study the party in isolation from its environment is to ignore one of the main means of political change in a communist system. This does not imply that the party adapts quickly, easily, or even inevitably to its environment. But just as problems in American schools are largely caused by the social environment of which they are a part, so too are the CCP's problems caused in part by the environment around it, which it helped create, and which it has tried to change.

The difference is that Leninist parties, unlike most organizations, have organizational resources that limit their dependence on the environment. They have a monopoly on legitimate political organization, which they defend zealously. They do not have to defend their record in the court of public opinion, although the shift toward inclusion and adaptation suggests they are interested in the views and support of at least some key groups in society. They control access to key jobs, financial resources, and nearly all political appointments. In short, they are the only game in town, politically speaking, and they use the resources they control to reward supporters and punish opponents.

---

[5] Ken Jowitt, "Inclusion," in *New World Disorder: The Leninist Extinction* (Berkeley: University of California Press, 1992), pp. 88–120 (originally published in *World Politics*, vol. 28, no. 1 (October 1975), pp. 69–97); the quote is from pp. 91–92; Samuel P. Huntington, "Social and Institutional Dynamics of One-Party Systems," in Samuel P. Huntington and Clement H. Moore, eds., *Authoritarian Politics in Modern Society: The Dynamics of Established One-Party Systems* (New York: Basic Books, 1970), pp. 3–47. Jowitt offered these stages of development as an alternative to other models of change in communist systems, including Lowenthal's, which he criticized for positing "a unilinear . . . de-utopianization of Leninist regimes." In China, however, neither the transition from utopianism to development nor the stages of transformation, consolidation, and inclusion/adaptation proceeded in a linear fashion. Both approaches hold useful insights and should be seen as complementary.

[6] W. Richard Scott, *Organizations: Rational, Natural and Open Systems*, 4th ed. (Englewood Cliffs, NJ: Prentice-Hall, 1998).

The CCP's emphasis on economic development in its policy agenda has inevitably created contradictions between the norms that are needed to manage the marketplace and the norms that are necessary to sustain a Leninist system. Where the Leninist system emphasizes hierarchy, the market requires horizontal ties and reciprocal networks; where the Leninist system entails a closed decision-making system and strict secrecy about even elemental forms of information, the market requires openness and the free flow of information; where the hallmark of a Leninist system is party dominance over the state and society through its network of party cells, the market requires minimal state involvement, especially the use of political criteria for economic decisions; where the Leninist system makes the distribution of most goods and services dependent on political decisions, the market entails the exchange of goods and services on the basis of equal value; above all, where most Leninist parties claim to promote the interests of the working class over those of the capitalists, the market operates primarily for the benefit of capitalists. When we recall that this party formerly waged violent class warfare against China's industrial and commercial classes, we can understand why the decision to admit entrepreneurs into the party is so momentous, and why it was hotly contested within the party for so long.

Even in party recruitment policies, there has been a debate on whether the emphasis should be on the "production standard" (i.e., promoting greater economic growth, either through hard work or especially entrepreneurship) or the "party standard" (loyalty to the party and adherence to its official ideology). Party journals often juxtapose these two standards to show their contradictory nature. Whether they can be reconciled is beside the point: critics claim that the production standard is displacing the party standard as the top criterion of party membership; adherents claim it should be given even greater priority. Although the party is pursuing policies of inclusion, not all in the party agree that inclusion should include allowing capitalists into a communist party or abandoning all the party's ideological traditions.

## THE POLITICAL CONSEQUENCES OF ECONOMIC REFORM

It has become a truism that continued economic reform in China, and privatization in particular, will lead to political change. Policy makers as well as many scholars expect that formation of a private sector will lead, directly or indirectly through the emergence of a civil society, to political change and ultimately democratization. The rapidly growing numbers of private entrepreneurs, the formation of business associations, and the cooperative relationships between entrepreneurs and local officials are seen as initial indicators of a transition from China's still nominally communist political system. This expectation, often stated by politicians and those in the policy community, is based on a simplified version of modernization theory. For instance, it was the rationale given by Presidents Bush and Clinton for annually renewing China's most favored nation status (later renamed normal trade relations) and for admitting China into the World Trade Organization: Increased trade will promote economic development, leading to the formation of a civil society that will push for political change. The result will be a democratic China that will promote peace and stability in the Asia-Pacific region, thus benefiting American security interests.[7]

This perspective is shared by many scholars. The influential works of Lipset, Almond and Verba, Dahl, Inglehart, and others showed the close correlation between economic development and democracy.[8] Although the specific cause and effect relationships are often disputed, economic development is clearly correlated with industrialization, urbanization, higher rates of literacy, improved communications, value changes, and the creation of a middle class. These attributes of modernization in turn promote democratization. In her study of democracy in East Asia, Samantha Ravich offers an even more multifaceted depiction of the link between economic and political change. She argues that marketization gives rise to prosperity, experience with competition and choice, reduced levels of corruption, and the dispersal of power away from the state as private citizens gain economic autonomy and private firms gain better bargaining power against the government. "A private sphere that exists, separate and distinct from a public domain, erodes the ability of the government to exert coercive power over the populace."[9]

The connection between economic development and democracy has led some scholars to offer unusually precise predictions about the advent of democratization in China. Henry Rowen, an economist at Stanford University, predicted

---

[7] This benign scenario is not held by all. A vocal minority in the United States argues forcefully that China's economic development is also leading to its military modernization and a security strategy that poses a challenge to American interests in Asia and elsewhere in the world. This is the perspective of the "blue team," a loosely organized group of Congressional staff, think tank scholars, and journalists. See Richard Bernstein and Ross H. Munro, *The Coming Conflict with China* (New York: Knopf, 1997).

[8] Seymour Martin Lipset, "Some Social Requisites of Democracy: Economic Development and Political Legitimacy," *American Political Science Review*, vol. 53, no. 1 (March 1959), pp. 69–105; Gabriel Almond and Sidney Verba, *Civic Culture: Political Attitudes and Democracy in Five Nations* (Princeton: Princeton University Press, 1963); Robert A. Dahl, *Polyarchy: Participation and Opposition* (New Haven: Yale University Press, 1971); Ronald Inglehart, *Modernization and Post-Modernization: Cultural, Economic, and Political Change in 43 Societies* (Princeton: Princeton University Press, 1997).

[9] Samantha F. Ravich, *Marketization and Democracy: East Asian Experiences* (Cambridge: Cambridge University Press, 2000), p. 19.

that China will be democratic by 2015, based solely on economic projections.[10] Shaohua Hu is even more optimistic, anticipating China will be democratic by 2011 because the obstacles to democracy, including socialist values and limited economic development, are breaking down.[11] These types of arguments, based on a linear and deterministic approach to political development, ignores the weak link between economic development and democracy. Adam Przeworski and Fernando Limongi tested some of the main elements of modernization theory using time series data from a wide range of countries and found that there was no simple correspondence between economic change and the timing of democratization.[12] Moreover, despite the obvious trend of economic growth in China, other trends suggest that liberalization will not be as immediate or as smooth as some scholars and policy makers suggest. Among the factors that may prevent liberalization in China are unclear property rights, the state's ambivalence over privatization, local protectionism, labor unrest, and the common backgrounds and shared interests of the emerging middle classes and state officials.[13] Despite the many critiques of modernization theory, the simple and intuitive logic linking economic and political change is too seductive for many scholars and policy analysts to ignore.

Economic development and modernization may facilitate democratization, but not directly and not always immediately. Democratization is not a natural result of economic growth, it is a political process fraught with conflict, negotiations, and occasionally setbacks. Scholars looking at democratic transitions tend to focus not just on economic and social preconditions but more importantly on the actors who influence the process. One corollary of the modernization argument is that privatization in the economy creates a new class of entrepreneurs who can be agents of change. This is particularly pertinent in China. According

---

[10] Henry S. Rowen, "The Short March: China's Road to Democracy," *The National Interest*, no. 45 (Fall 1996), pp. 61–70.

[11] Shaohua Hu, *Explaining Chinese Democratization* (Westport, CT: Praeger, 2000).

[12] Adam Przeworski and Fernando Limongi, "Modernization: Theories and Facts," *World Politics*, vol. 49, no. 2 (January 1997), pp. 155–183. See also Ross E. Burkhart and Michael A. Lewis-Beck, "Comparative Democracy: The Economic Development Thesis," *American Political Science Review*, vol. 88, no. 4 (December 1994), pp. 903–910, who conclude that economic development leads to democratization, but also that democracy does not lead to economic development.

[13] David Zweig, "Undemocratic Capitalism: China and the Limits of Economism," *The National Interest*, no. 56 (Summer 1999), pp. 63–72; David S.G. Goodman, "The New Middle Class," in Merle Goldman and Roderick MacFarquhar, eds., *The Paradox of China's Post-Mao Reforms* (Cambridge: Harvard University Press, 1999), and Goodman, "The Interdependence of State and Society: The Political Sociology of Local Leadership," in Chien-min Chao and Bruce J. Dickson, eds., *Remaking the Chinese State: Strategies, Society, and Security* (London and New York: Routledge, 2001).

to Kristen Parris, as more and more private entrepreneurs are recruited into the CCP, they are likely to be a "force for change within the party rank and file."[14] Others see private entrepreneurs as the leading edge of an emerging civil society that will eventually transform China's political system. These are exactly the fears of leftists in the party, who use a similar logic to argue that capitalists should be kept out of the party, rather than co-opted into it. This emphasis on the political role of entrepreneurs, apart from the economic development process, is based on the important part entrepreneurs have historically played in shaping and changing their political systems. Barrington Moore's oft-cited phrase "no bourgeoisie, no democracy" succinctly states one of their important roles in a nation's political transformation. Samuel Huntington found that one of the main threats to an authoritarian regime is the "diversification of the elite resulting from the rise of new groups controlling autonomous sources of economic power, that is, from the development of an independently wealthy business and industrial middle class."[15]

However, the contribution of entrepreneurs to the transition from authoritarianism is complex and ambiguous. Entrepreneurs may prop up an authoritarian regime because they benefit materially or because they are worried that political change will harm their property interests. Their political activism is often limited to economic issues that directly affect their immediate interests and does not include broader political issues. The literature on business associations in developing countries also emphasizes collective action efforts on economic and commercial matters, while paying less attention to strictly political matters.[16] But once they perceive that the regime is under challenge by broader elements of civil society, especially if this opposition is triggered by an economic downturn, businesspeople may turn from regime supporters (or at least political neutrality) to more overt opposition.[17] In countries as diverse as South Korea, the Philippines, Brazil, Peru, Ecuador, and Spain, democratization was facilitated when businesspeople and the broader middle classes shifted their support from

---

[14] Kristen Parris, "Local Initiative and National Reform: The Wenzhou Model of Development," *China Quarterly*, no. 134 (June 1993), p. 261.

[15] Samuel P. Huntington, *Political Order in Changing Societies* (New Haven: Yale University Press, 1970), p. 20.

[16] See for example Leroy Jones and Il Sakong, *Government, Business, and Entrepreneurship in Economic Development* (Cambridge: Harvard University Press, 1980) and Sylvia Maxwell and Ben Ross Schneider, eds., *Business and the State in Developing Countries* (Ithaca: Cornell University Press, 1997).

[17] Guillermo O'Donnell and Philippe C. Schmitter, *Transitions from Authoritarian Rule: Tentative Conclusions about Uncertain Democracies* (Baltimore: Johns Hopkins University Press, 1986); Yanqi Tong, "State, Society, and Political Change in China and Hungary," *Comparative Politics*, vol. 26, no. 3 (April 1994), pp. 333–353.

the government to the opposition.[18] It is this possibility, that China's red capitalists will one day be supporters of democratization and not simply regime supporters, that gives hope to those who advocate political change and nightmares to those who fear the demise of the CCP.

In sharp contrast to those who see economic development leading directly or indirectly to democratization, others foresee a coming collapse into chaos. This prediction is supported by regular reports of rural protests, labor unrest, environmental degradation, and rampant corruption. The central state's authority has been steadily eroded by the decentralization of authority and the privatization of the economy. According to this perspective, the ultimate, albeit unintended, consequence of the post-Mao economic reforms will be the hollowing out of the state, with its collapse at some unspecified date in the not too distant future. As opposed to expectations that economic development is laying the foundation for an imminent and smooth transition to democracy, this perspective sees an extended period of decay and disunity, leading perhaps even to the breakup of China into separate countries.[19]

A less dramatic version of what may be called the "disintegration thesis" emphasizes how the transition to a market economy erodes what Andrew Walder calls the "institutional pillars" of a communist system: the Leninist style of party organization and central planning over the economy.[20] As a consequence of these two factors, the party was able to monitor the activities of managers, workers, farmers, and all others in society, rewarding proper conduct with career advances and access to essential goods and services and punishing improper

---

[18] Samuel Huntington, *The Third Wave: Democratization in the Late Twentieth Century* (Norman: University of Oklahoma Press, 1991), pp. 67–68.

[19] Gordon G. Chang, *The Coming Collapse of China* (New York: Random House, 2001). For a more succinct enunciation of this perspective, see Jack A. Goldstone, "The Coming Chinese Collapse," and the rejoinder by Yasheng Huang, "Why China Will Not Collapse," *Foreign Policy*, no. 99 (Summer 1995), pp. 35–52 and 54–68, respectively. This viewpoint runs counter to the "blue team" perspective that economic development is leading to a strong, unified, and aggressive China. When looking at China from the inside, that viewpoint is harder to see. For a discussion of alternative scenarios of China's future and their implications for U.S. policy, see Kenneth Lieberthal, "U.S. Policy Toward China," *Brookings Policy Review*, no. 72 (March 2001).

[20] Andrew G. Walder, "The Decline of Communist Power: Elements of a Theory of Institutional Change," *Theory and Society*, vol. 23, no. 2 (April 1994), pp. 297–323; see also Walder's "The Quiet Revolution from Within: Economic Reform as a Source of Political Decline," in Walder, ed., *The Waning of the Communist State: Economic Origins of Political Decline in China and Hungary* (Berkeley: University of California Press, 1995). Other studies also assert the erosion of the party's power, for instance Hsi-sheng Ch'i, *Politics of Disillusionment: The Chinese Communist Party under Deng Xiaoping, 1978–1989* (Armonk, NY: M. E. Sharpe, 1991) and Murray Scot Tanner, "The Erosion of Central Party Control over Lawmaking," *China Quarterly*, no. 138 (June 1994), pp. 381–403.

behavior by withholding these same things. The emergence of markets in the post-Mao era eroded the "organized dependence" created by central planning and party dominance in the Maoist era. Markets provide the ways and means for workers and farmers to obtain the necessary goods and services (e.g., food, clothing, housing), limiting the party's ability to shape their behavior with positive and negative sanctions. In addition, the expansion of the private sector weakened the monitoring capacity of the CCP, because most private firms do not have party organizations, the nominal (but not fully effective) ban on recruiting entrepreneurs has limited the party's direct link with that group, and the relationship between local officials and entrepreneurs is more symbiotic than dependent. If the capacity to monitor and sanction economic and social behavior are key elements of a Leninist system, then as that capacity declines, so too does the stability of the system. As Huntington noted, the strength of any authoritarian regime depends in large part on the strength of its party. As the party weakens, the stability of the regime it governs also comes into question.[21]

The change in the party's work from class struggle to economic development also contributed to a reorientation of inner party norms. The emphasis on maximizing economic growth can and often does conflict with other central directives. As Walder showed, the introduction of markets made local officials less dependent on their superiors. The non-state owned sectors of the economy created new sources of revenue and investment funds. Ill-defined property rights also allowed local officials to use "public" property for personal use, for instance by opening so-called collective enterprises that were in fact wholly owned by state owned enterprises (SOEs), or by entering into joint ventures. The transition to a market economy also created new sources of personal income. In addition to blatant corruption, local officials earn income by being partners or board members of local enterprises, by opening their own enterprises, by extorting taxes and fees from farmers and firms, or requiring matchmaker fees to facilitate joint ventures and trade. The emphasis on achieving faster rates of growth as a criterion for promotion also makes these officials pay more attention to local needs and less to strict compliance with non-economic orders from above. As will be shown throughout this book, local officials were willing to co-opt successful entrepreneurs into the party even when it violated central party policy to do so. Forging links with local economic elites had "horizontal" advantages even if they did not conform to "vertical" guidelines. Under these circumstances, local officials have less incentive to be loyal agents of higher

---

[21] Huntington, "Social and Institutional Dynamics," p. 9.

levels of the state.[22] This reduced ability to sanction the behavior of local officials also reduced the political cohesion of the Leninist system in China.

To some extent, these different scenarios are potentially compatible. The disintegration of the CCP need not mean the disintegration of the country. The institutional pillars of China's communist system may be undermined, but if they are replaced by alternative institutional arrangements, then the CCP may disintegrate, but the country may remain intact. In other words, the "disintegration thesis" refers to the implications for the CCP and the communist political system in China; the predictions for either democratization or decay and disunity focus more on the economy and society and less on the communist system itself. Obviously, economic, social, and political trends are closely related, but they are not so tightly bundled as to be synonymous. Economic and social development may spell danger for the CCP, but need not spell disaster for the country at large. That is the expectation, and indeed the hope, of many observers, both inside and outside China.

DYNAMICS OF CIVIL SOCIETY

As noted in the previous section, the prospects for political change in China are generally predicated on the role of civil society. The existence of civil society in China has fostered heated debates among scholars. Historians have argued over whether the economic and social changes of the late Qing and Republican periods led to the emergence of a civil society, at least in some of the main cities of the time.[23] During the late Qing, associations of various kinds formed, including guilds for merchants and tradesmen and organizations for immigrants and sojourners from the same place of origin (tongxianghui). By the Republican period, guilds for bankers, lawyers, and other professions were also common. Initially, guilds concentrated on commercial regulations and worship activities.

---

[22] For other examples of how economic reform weakened the center's control over local governments, see Jia Hao and Lin Zhimin, eds., *Changing Central-Local Relations in China* (Boulder: Westview, 1994), and Wang Shaoguang, "The Rise of the Regions: Fiscal Reform and the Decline of Central State Capacity in China," in Walder, ed., *Waning of the Communist State*. Others argue that the power of the center grew as a consequence of reform policies: see Dali Yang, "Reform and Restructuring of Central-Local Relations," in David S. G. Goodman and Gerald Segal, eds., *China Deconstructs: Politics, Trade, and Regionalism* (London: Routledge, 1994) and Yasheng Huang *Inflation and Investment Controls in China: The Political Economy of Central-Local Relations during the Reform Era* (New York: Cambridge University Press, 1996).

[23] William T. Rowe, *Hankow: Commerce and Society in a Chinese City, 1796–1889* (Stanford: Stanford University Press, 1984); Mary Backus Rankin, *Elite Activism and Political Transformation in China: Zhejiang Province, 1865–1911* (Stanford: Stanford University Press, 1986); David Strand, *Rickshaw Beijing: City People and Politics in the 1920s* (Berkeley: University of California Press, 1989).

By the late Qing, they assumed a variety of social regulatory and welfare functions that continued into the Republican period. They organized philanthropic efforts, local construction projects such as water-works, schools and temples, fire-fighting, police and public order, and in some cases even tax collection. Over time, the separate guilds and associations combined to form larger chambers of commerce which assumed larger public roles, including debating public policy issues. As a result of these developments, some historians have argued that these guilds, associations, and chambers of commerce constituted a "public sphere," an intermediate realm between the official world of the state and the private world of society. This concept of a public sphere was influenced by Jürgen Habermas, whose writings were being translated and published in English as these new works of social history appeared.[24] The notion of a public sphere of autonomous guilds and associations challenged the conventional paradigm of Weber, which argued that China failed to develop capitalism and fell behind the West in its development because the Confucian state was the guardian of agrarian society and culture but hostile to urban industry and commerce.[25]

The search for signs of civil society in contemporary China is driven, in contrast, by the expected link between civil society and democratization. Scholars have debated whether a civil society was created as a consequence of the early post-Mao reforms, what role it played in the 1989 demonstrations, and what prospects it holds for China's future.[26] The rise of civil society received a large share of the credit for the "velvet revolutions" that brought down communist governments throughout central and eastern Europe in 1989.[27] As Martin King Whyte wrote, "To the extent that a civil society develops within a Leninist system, it will produce pressure on elites for democratic reforms." If the state actively represses civil society, "elites may feel that they can conduct business

[24] See especially Jurgen Habermas, *The Structural Transformation of the Public Sphere* (Cambridge, MA: MIT Press, 1989).
[25] For a careful comparison of the developmental trajectories of China and the West, see R. Bin Wong, *China Transformed: Historical Change and the Limits of European Experience* (Ithaca: Cornell University Press, 1997).
[26] Thomas B. Gold, "The Resurgence of Civil Society in China," *Journal of Democracy*, vol. 1, no. 1 (Winter 1990), pp. 18–31; Martin King Whyte, "Urban China: A Civil Society in the Making?" in Arthur Lewis Rosenbaum, ed., *State and Society in China: The Consequences of Reform* (Boulder: Westview Press, 1992); Heath B. Chamberlain, "On the Search for Civil Society in China," *Modern China*, vol. 19, no. 2 (April 1993), pp. 199–215; Baogang He, *The Democratic Implications of Civil Society in China* (New York: St. Martin's Press, 1997).
[27] Timothy Garton Ash, *The Uses of Adversity: Essays on the Fate of Central Europe* (New York: Vintage, 1990); Marcia A. Wiegle and Jim Butterfield, "Civil Society in Reforming Communist Regimes: The Logic of Emergence," *Comparative Politics*, vol. 25, no. 1 (October 1992), pp. 1–24; Vladimir Tismaneanu, *Reinventing Politics: Eastern Europe from Stalin to Havel* (New York: The Free Press, 1992).

as usual, but they may learn to their surprise and sorrow, as [former Romanian leader Nicolae] Ceausescu did, that a nascent civil society nurturing and spreading protodemocratic views lies just below the surface of official controls."[28] The implication is clear: if a civil society emerges, the prospects for democratization in China will improve.

The historical and contemporary debates center on whether key elements of a civil society existed, either in the past or in the present. Did organizations of various kinds exist that enjoyed relative autonomy from the state? Were they able to represent the interests of their members and the community at large? Were they able to influence government policy? Critics of the approach find little evidence in support of any of these questions. They also note that the concept of civil society and the public sphere were originally tied to the development of liberalism and bourgeois society in the West, and may therefore be inappropriate in the Chinese context.[29] Even advocates of a civil society perspective acknowledge that the degree of autonomy, representation, and influence varied considerably over time, in different areas of the country, and among different types of organizations. William Rowe claimed that the "balance between autonomy and state control was thus never clearly defined, but it was in practice the result of a process of continual negotiation."[30] Most studies of civil society in contemporary China are qualified by words such as "nascent," "embryonic," or "emerging." These modifiers acknowledge the limits on the autonomy, influence, and even the durability of social and economic organizations created in the post-Mao era.

Much of the debate about the applicability and the implications of civil society in contemporary China revolves around the presumed goals of civil society. Social changes have led to an explosion of civic and professional associations of all kinds, but to what ends? This is where the debate rests. We can agree that there is a growing number of associations. But do they intend to challenge the state, demanding that it either become more responsive and more representative? For some, this adversarial stance is the true test of civil society. Or do these groups hope to produce stability at a time of great change and uncertainty? A civil society may be cooperative with the state, more concerned with issues of good governance and economic performance than the promotion of liberal democracy. There are different strands of thinking within civil society, and they

---

[28] Whyte, "Urban China," pp. 79–80.

[29] Frederic Wakeman, "The Civil Society and Public Sphere Debate: Western Reflections on Chinese Political Culture," *Modern China*, vol. 19, no. 2 (April 1993), pp. 108–138; Timothy Brook and B. Michael Frolic, eds., *Civil Society in China* (Armonk, NY: M. E. Sharpe, 1997).

[30] William T. Rowe, "The Problem of 'Civil Society' in Late Imperial China," *Modern China*, vol. 19, no. 2 (April 1993), p. 148.

may be present in varying degrees at any given point in time because there are different interests within civil society.[31]

What impact will the rise of private entrepreneurs have on China's still nominally communist system? Scholars looking for an emerging civil society in China typically look for evidence of autonomy for individuals and especially groups. But most individuals and groups in China do not seek autonomy but rather closer embeddedness with the state. They recognize that to be autonomous is to be "outside the system" (*tizhiwai*), and therefore powerless. Instead they seek to be part of the system (*tizhinei*) in order to better pursue their interests and maximize their leverage. To be able to assess the political impact of China's entrepreneurs, we need to use a nuanced notion of civil society, one that acknowledges that civil society is not necessarily antagonistic toward the state. The present study is not focused on whether a civil society exists in China. Instead, the inquiry is on the dynamics that lead to its emergence and more importantly the implications for the CCP. In their search for signs of civil society in China, Gordon White, Jude Howell, and Shang Xiaoyuan describe two separate dynamics that lead to the emergence of civil society. The political dynamic is the most familiar one. It entails the "resistance to state control on the part of groups and organizations with implicit or explicit political agendas."[32] This dynamic can be seen as early as the 100 Flowers movement and later in the Red Guards, the anti-Gang of Four protests in April 1976, the Democracy Wall movement of 1978–9, and most vividly to foreign audiences in the 1989 demonstrations in Tiananmen Square. Its most dramatic impact on political change within a socialist system was seen in Poland's Solidarity movement, which after nearly a decade of popular support and official repression finally replaced the communist government. The political dynamic gives rise to what Yanqi Tong calls the "critical realm" of civil society, a political sphere that is critical of the state and represents a challenge to it.[33]

In addition to this political dynamic, there is a separate market dynamic that gives rise to a "non-critical realm" which is primarily concerned with the management and regulation of collective goods and services but less interested in changing the political system itself. With the rise of a market economy and

---

[31] We also need to recognize that society can be just as vicious as the state. Replacing an authoritarian government does not automatically open the doors to civil society or liberal democracy. Islamic revolutions have often replaced one form of despotism with another and occasionally even more ruthless one. An entirely capitalist oriented polity would also lead to a rather uncivil society.

[32] Gordon White, Jude Howell, and Shang Xiaoyuan, *In Search of Civil Society: Market Reform and Social Change in Contemporary China* (Oxford: Oxford University Press, 1996), p. 7.

[33] Tong, "State, Society, and Political Change in China and Hungary."

the shift of social power away from the state toward new economic strata (viz., the private sector) comes a clearer separation of state and society. Whereas the political dynamic has taken place within a relatively static institutional context, "the market dynamic contains the potential for creating new institutions and shifting the balance of power between the state and society in the latter's favor. To that extent, the market dynamic can be seen as constructing a material or structural basis for the development of civil society."[34] The state needs, and indeed encourages, this market dynamic and cannot suppress it entirely. Whereas the "critical realm" arising from a political dynamic is a direct threat, the "non-critical realm" resulting from the market dynamic creates a more complementary relationship between state and society, presenting costs and benefits to both. To fully understand the potential for political change in China, it is necessary to appreciate these separate dynamics and the three-way relationships between the critical realm, the non-critical realm, and the state. In determining the ultimate political implications of economic reform in China, the non-critical realm may have the decisive role.

The potential for political change comes in the potentially complementary and reinforcing relationship between the political and market dynamics, and the critical and non-critical realms they create. This interactive relationship is the flip side of the disintegration thesis noted above. Whereas Walder described how the winnowing away of the "institutional pillars" of communism weakened its capacity to monitor and control developments in society, the political and market dynamics add external pressure on those pillars. *If* (and that is the main qualifier) the political dynamic offers an alternative more conducive to the market dynamic and the new strata emerging therefrom, a powerful coalition in opposition to the state is possible. The market dynamic may reinforce the political dynamic by weakening "the ideological authority and organizational reach of the state, thereby reducing its generalized capacity to repress political alternatives."[35] According to Liu Junning, a leading advocate of liberalism in China, "The case of China shows that a free market in commodities will ultimately result in a free market of ideas and a demand for liberal ideas. As long as people are free to choose, most people will choose liberty and liberalism."[36] The market can also provide resources and potential allies to the political dynamic, and safe haven in times of trouble. On the other hand, if the critical

---

[34] White, Howell, and Shang, *In Search of Civil Society*, pp. 7–8.
[35] White, Howell, and Shang, *In Search of Civil Society*, p. 9.
[36] Liu Junning, "Classical Liberalism Catches On In China," *Journal of Democracy*, vol. 11, no. 3 (July 2000), pp. 48–57. Liu is the founder and former editor of *Res Publica*, a journal devoted to the promotion of liberalism in China. In 2000, he was fired from the Chinese Academy of Social Sciences for his liberal views.

and non-critical realms do not join together in common cause against the state, the state has more leeway to repress the political dynamic while supporting the market dynamic. As Adam Przeworski noted, it is not the legitimacy of the state but the presence of a feasible alternative to the status quo that determines whether the authoritarian state survives or is replaced.[37]

This concept of dual dynamics and separate but potentially reinforcing realms of civil society is tantalizing, and as noted above the non-critical realm of businessmen has joined with the critical realm to promote democratization in a variety of other countries. In China, however, the evidence is more ambiguous. For one thing, the political dynamic is not necessarily antagonistic to the state. Intellectuals in modern China, beginning with the late imperial era up to the present, have had a complex relationship with the state. While critical of official policy and the performance of political institutions, they are more likely to be reformers trying to improve both the efficiency and the responsiveness of the state than to offer a dramatic alternative to the status quo.[38] They see themselves, and want to be seen by state leaders, as loyal remonstrators fulfilling their patriotic duty to point out the government's shortcomings, not revolutionaries (or worse counter-revolutionaries) bent on overthrowing the system. Many hold official positions, or have close ties with party and government leaders in order to get their voices heard. The truly dissident voices are relatively small in number and are perhaps held in higher regard abroad than they are within China.

While economic reforms have fueled a market dynamic in China and created a non-critical realm made up of entrepreneurs, professionals, high tech specialists and others, most observers have noted the apolitical, even anti-political, character of these groups. Although White, Howell, and Shang reach provocative conclusions about the potential influence of business associations, the evidence they provide does not match their enthusiasm. Claims of desired autonomy, of new and unofficial or semi-official associations created to supplant the official ones, are asserted with little or no supporting evidence. Some examples are given in footnotes, but they do not receive sustained investigation. Other studies of

---

[37] Adam Przeworski, "Some Problems in the Transition to Democracy," in Guillermo O'Donnell, Philippe C. Schmitter, and Laurence Whitehead, eds., *Transitions from Authoritarian Rule, vol. 3: Comparative Perspectives* (Baltimore: Johns Hopkins University Press, 1986).
[38] Merle Goldman and Timothy Cheek have written extensively on these themes. See Goldman, *China's Intellectuals: Advise and Dissent* (Cambridge: Harvard University Press, 1981); Carol Lee Hamrin and Timothy Cheek, eds., *China's Establishment Intellectuals* (Armonk, NY: M. E. Sharpe, 1986); Cheek, "From Priests to Professionals: Intellectuals and the State under the CCP," in Jeffrey Wassertrom and Elizabeth J. Perry, eds., *Popular Protest and Political Culture in Modern China* (Boulder: Westview Press, 1992); Goldman, *Sowing the Seeds of Democracy in China: Political Reform in the Deng Xiaoping Era* (Cambridge: Harvard University Press, 1994).

entrepreneurs and their associations emphasize that private entrepreneurs are not engaged in political activities (beyond those that directly affect their business interests). Although Wan Runnan, the former head of Beijing's influential Stone Corporation, offered material and moral support to students demonstrating in Tiananmen Square in 1989, he was the exception, not the rule.[39] Most private businessmen did not support the 1989 demonstrations; many of those who did later regretted doing so because it led to a temporary retreat from Deng's reform and opening policies and damaged the business environment in China.[40] Rather than seeing the rise of entrepreneurs as the vanguard of an autonomous civil society, Solinger saw the result being the merger of state and society, "a bonding and incipient interdependence between the bureaucrat and merchant."[41] Still, expectations continue to run high that continued privatization will lead to a stronger and more autonomous civil society, which in turn will bring about political change. The logic that underlies the link between civil society and political change is very intuitive and persuasive, supported by the experience of other countries, even if it has not yet been demonstrated in China.

The state is not a passive actor in this process. The implications of the market dynamic and the emergence of the non-critical realm in China are not lost on China's leaders, who have been debating the issue throughout the reform era. The CCP is determined to maximize the benefits of the market dynamic and minimize the risk of the political dynamic. As this book will detail, the CCP has adopted inclusive policies toward members of the non-critical realm, particularly private entrepreneurs and technical specialists, while continuing to exclude and repress those from the critical realm who push for democratization and liberalizing reforms. In particular, it has created links with organizations representing entrepreneurs and has co-opted individual entrepreneurs directly into the party. Both of these strands of inclusion, and the more general emphasis on economic growth in the work of the party, have been harshly criticized by

---

[39] Wan was forced to flee China after the Tiananmen demonstrations because his very visible support angered party leaders who ordered the crackdown. He was named as one of the "black hands" behind the movement. For Wan's leadership of Stone and support of political activists, see Scott Kennedy, "The Stone Group: State Client or Market Pathbreaker?" *China Quarterly*, no. 152 (December 1997), pp. 746–777.

[40] David L. Wank, "Private Business, Bureaucracy, and Political Alliance in a Chinese City," *Australian Journal of Chinese Affairs*, no. 33 (January 1995), pp. 55–71; Margaret M. Pearson, *China's New Business Elite: The Political Consequences of Economic Reform* (Berkeley: University of California Press, 1997); He, *Democratic Implications of Civil Society in China*.

[41] Dorothy Solinger, "Urban Entrepreneurs and the State: The Merger of State and Society," in Rosenbaum, ed., *State and Society in China*, p. 136.

conservative leaders within the party, but the consensus has been that such institutional and individual links are necessary to promote the party's agenda and prevent the non-critical realm from presenting a challenge to the state by aligning with the critical realm. The success of this strategy may decide the fate of the party itself.

In the current political context in China, it is probably unrealistic to expect to find explicit evidence of determined efforts on the part of private entrepreneurs to change the political system. China's entrepreneurial class is barely a decade old with a precarious legal identity and poorly protected property rights. Private entrepreneurs are more likely to be partners with the state, rather than adversaries of it, and more likely to focus on local and procedural issues, rather than abstract notions of civil, political, and social rights. According to Margaret Pearson, China's entrepreneurs have not turned their economic power into political power for several reasons: They are uninterested in politics; political action is unnecessary to solve individual problems because they have the viable option of engaging in clientelism; and the "socialist corporatist strategy of the state is designed to prevent" organized political action.[42] She argues that it is "less likely that business associations . . . will be at the forefront of systemic change than that they will be available to lend support if others take the lead in pressuring for economic and political reform."[43] The close and symbiotic relationship between entrepreneurs and local officials may make the state more sympathetic to the views of businesspeople, and more willing to listen when they advocate political reforms. At the same time, they hold the option of shifting their support from the state to the critical realm if their concerns are not met. This is what enhances their "king maker" potential.

THE CORPORATIST PERSPECTIVE ON STATE–SOCIETY RELATIONS

While the environment for a civil society looked quite promising in the 1980s, the June 4th tragedy led most people to tone down their immediate expectations. Even if a civil society was emerging in China, it would take more time for its full effects to be felt. Because the obviously limited autonomy available in China casts doubt on the relevance of the civil society concept, some scholars have adopted the corporatist framework as a way of explaining

---

[42] Pearson, *China's New Business Elite*, p. 141.
[43] Margaret M. Pearson, "The Janus Face of Business Associations in China," *Australian Journal of Chinese Affairs*, no. 31 ( January 1994), p. 45; see also her "China's Emerging Business Class: Democracy's Harbinger?" *Current History*, vol. 97, no. 620 (September 1998), pp. 268–272.

state–society relations.[44] In the classic definition offered by Philippe Schmitter, corporatism is

a system of interest representation in which the constituent parts are organized into a limited number of singular, compulsory, noncompetitive, hierarchically ordered and functionally differentiated categories, recognized or licensed (if not created) by the state and granted a deliberate representational monopoly within their respective categories in exchange for observing certain controls on their selection of leaders and articulation of demands and supports.[45]

On each element of this definition, the contrast with the more familiar concept of pluralism is immediately apparent. As Alfred Stepan noted, corporatism is an attractive concept because it gives a key role to the state as an independent and autonomous (although not unitary) actor. Whereas the civil society perspective based on pluralism and even Marxist theories looks primarily at divisions within society to explain political dynamics, corporatism looks at the relative strength of the state and social groups. When corporatism is created by the state from above, the autonomy and participation by the other parts of the corporatist system are severely restricted. Although there are limits to the applicability of the corporatist model to China, as will be discussed in Chapter Three, it does capture important elements of China's political economy and state-society relationship and therefore may have important insights regarding the prospects for political change.[46]

---

[44] For a thoughtful synthesis and analysis of the corporatist, civil society, and other models of the contemporary Chinese state, see Richard Baum and Alexei Shevchenko, "The 'State of the State,'" in Merle Goldman and Roderick MacFarquhar, eds., *The Paradox of China's Post-Mao Reforms* (Cambridge: Harvard University Press, 1999).

[45] Philippe C. Schmitter, "Still the Century of Corporatism?" in Schmitter and Gerhard Lehmbruch, eds., *Trends towards Corporatist Intermediation* (Beverly Hills: Sage, 1979), p. 13.

[46] Jonathan Unger and Anita Chan, "Corporatism in China: A Developmental State in an East Asian Context," in Barrett L. McCormick and Jonathan Unger, eds., *China after Socialism: In the Footsteps of Eastern Europe or East Asia* (Armonk, NY: M. E. Sharpe, 1996); Kristen Parris, "Private Entrepreneurs as Citizens: From Leninism to Corporatism," *China Information*, vol. 10, nos. 3/4 (Winter 1995/Spring 1996); Yijiang Ding, "Corporatism and Civil Society in China: An Overview of the Debate in Recent Years," *China Information*, vol. 12, no. 4 (Spring 1998), pp. 44–67. B. Michael Frolic critiques four variants of civil society and offers an alternative, state-led civil society that closely resembles state corporatism; see his "State-led Civil Society," in Brook and Frolic, eds., *Civil Society in China*. Other critiques include Steven M. Goldstein, "China in Transition: The Political Foundations of Incremental Reform," *China Quarterly*, no. 144 (December 1995), pp. 1122–1126, and Scott Kennedy, *In the Company of Markets: The Transformation of China's Political Economy*, Ph.D. dissertation (George Washington University, 2001).

The empirical work on civil society and corporatism in recent years turned from macro trends to a closer look at local and sectoral trends, particularly the expansion of associations for civic, social, professional, and commercial affairs.[47] The rationale for expanding the scope of social organizations was the recognition that mass organizations of the Maoist era did not serve the purpose of the CCP's new mission. They worked well in the era of class struggle, where the goal was control and dictatorship, but did not work to promote the entrepreneurship, creativity, and progress needed in the reform era. The Organization Law, passed in draft form in 1989 and revised in its final version in 1998, codified the implicit corporatist strategy of the CCP. The law mandated that every organization must register with the government and have a party or government unit as its supervisory organization, responsible for its daily affairs. The law also granted organizations a representational monopoly: there can be only one organization for each profession, interest, or activity. In practice, of course, reality has not been so clear cut. Some organizations operate with little oversight, and the profusion of business associations has led to inevitable overlap and the widespread practice of having firms belong to multiple associations. Nevertheless, the Organization Law established the framework in which China's civic and professional associations must operate, including limits on their autonomy and range of membership.[48]

Like all corporatist organizations, China's associations have a dual function: they are designed to give the state control over organized interests in society, and also to represent their members' interests. While many Western scholars see these two functions in conflict, that seems not to be the case in China or elsewhere in East Asia. The two functions are not mutually exclusive in a context that does not assume that state–society relations are inherently adversarial. Replacing the class struggle policies of the Maoist era, which did assume hostile relations, corporatist institutions provide the basis for a more harmonious relationship between the party and society, and with business in particular. As will be shown in Chapter Three, both local officials and private entrepreneurs surveyed for this project indicate the compatibility of these two functions.

---

[47] Christopher Earle Nevitt, "Private Business Associations in China: Evidence of Civil Society or Local State Power," *China Journal*, no. 36 (July 1996), pp. 25–45; Jonathan Unger, "'Bridges': Private Business, the Chinese Government and the Rise of New Associations," *China Quarterly*, no. 147 (September 1996), pp. 795–819; Minxin Pei, "Chinese Civic Associations: An Empirical Analysis," *Modern China*, vol. 24, no. 3 (July 1998), pp. 285–318.

[48] Tony Saich, "Negotiating the State: The Development of Social Organizations in China," *China Quarterly*, no. 161 (March 2000), pp. 124–141.

One of the peculiar features of the literature on corporatism in China is that it primarily focuses on business groups, as opposed to labor.[49] Most of the literature on corporatism in Latin America, in contrast, looks at the role of labor unions. This is a curious twist: studies of corporatism in capitalist states have labor as a focus, but for China's communist state, the focus is on business. The CCP originally represented proletarian interests and persecuted business interests, but in the reform era it redefined the nature of regime goals. As a consequence, it began to rely on individuals and groups it had previously repressed. Although the political role of labor groups has been a primary focus in studies of Latin America and Europe, it has had not received as much attention in studies of contemporary China.

Rather than trying to accurately define the institutional features of China's corporatism, recognizing the tremendous variety across different sectors of the economy and the yawning gap between theory and practice, it may be more useful to consider what the state's intentions are and how well it has been able to implement its strategy. That will be one of the primary tasks of the remainder of this book.

PRÉCIS OF STUDY

The ideas and debates outlined in this introduction will be examined in more detail in subsequent chapters. Chapter 2 describes how the change in the CCP's core task – from waging class struggle to promoting economic modernization – led to changes in the basic organization and personnel of the party. It contrasts these new policies with those of the Maoist era and shows the intended consequences of these changes, such as improved qualifications of party and government officials and younger and better educated members. It also identifies some of the unintended consequences: the declining prestige of the CCP and its members; the challenge of party building in the expanding private sector; the decay of party organizations in the countryside; and the resurgence of clans, traditional religion and local strongmen. Problems in the party were often a reflection of more wide-spread problems in society. For instance, young and middle-aged party members left their hometowns to seek new jobs in the cities, leaving mostly elderly members in the party's grass-roots units. With

---

[49] Exceptions to this observation include Anita Chan, "Revolution or Corporatism? Workers and Trade Unions in Post-Mao China," in David S. G. Goodman and Beverly Hooper, eds., *China's Quiet Revolution: New Interactions between State and Society* (New York: St. Martin's Press, 1994) and Yunqiu Zhang, "From State Corporatism to Social Representation: Local Trade Unions in the Reform Years," in Brook and Frolic, eds., *Civil Society in China*.

SOE reform, the number of unemployed party members grew, as did the general unemployment rate. The CCP does not intend to protect its members from unemployment nor to discourage them from joining the "floating population" to find new jobs, but it is wrestling with how to combine its interests in party building with the new realities of privatization and social mobility.

Chapter 3 analyzes the CCP's corporatist strategy of developing business associations in order to link itself to the expanding private sector. The logic of this strategy is described using insights of scholarly literatures on the corporatist model, civil society, democratization, and organizational change. The pre-1949 patterns of relations between the Chinese state and business associations is also presented to compare and contrast with the contemporary experience. In this chapter, the findings of previous research on the relationship between local party and government officials, on the one hand, and private entrepreneurs and their business associations, on the other, are examined with survey data. The survey data allow me to test the generalizability of previous scholarship based on case studies of single cities or specific sectors of the private economy.

Chapter 4 examines the logic of co-optation as a strategy of adaptation. This chapter will examine both the benefits and potential dangers of co-optation, as well as the controversies it can generate within political parties and other organizations. The examples of Hungary and Taiwan, two other countries formerly ruled by Leninist parties, will be compared to China. Co-optation of new elites into the ruling parties in Hungary and Taiwan eventually led to their democratization, but these parties co-opted members of the critical realm of civil society, whereas the CCP is co-opting only those from the non-critical realm. This comparison will demonstrate that who gets co-opted has important implications for how the party adapts. Next, this chapter will review the inner-party debate created by the decision to recruit intellectuals and entrepreneurs. While some in the party saw this strategy as necessary to fulfill the party's economic goals, others felt that co-opting these former "class enemies" into the party undermined its integrity, betrayed the interests of its traditional base, the workers and peasants, and threatened its survival. Finally, it looks more closely at the "red capitalists," comparing the characteristics of entrepreneurs who were co-opted into the party with those who were already party members before going into business and those who are not party members.

Chapter 5 looks at the political beliefs and behaviors of China's red capitalists. The ultimate test of what impact the co-optation of private entrepreneurs into the CCP will have on the party itself, and ultimately on China's political system, requires an examination of their basic political beliefs and patterns of political behavior. Will they serve as "agents of change" either within the CCP or as an external force, or will they be a conservative force that upholds the political status quo? That is the subject of this chapter, again comparing my survey data against the findings of previous studies. In addition, this chapter looks at the types of political behavior that entrepreneurs engage in, such as philanthropic activities, serving in local people's congresses, and most importantly competing in village elections.

Finally, the concluding chapter will summarize the main findings of the book, assess both their generalizability and limitations, and will emphasize the significance of the evolving relationship between the CCP and the "red capitalists," both for scholars of contemporary China and for policy analysts and general readers who are concerned about the possible direction of Chinese politics.

# 2

# Challenges of Party Building in the Reform Era

Traditionally, party building has been linked to the party's historical tasks and to the theories and lines established by the party in order to accomplish the tasks . . . [We] must firmly establish the guiding idea that party building serves the implementation of the basic line and put an end to the practice of tackling party building for the sake of party building in isolation from the center of economic construction. We must make the implementation of the basic line the be all and end all in party building and let it permeate all parts of party building, all manner of work in party building.[1]

T HE CCP has been highly selective about the kinds of people it recruits, although the criteria for membership has changed over time. The qualities of the party's key personnel and rank-and-file membership as well as the integrity of the party's organization have been key elements of elite strategies for successful policy implementation, regardless of the content of their policy agenda. As is the case for most complex organizations, the criteria for membership has changed along with the party's main goals. For example, different types of skills were needed during the Great Leap Forward than are sought today when the party is pursuing "reform and opening" (*gaige kaifang*) policies. Mass mobilization and propaganda skills are appropriate for one set of policy goals, but technical expertise and entrepreneurship are necessary for others.

This chapter highlights the changing criteria of party membership caused by changes in the key task of the party. With the emphasis on economic modernization in the post-Mao era, the party has encountered new challenges in its party building, including controversies within the party about the proper political and professional qualities of party members; the large number of enterprises in

[1] *Qiushi*, February 1, 1999, pp. 23–27, in *Foreign Broadcast Information Service: Daily Report – China* (hereafter FBIS), February 16, 1999.

the non-state sector that lack party organizations; the mobility of party members who join the "floating population" in search of better jobs, and as a result become inactive in party life; and the declining recruitment of new members and the weakness of party organizations in the countryside. This chapter will also show how some localities are experimenting with new forms of party building to adapt the party's traditional practices to the new situation brought about by more than two decades of economic reform. This discussion of the new challenges in party building will provide the necessary background for the subsequent chapters which will explore how the CCP is creating new institutional links with business associations and co-opting private entrepreneurs into the party. These alternatives to traditional party building are designed to better integrate the party with the growing private sector.

### CHANGING CRITERIA FOR PARTY RECRUITMENT

Since its arrival as the ruling party of China in 1949, a key and divisive issue confronting the CCP has been the appropriate skills and political backgrounds of potential party members. During the Maoist era, the party alternated between periods of radicalist upsurges designed to transform the economy and society and periods of recovery designed to resume economic production and social order.[2] As policies changed, so too did criteria for recruitment. During periods of radicalism, when the party pursued utopian goals in its economic and social policies and promoted class struggle in its relations with society, the party rewarded political reliability and ideological fervor, while downgrading – and in some cases persecuting – technical expertise and intellectual freedom. Mao's calls in 1962 to "never forget class struggle" and in 1966 to seize power from capitalist roaders within the party therefore defined the key goal in party work and also shaped the state–society relationship in those years. In the eyes of Mao and his supporters, the continued presence of class enemies and the consequent ongoing need for class struggle meant that some people were not fit to be a part of the political system, and certainly not to be members of the CCP. In contrast, when the party emphasized economic development during periods of recovery from radical policies, the party targeted for advancement those with the experience and skills needed to manage the economy and impose order. Most

---

[2] Richard Lowenthal, "Development versus Utopia in Communist Policy," in Chalmers Johnson, ed., *Change in Communist Systems* (Stanford: Stanford University Press, 1970); G. William Skinner and Edwin A. Winckler, "Compliance Succession in Rural China: A Cyclical Theory," in Amitai Etzioni, ed., *A Sociological Reader on Complex Organizations* (New York: Holt, Rinehart, and Winston, 1969).

often, these types of people had to be "rehabilitated," that is restored to office and public life, after suffering persecution during a previous radical phase.

Rather than evolving in a linear fashion, therefore, the CCP remained stuck in recurring cycles of transformation and consolidation in its political and economic policies. This was so largely because Mao resisted the institutionalization of the party.[3] As a result, the debate over the proper qualities of party members and cadres was never decisively resolved and the criteria for recruitment periodically shifted between "redness" and expertise. The alleged presence of class enemies and the consequent ongoing need for class struggle meant that some people were excluded from the political system and from the CCP in particular. This is the essence of an exclusionary recruitment policy, appropriate for both the periods of transformation and consolidation.

Not only did the quality of party members and officials change with the party line, so too did the quantity of those recruited. During periods of radicalism, recruitment standards were dropped and the number of new recruits blossomed; during periods of recovery, the party typically froze new recruitment and weeded out the unqualified members or gave them the necessary training. For instance, the party grew by over 50 percent during the Great Leap Forward: it recruited 6.42 million new members during 1958–60, including 3.23 million in 1958 alone. Between 1961 and 1964, however, the party grew only from 17.38 million to 18.01 million as the party again emphasized quality standards and imposed a virtual freeze on new recruitment. The beginning of the Cultural Revolution signaled the beginning of another "high tide," with recruitment characterized by political criteria and leftist loyalties at the expense of technical expertise. As a result, the party doubled in size during the Cultural Revolution decade.[4]

Over time, however, the "red versus expert" debate took its toll on the party's organization. Most members had been recruited during periods of radicalism; their loyalty to the party and skills at mass mobilization did not compensate for their deficiencies in education and professional competence. Moreover, the party at all levels was divided by factionalism: experts were forced to work

---

[3] For the phases of transformation, consolidation, and adaptation for one-party systems, see Samuel P. Huntington, "Social and Institutional Dynamics of One-Party Systems," in Samuel P. Huntington and Clement H. Moore, eds., *Authoritarian Politics in Modern Society: The Dynamics of Established One-Party Systems* (New York: Basic Books, 1970), p. 9; for its relevance to China's political evolution under Mao and afterwards, see my *Democratization in China and Taiwan: The Adaptability of Leninist Parties* (Oxford and New York: Oxford University Press, 1997).

[4] Zhao Shenghui, *Zhongguo gongchandang zuzhi shi gangyao* (Outline of the CCP's Organizational History) (Anhui: Anhui renmin chubanshe, 1988), p. 338; Li Lieman, "*Gongchandang 70 nian dangyuan fazhan gailue yi qishi*" (Outline and Revelation of 70 Years of CCP Recruitment), *Lilun xuexi yuekan* (Fuzhou), August 30, 1991, pp. 30–33.

in the same office as the reds who had attacked them in previous campaigns. By the end of the Maoist era, the party organization was too divided to govern effectively or to maintain a coherent policy direction.

The transition to the post-Mao era of reform and opening led to a fundamental change in the party's work. In December 1978, the CCP's central committee decreed that the period of class struggle was over, and that the CCP would begin to concentrate on economic modernization as its key task. This change in the party's main mission brought about changes in its priorities for recruiting new members and appointing key personnel. These priorities changed for two reasons. First, the goals of the regime changed and new skills were now needed to perform new tasks. This is functional adaptation, resulting from a simple means-ends calculation about the party's work. Better educated, more professionally competent people and those with the types of technical skills needed for economic modernization were recruited in large numbers and appointed to key posts. The party also tried to reconcile its relations with society, damaged during the Cultural Revolution decade and previous periods of radicalism. Victims of previous political campaigns were released from prison and exonerated; former "class enemies" had their political labels removed and were welcomed into the definition of the "people." The party's reconciliation policies included the end of persecution of alleged class enemies, the release of political enemies from prison camps, expanded exposure to foreign media, greater travel and education opportunities, and enhanced artistic creativity and labor mobility.[5] In this sense, recruitment policies changed as a rational response to new goals, and the change was apparent from the very beginning of the reform era.

The second reason for the CCP's new recruitment policy is more overtly political, and did not become apparent until after the reforms were well underway. The party's new goal of economic modernization created new social and economic elites. The CCP had to cooperate with these elites in order to succeed with modernization and in some cases had to compete with them for local support. They thus represented potential threats to the regime if left outside the party. The CCP chose to co-opt some of these emerging elites to take advantage of their popular prestige, accomplishments, and above all their contributions to the party's preeminent goal of economic growth. This policy of co-optation symbolized a shift in the party's recruitment toward more inclusionary practices. It also prompted a debate within the CCP between those who argued the party had to adapt to survive and those who felt this particular form

---

[5] In Hungary, similar policies of reconciliation were used to improve the ruling communist party's relations with society. See Yanqi Tong, "State, Society, and Political Change in China and Hungary," *Comparative Politics*, vol. 26, no. 3 (April 1994), pp. 333–353.

of adaptation undermined party traditions and thereby reduced its long-term survivability rather than enhanced it. This debate exemplified the challenge all organizations face as they adopt new tasks and confront new challenges. The evolution of this debate and its implications for the party's adaptation will be detailed in Chapter 4.

## THE INTENDED CONSEQUENCES OF NEW RECRUITMENT POLICIES

As the CCP abandoned class struggle as its core task and shifted to economic modernization, it first weeded out those whose radical tendencies made them unlikely supporters of reform and also rehabilitated the victims of past political campaigns, especially the anti-rightist movement of 1956–7 and the Cultural Revolution of 1966–76. These victims were generally too old and poorly educated to guarantee the success of reform, so the party first rehabilitated and exonerated them and then eased them into retirement.[6] To replace these aging cadres, the CCP also recruited those who were "more revolutionary, younger, better educated, and more professionally competent." Despite some initial reluctance by recruiters to accept intellectuals, especially those still in college, into the party, eventually the new criteria transformed the membership of the party.[7] By the 15th Party Congress in 1997, the percentage of party members with a senior high school or better education was 43.4 percent, up from 12.8 percent in 1978, and 92 percent of central committee members had at least some college education. The proportion of cadres with college education was 93.5 percent at the provincial level, 91.5 percent at the prefectural level, and 83.6 percent at the county level.[8] To paraphrase the title of Hong Yung Lee's book on the subject, this led to a transformation of the party from revolutionaries to technocrats.[9] Cheng Li describes this transformation, with a touch of hyperbole, as "not only the largest peaceful elite turnover in Chinese history, but it is probably the most massive, rapid change of elites within any regime in human history."[10] The CCP was less successful recruiting youth and therefore in the mid-1980s adopted

---

[6] Melanie Manion, *Retirement of Revolutionaries in China: Public Policies, Social Norms, Private Interests* (Princeton: Princeton University Press, 1993).

[7] Stanley Rosen, "The Chinese Communist Party and Chinese Society: Popular Attitudes toward Party Membership and the Party's Image," *Australian Journal of Chinese Affairs*, no. 24 (July 1990), pp. 51–92; Hsi-sheng Ch'i, *Politics of Disillusionment: The Chinese Communist Party under Deng Xiaoping, 1978–1989* (Armonk, NY: M. E. Sharpe, 1991).

[8] *Qiushi* (February 1, 1999), pp. 23–27, in FBIS (February 16, 1999).

[9] Hong Yung Lee, *From Revolutionary Cadres to Party Technocrats in Socialist China* (Berkeley: University of California Press, 1991).

[10] Cheng Li, *China's Leaders: The New Generation* (Lanham, MD: Rowman and Littlefield, 2001), p. 34.

the standard that two-thirds of new recruits had to be less than 35 years old. However, the party as a whole continued to age and the percentage of all party members under 35 actually fell from 27.3 percent in 1987 to 22.4 percent in 1997.[11] When the CCP celebrated its 80th anniversary in 2001, it had grown to 64.5 million members, approximately 5 percent of China's total population. Of that number, 17.4 percent were women, and 6.2 percent belonged to China's ethnic minorities. Almost half were under 45 years old. This numerical growth and improvements in levels of education, however, masked signs of organizational decay which will be described below.

By the late 1980s, more orthodox leaders began to argue that the exclusive reliance on expertise had pushed aside political reliability as a criterion for recruitment and promotion.[12] From their perspective, the proletariat was being squeezed out by economic and technical elites: "progressive" forces (i.e., workers and peasants) were declining in numbers and influence, while those who until recently had been persecuted as "reactionary" forces (intellectuals and entrepreneurs) were on the rise. A 1990 study of over 30,000 workers in 50 enterprises found that 8.3 percent of front-line workers were party members, less than half of the 17.9 percent found in a 1982 survey.[13] In contrast, a separate study found that one quarter of technical specialists in state-owned enterprises (SOEs) were party members in 1987.[14] Although this latter group had contributed immeasurably to the success of the post-Mao economic reforms, they also threatened the party's traditional base. Renewed efforts to recruit workers was not intended to replace the need for expertise, but simply to restore the proletariat to its previous position of status within the party.

Concerns about emphasizing expertise over political reliability became especially prominent after the Tiananmen demonstrations of 1989. Many party members and cadres openly participated in these protests, demonstrating that the

---

[11] *Xinhua*, June 22, 1988, in FBIS, June 24, 1988, p. 19; *Xinhua*, October 6, 1992, in FBIS, October 6, 1992, p. 29; *Xinhua*, July 7, 1997, in FBIS (online service), July 7, 1997.

[12] For instance, see Li Yanxi, *"Shelun dangyuan duiwu de shuliang kongzhi"* (Limit the Number of CCP Members), *Xuexi yu shixian* (Wuchang) (January 1989), pp. 49–51; Zhou Peng, *"Shinian lai fazhan dangyuan gongzuo de huigu"* (Review of the Past Ten Years of Party Recruitment), *Dangzheng wenhui* (Luoyang) (January 1989), p. 12; Dong Wanmin, *"Yange anzhao biaozhun fazhan dangyuan"* (Recruit Party Members Strictly According to Standards), *Henan ribao*, January 7, 1991.

[13] The 1982 survey was conducted by the CCP's central secretariat research office; The 1990 survey was conducted by the Chinese Mechanical and Electrical Industry Staff and Workers Ideological and Political Work Society. See Gong Kaijin, *"Qiye lingdao tizhi yu dang zuzhi zai qiyezhong de diwei"* (The Enterprise Leadership System and the Role of Party Organizations within Enterprises), *Qiye wenming* (Chongqing) (March 1995), pp. 25–28.

[14] Zhou Peng, *"Shinian lai fazhan dangyuan gongzuo de huigu"* p. 12.

party was losing not only its external support but more importantly its internal cohesion. In a December 1989 speech at the central party school, CCP general secretary Jiang Zemin said, "We must make sure that the leading authority of all party and state organs is in the hands of loyal Marxists."[15] A commentator's article in *People's Daily*, the CCP's official paper, criticized two errors in recruiting cadres: first, focusing on education and professional competence at the expense of being more revolutionary, and second, giving exclusive priority to intellectuals and ignoring workers, peasants, and others at the grass-roots level.[16]

After the June 1989 crackdown, the CCP changed its recruitment policies to match its orthodox rhetoric. It banned the recruitment of private entrepreneurs, denouncing them as exploiters of the working class and asserting that their interests were inimical to the party's. At the same time, the CCP paid new interest to recruiting "workers at the forefront of production." Age and education remained key criteria for new recruits, but now the party also sought out those directly involved in agricultural and industrial production and de-emphasized those engaged in administrative or intellectual pursuits. For instance, although 69.2 percent of the 1.87 million new party members recruited in 1994 reportedly were under 35 years old and 70.8 percent had a senior high school education or better, 854,000 (45.7 percent) were "forefront" farmers and workers, and only 328,000 (17.6 percent) were technical experts.[17] The CCP did not end its efforts to co-opt expertise, but tried to balance the new elites in the organization with its traditional supporters. In fact, beginning in the mid-1990s, as the pace of economic reform began to accelerate again, the CCP re-emphasized the value of entrepreneurial skills, especially for cadres.

The renewed emphasis on recruiting those workers at the "forefront of production" was meant to reduce the influence of "non-productive" trades, especially intellectuals and teachers, who were blamed for contributing to the 1989 demonstrations. One result was the reassertion of stricter party control over universities. The party is well represented among those employed in higher education; whereas roughly 5 percent of the general population belongs to the CCP, almost 40 percent of college teachers and administrators are party members.[18] But the 1989 demonstrations showed that party membership alone did not result in party loyalty. Consequently, the CCP took several steps to regain control over China's campuses. First, it abandoned the responsibility

---

[15] *Xinhua*, December 29, 1989, in FBIS, January 10, 1990, pp. 17–19.
[16] *Renmin ribao*, March 11, 1990, p. 1, in FBIS, April 5, 1990, p. 29.
[17] *Xinhua*, June 29, 1995, in FBIS, June 30, 1995, pp. 12–13.
[18] The exact figure in the early 1990s was 37.4 percent; see *Xinhua*, June 20, 1991, in FBIS, June 21, 1991, p. 22.

system for college presidents and returned leadership authority to the party committees. In June 1990, the party issued a "Circular on Strengthening Party Building in Higher Education Institutions," which emphasized the leading role of party committees. This was necessary, according to Li Tieying, member of the Politburo and minister of the State Education Commission, "to ensure that leadership positions remain in the hands of people who are loyal to Marxism."[19]

Second, special organizations were created throughout the country to handle the work of party building on campuses. Many colleges established party schools for the ideological training of their party members.[20] The most extreme example of this was at Peking University. Because of its prominent and visible role in the democracy movement, its incoming freshmen were forced to undergo a year of military training and ideological study before beginning regular classes.

Third, new emphasis was given to recruitment among college students. Party membership among college students dropped from 23,000 in 1982 to 16,000 in 1990 (put differently, from 1.9 percent to .8 percent of all college students). Following a recruitment drive, by mid-1995, there were 70,000 students who were party members (2.5 percent of all college students) in the more than 1000 colleges and universities nationwide.[21] At Peking University, 11.7 percent of all students (and 22.2 percent of graduate students) were party members by the end of 1998, up from 5.3 percent in 1991. Among all of Beijing's universities, 10.1 percent of students were party members.[22] In 2001, Xinhua reported that one-third of college students nation-wide had applied for party membership.[23] This rapid and dramatic increase among university students demonstrated the CCP's desire to gain a foothold among the student body. In short, through the reassertion of the party committee's authority, ideological training, and increased student recruitment, the CCP attempted to regain its control over China's campuses. After seeing large numbers of intellectuals engage in exit and voice during 1989, the CCP began to demand loyalty from them. In the views of most observers, however, the interest in party membership among

---

[19] Of the more than 1000 colleges and universities, only some 40 still experimented with the presidential responsibility system. See *Xinhua*, June 5, 1991, in FBIS, June 10, 1991, p. 30. Quote by Li Tieying is in *South China Morning Post*, April 13, 1990, p. 10, in FBIS, April 13, 1990, p. 25.

[20] Xinhua, September 26, 1990, in FBIS, October 3, 1990, pp. 14–15.

[21] Ch'i, *Politics of Disillusionment*, p. 142; Xinhua, June 27, 1995, in FBIS, June 28, 1995, p. 44.

[22] *Xinhua*, April 30, 1999. See also Erik Eckholm, "At China's Colleges, a Rush To Party, as in Communist," *New York Times* (January 31, 1998).

[23] *Xinhua*, June 2, 2001.

university students was driven by the desire to make connections that would be useful in business, not by the appeal of the party's ideology or image.

But as the economy shifted more and more away from the state sector during these years, the orthodox concerns over the qualities of party members and cadres conflicted with the economic priorities set by the party and especially with the interests of local party committees. Some local officials, and even more rank-and-file party members, chose to take the plunge into the private sector, and in doing so they lost touch with their original party organization and ceased being active party members. Others attempted to ally themselves with local elites, primarily successful entrepreneurs and leaders of clans and triads, which reemerged with the decline of party controls over society and now compete with local party committees for influence and prestige. Although central policy forbade those actions, local party committees nevertheless sought out these local elites in order to preserve the party's influence.

The CCP's adoption of new recruitment policies to match its shift from class struggle to economic modernization was generally successful, as seen in the aggregate statistics of party members and cadres noted above. However, other aspects of party building have been more problematic, as will be seen below.

## THE UNINTENDED CONSEQUENCES OF ECONOMIC REFORM FOR PARTY RECRUITMENT

The creation of a market economy has created new opportunities for pursuing personal goals that do not require joining the party. Indeed, party membership is now seen by many as detrimental to fulfilling individual interests.[24] The non-state sector (especially private enterprises and foreign joint ventures) is expanding so rapidly that the party's traditional party building efforts cannot keep pace. Party organizations in the countryside have weakened, and recruiting new members has become increasingly difficult. Moreover, many party members in rural areas have joined the "floating population" of migrant workers seeking jobs in coastal cities, further reducing the party's presence in the countryside. These threats to the party's integrity are indicators of the political decay of China's Leninist system. The tension between the party's attempts at adaptation and its traditional ways of recruitment and integration with various sectors of society

---

[24] For analysis of how the post-Mao reform policies have changed career strategies in China, see Andrew G. Walder, "Career Mobility and the Communist Political Order," *American Sociological Review*, vol. 60, no. 3 (June 1995), pp. 309–328; Bruce J. Dickson and Maria Rost Rublee, "Membership Has Its Privileges: The Socioeconomic Characteristics of Communist Party Members in Urban China," *Comparative Political Studies*, vol. 33, no. 1 (February 2000), pp. 87–112.

is becoming more pronounced in the course of economic modernization, resulting in unwanted and unintended consequences for the party's organization.

### Enterprises Without Party Organization

One hallmark of a Leninist party is the penetration of both state and society with a network of party cells, but this is now being challenged with the explosion of new enterprises. The new collectively and privately owned and foreign-funded enterprises are being created so fast that the party cannot create organizations within most of them, and many do not even have party members in them. This rapid expansion of the non-state sectors has weakened the CCP's ability to monitor and control what goes on there. As Andrew Walder notes, monitoring capacity is one of the key elements of a communist system. As it declines, so too does the stability of the political system.[25] An additional problem arising from the weak presence of the party in the non-state sectors of the economy is that these are sources of some of China's best talent. The people who are attractive to private enterprises and joint ventures as prospective managers and workers are also attractive to the party as potential future members. If the party is not actively recruiting in these growing sectors of the economy, it will shut itself off from the best supply of human resources.

China's media and party journals report the weak presence of the party within the non-state sector. According to national statistics in late 1988, there were only 180,000 party members among the roughly 18 million *getihu*[26] (1 percent), and in Shanghai there were only 1135 party members among the 160,000 *getihu* (.7 percent); the vast majority of these *getihu* party members were old and middle-aged who had resigned from their original units, with very few new recruits.[27] At the end of 1993, Anhui had over 1.66 million township and village enterprises (TVEs), but around 90 percent had no party organization, and almost half had no party members. In 1994, only 171 of Tianjin's over 7000 village-run or jointly-run enterprises had a party branch and less than 2000 had party cells; in other words, roughly two-thirds of these enterprises had no party organization. Heilongjiang had almost 43,000 township, collective, and

---

[25] Andrew G. Walder, "The Decline of Communist Power: Elements of a Theory of Institutional Change," *Theory and Society*, vol. 23, no. 2 (April 1994), pp. 297–323.

[26] *Getihu* are individually owned enterprises and are allowed to hire no more than seven workers. Firms classified as "private enterprises" do not have restrictions on the number of workers they employ.

[27] *"Bixu jiaqiang geti laodongzhe zhong dang de zuzhi jianshe"* (Must Strengthen the Party's Organization Building among Private Workers), *Dangzheng luntan* (Shanghai) (October 1988), pp. 28–31.

cooperative enterprises in late 1994, but 54.7 percent had no party members. In Guizhou, 63.5 percent of TVEs had no party organization, and the figure rose to 75 percent for commercial, service, and food collectives.[28] In Zhejiang's Shaoxing city, only 696 of 8,838 private enterprises had party organizations (7.9 percent) as of June 1999. Moreover, 85 percent of private enterprises were family firms, and in some of them the only party members were relatives of the owner, suggesting their primary interests lay with the firm (and by extension the family), not the party.[29] In Shenzhen, the party acknowledged that party building in private enterprises was the weakest part of party building: of the more than 13,000 private enterprises in 1995, only 17 had basic level party organizations and less than 1 percent of workers in private enterprises were party members.[30]

The weakness of party building in the private sector was closely tied to the ban on admitting private enterprise owners into the party. Although some feared that the presence of private entrepreneurs in the party would be a bad influence and weaken the party from within, others argued they represented a new productive force and were the source of new jobs and economic growth. Each view is one-sided, and ignores the fact that the ban had the unintended consequence of inhibiting party building in the private sector. The ban made entrepreneurs less than enthusiastic about creating party organizations in their enterprises. Staff and workers could be recruited into the party, but the owners could not. Under those circumstances, the party made little progress in expanding its organizations into the private sector.[31]

The weakness of party organizations within foreign joint ventures presents a stickier problem. Many foreign investors do not want to have party members

---

[28] For Anhui, see Yang Yongmin, *"Ba nongcun dangjian gongzuo tigao dao xin de shuiping"* (Raise Rural Party Building Work to New Levels), *Dangjian yanjiu* (Beijing) (July 1994), pp. 13–16; for Tianjin, see Zheng Yusheng, *"Dui shichang jingji tiaojian xia cunji dang zuzhi jianshe de wudian"* (Five Suggestions for Village Level Party Organization Work under Market Economy Conditions), *Qiuzhi* (Tianjin) (September 1994), pp. 27–28; for Heilongjiang, see Harbin Heilongjiang People's Radio, November 8, 1994, in FBIS, November 10, 1994, p. 74; for Guizhou, see Huang Jun, *"Kaichuang nongcun dangjian gongzuo xin jumian"* (Initiate a New Phase in Rural Party Building Work), *Lilun yu dangdai* (Guiyang) (July 1994), pp. 20–21.

[29] Zhao Dingguo, Wang Yonghuo, and Xu Di, *"Jiji wentuo di tuijin feigong youzhi qiye dangjian gongzuo"* (Actively Promote Party Building in Non-State Owned Enterprises), *Shaoxing wenli xueyuan xuebao: Zhe-she ban* (April 1999), pp. 66–73.

[30] Lu Ruifeng, Zhong Yinteng, Xu Libin et al. *"Shenzhen shi siying qiye dangde jianshe wenti yu duice"* (Problems and Countermeasures in Party Building in Shenzhen's Private Enterprises), *Tequ lilun yu shixian* (Shenzhen) (December 1995), pp. 37–39.

[31] Zhou Linghua and Zheng Hefu, *"Siying qiye: Dangjian luohou de yuanyin ji duice"* (Private Enterprises: The Causes and Policies toward Sluggish Party Building), *Dangzheng luntan* (Shanghai) (January 1995), pp. 29–30.

as employees, much less have a party organization within their enterprise. As a result, the party has had to remain "underground" in many of these ventures in deference to the foreign partners' wishes. In addition, many party members either lack the necessary management expertise and sales techniques and are unable to find jobs in foreign-funded or joint ventures or, in a wonderful example of sour grapes, believe that "it would hurt the party's dignity to learn from foreign capitalists," and are therefore unwilling to work for them. As a result, most key posts are filled by the foreign partner's personnel.[32] Even when the party is allowed to organize itself within a foreign-funded enterprise, party life is weak because it is subordinate to economic and business interests. Except for the annual democratic appraisal meeting, all other party activities must take place in workers' spare time. As a result, party life is restricted to the circulation of documents, self-study, and one-on-one talks. A study of joint venture firms in Shanghai found that many had no formal party branch and no full time party officials. At best, party leaders served as chairmen of the state-authorized union and tried to conduct party activities from that post. Much of the party's work seemed more in keeping with union activities than monitoring compliance with party policies: mediation between labor and management in labor disputes and carrying out social functions within the enterprise, such as caring for sick workers. Although party members were still expected to attend study meetings, these meetings often focused on production and sales strategies or management skills rather than political education. These may be useful functions that benefit the enterprises' performance, but they turn the members of these party organizations into support staff instead of leading personnel.[33] In Shenzhen and other cities as well, party secretaries in joint ventures served as the heads of labor unions because the party could not be organized openly.[34]

---

[32] *Liaowang*, June 13, 1994, pp. 24–25, in FBIS, July 15, 1994, pp. 21–24. As always, the solution to these problems is said to be more education: to bring the practical skills of party members up to speed, on the one hand, and to correct the erroneous views toward foreign capitalists, on the other.

[33] "*Zhagen hezi qiye fahui dang de zhengzhi youshi*" (Establish Joint Ventures, Promote the Party's Political Superiority), *Dangzheng luntan* (Shanghai) (October 1999), pp. 21–23.

[34] Dong Lianxiang and Zu Qiang, "*Guanyu waishang touzi qiye dang de jianshe*" (Regarding Party Building in Enterprises with Foreign Investment), *Tansuo: Zhe-she ban* (Chongqing) (June 1995), pp. 11–13; Xu Genyi and Cheng Huiqiang, "*Qieshi jiaqiang waishang touzi qiye de dangjian gongzuo*" (Strengthen the Work of Party Building in Enterprises with Foreign Investment), *Lilun xuekan* (Jinan) (February 1995), pp. 31–34. Having the party secretary also serve as the head of the labor union was also used in SOEs like Shougang (Capital Steel) in order to give the party something to do within the enterprise. See Gong Kaijin, "*Qiye lingdao tizhi yu dang zuzhi zai qiye zhong de diwei*," (The Enterprise Leadership System and the Role of Party Organizations within Enterprises), *Qiye wenming* (Chongqing) (March 1995), pp. 25–28.

Some media stories report how these foreign partners become enlightened to the advantages of having hard-working party members as employees, but this propaganda does not refute a simpler truth: by the CCP's own admission, it is represented in a small minority of these joint ventures. In 3,092 foreign-funded enterprises created in thirty-four national level development zones as of late 1994, grass roots party branches had been set up in only 704. Moreover, little new party recruitment is taking place within these enterprises: of 8,278 party members, only 975 are new recruits; the rest transferred from other units.[35] In most foreign-funded enterprises, party members working within the enterprise remain on the rolls of their former department or firm. This makes party work in general difficult, and party building cannot be carried out in many of these enterprises.[36]

The party has identified these problems as increasingly serious and has proposed creating branches in new enterprises, or when they are too small to justify their own branch to form a joint branch with other small enterprises under the jurisdiction of the local party committee. A *People's Daily* report acknowledged that "we are faced with many new circumstances and new problems in building grass roots organizations in enterprises and cannot keep up with the needs of development of reform, opening up, and modernization." But the report also noted the resistance, even from within the party, to creating party organizations in private enterprises. Because the party's political aims are incompatible with economic aims, "some people advocated not establishing party organizations in enterprises and that party members in enterprises should be managed by local party organizations [e.g., a party branch under the municipal committee, instead of within the workplace]. This view is extremely erroneous and harmful."[37] Some party members, especially cadres and senior managers, also

---

[35] *Liaowang*, November 14, 1994, p. 13, in FBIS, December 21, 1994, p. 55. On the other hand, a Hong Kong newspaper reported that party organizations had been created in half of foreign-funded enterprises in operation in 1990; see *Ching chi tao pao*, September 13, 1990, pp. 12–13, in FBIS, September 17, 1990, pp. 17–18. Party organizations had reportedly been established in *all* of Tianjin's foreign-funded enterprises that had the appropriate conditions (this was not specified, but presumably refers to the number of party members working within the enterprise): of the 590 such enterprises in operation as of June 1994, there were 114 general party branches and party branches. See *Tianjin ribao*, June 24, 1994, p. 2, in FBIS, July 1, 1994, pp. 48–49.

[36] In contrast to these reports on the low number of party members and party organizations in foreign owned and joint ventures, the rise in party membership among university students was reportedly fueled in part by the perception that it would make it easier to find jobs in the foreign sector. Students thought party membership would demonstrate that they were hard working, on good terms with their teachers, and had good organizational skills, making them desirable employees. See Stanley Rosen, "Chinese Youth in the Year 2000: Internationalization, Nationalism, and Pragmatism," paper prepared for the China Times Conference on the Chinese Media, University of Minnesota, May 19–20, 2001, p. 29.

[37] *Renmin ribao*, October 15, 1994, p. 5, in FBIS, November 11, 1994, p. 22.

reportedly feel that party work in foreign-funded enterprises is not essential, and may even "frighten foreign investors away and adversely affect the inflow of foreign capital." In Shenzhen, the city party committee had to emphasize that it was a special economic zone, not a special *political* zone, and therefore party organizations must be set up wherever enterprises develop. Only 60 percent of Shenzhen's shareholding enterprises and 900 of its foreign-funded enterprises (no percentage given) had party members.[38]

The weakness of party organizations in economic enterprises was not a concern for some in the party. Party journals have contained an ongoing debate on the continued relevance of party organizations within enterprises, regardless of their type of ownership. As China's enterprises are encouraged to adopt modern (i.e., Western) management practices, what role is there for the party? Western firms do not have offices for political oversight or monitoring the political propriety of the firm or improving the consciousness of its workers. In China's private enterprises, most decisions are made by the owner; in joint-stock companies, the decisions are made by boards of directors. Even where party committees do have input, they may lack the specialized knowledge required for the operations of modern firms and therefore be incapable of making informed decisions.

The ability of enterprises to hire their own managers and staff through open competition, a staple of market logic, is seemingly in contradiction to the principle of party control over cadres (*dang guan ganbu yuanze*). When the party does not directly control the assets of a firm, it is hard to make managers comply with party policies or to influence the firm's personnel practices. For example, the enterprise law stipulates that only stockholders have the authority to hire and fire board members and managers. When the enterprise's party committee does not hold shares in the firm, it may have difficulty leading or controlling board members and managers. Higher level party organs have means to persuade or coerce owners and managers, but the party organization within the firm has more limited means at its disposal. Party committees may still wield some influence in setting the standards for selection, investigating the political backgrounds of candidates, and approving the decisions by owners and shareholders, but this is less direct control than they enjoyed before, when they could directly appoint and remove managers and other personnel. If the party committee's preferences conflict with the economic interests of the firm, they may have a difficult time retaining influence.[39]

[38] *Liaowang*, November 14, 1994, p. 13, in FBIS, December 21, 1994, p. 55; Bruce Gilley, "Party Cells Multiply in Shenzhen," *Eastern Express* (Hong Kong), October 8–9, 1994, p. 9, in FBIS, October 24, 1994, pp. 58–59.

[39] See for instance, Organization Department of the Sichuan Provincial Party Committee, "*Shilun 'sankua' qiye jituan dang zuzhi zhengzhi hexin zuoyong de shixian xingshi he jiben tujing*"

Where party organizations have been created, they have often been staffed with surplus cadres from overstaffed party and government organs or by retired cadres. In Shenzhen, there has been resistance to accepting these "unproductive staff" in new enterprises. Moreover, the practice of using surplus personnel to build new party organizations also raises questions about their competence, ability, and vitality. Instead of being retired, these redundant personnel are being reassigned to areas already plagued by weak organization. Their arrival does not bode well for the invigoration of these new posts.

The relationship between party committees and management has also been a problem for SOEs, especially after the adoption of the so-called modern enterprise system of management. As one study pointed out, with the separation of the party from government and administration, party organizations in SOEs were stripped of their social function powers in the enterprise, and at the same time they were less able to perform their traditional political functions. Without being able to perform social functions, the party's political functions are empty.[40] The propriety and continued relevance of party committees within SOEs has also been a source of debate. To make sure that the party continued to play an active and influential role in SOEs, most SOEs in Shanghai adopted internal regulations that half of the members of the party committee must also be members of the board of directors and that at least one-third of the members of the party committee be managers with the enterprise. In one survey of Shanghai SOEs, party secretaries also served as chairmen of the board in 49 of 59 firms, and deputy party secretaries served as chairmen in another 7.[41] A subsequent report concluded that this arrangement worked fine when the state was the major stockholder, but not when the state had less influence, as in foreign and private joint ventures.[42]

---

(On the Practical Form and Basic Means of the Party's Organizational and Political Core Role in 'Three Trans' Enterprises), *Zuzhi renshixue yanjiu* (Lanzhou) (June 1998), pp. 35–39; Lou Ximing and Wu Jian, "*Dang guan ganbu yuanze yu jingyingzhe jingzheng shanggang*" (The 'Party Controlling Cadres' Principle and the Advantages of Competitive Recruitment of Enterprise Managers), *Xingzheng yu renshi* (Shanghai) (January 1999), pp. 26–27; Chen Shaoyi, "*Dui guoyou gongsizhi qiye jianchi dang guan ganbu yuanze de sikao*" (Thoughts on the 'Party Controlling Cadres' Principle in State Owned Enterprises), *Lilun tantao* (Harbin) (February 1999), pp. 88–90.

[40] Gong, Kaijin "*Qiye lingdao tizhi yu dang zuzhi zai qiye zhong de diwei.*"

[41] "'*Shuangxiang jinru jiaocha renshi' shi yizhong youxiao de jizhi*" ('Two-way Entry and Overlapping Personnel' Is an Effective Mechanism), *Dangjian yanjiu* (September 1999), pp. 15–17.

[42] Zhou Heling, "*Dangqian jiceng dang zuzhi he dangyuan duiwu jianshe de jige wenti*" (Several Problems Regarding Grass Roots Party Organizations and Party Members), *Dangzheng luntan* (Shanghai) (April 2000), pp. 4–7.

43

## Mobile Party Members

Many CCP members have joined the "floating population" for the same reason as the general population: the promise of better and higher paying jobs elsewhere. Estimates are that roughly 2.5 million CCP party members are mobile, constituting about 4 to 5 percent of all party members and about 2 to 3 percent of the estimated floating population of 80 to 100 million. In more economically developed areas, mobile party members make up close to 10 percent of the total floating population.[43]

From the party's standpoint, this creates two problems. First, most mobile party members are young and middle-aged and either business oriented or "back-bone workers," precisely the kinds of people the party is trying to attract. Second, mobile party members lose touch with their original party unit and usually do not register with the party committee in their new location, thus, they cannot perform their responsibilities or "vanguard role." The absence of party organization makes it easy for them to avoid party discipline, not pay party dues and taxes, and engage in criminal or disruptive activities, thereby setting a poor example for other vendors and workers.

The mobility of party members also contributes to the weakness of party building in the private sector. Most mobile party members come from rural areas and are unwilling to join party branches in their new workplaces or neighborhoods. They believe that if they encounter difficulties, they are more likely to get assistance from party organizations in their hometowns, where they have some degree of status and connections, than in their new and often temporary working and living arrangements.[44] Local party committees therefore have tried to organize these mobile party members and monitor their activities. Mobility certificates are given to party members who have been away from their villages for more than six months. They are supposed to register with the party committee in their new locale, take part in meetings and study sessions, and pay dues.[45] To prevent its party members from becoming inactive, one village organized its own party branch for eight party members who had migrated from the village to Shanghai. They were required to meet once a month for a party group activity, but received no oversight and were not affiliated with any party

---

[43] Liang Yanjia and Li Kaisheng, *"Jiguan qishiye danwei dangyuan liudong de diaocha he sikao"* (Investigation and Reflection on Mobile Party Members in Administrative and Enterprise Units), *Lingnan xuekan* (Guangzhou) (January 1994), pp. 53–56; *Hong Kong Standard*, December 29, 1994, p. 5, in FBIS, pp. 33–34; *Ming Pao* (Hong Kong), February 3, 1995, p. A4, in FBIS, February 6, 1995, p. 24.

[44] Zhou Linghua and Zheng Hefu, *"Siying qiye: Dangjian luohou de yuanyin ji duice."*

[45] *Ming Pao* (Hong Kong), February 3, 1995, p. A4, in FBIS, February 6, 1995, p. 24.

organization in Shanghai.[46] However, these new regulations seem weak and unlikely to entice mobile party members back into party life, especially when the cadres responsible for their organization are already retired and have little appreciation for the economic interests that motivate the migrants' behavior.[47] These mobile party members have already decided that their economic interests outweigh their obligation to the party, and has been noted above, these party obligations interfere with getting rich because time lost in party meetings is time lost earning money. Adding new responsibilities to the mobile party members in the new locale is unlikely to return them to active party life. Moreover, the CCP is already having large problems recruiting youth from the countryside (see below); adding to the burden of party members is unlikely to help the recruitment efforts.

### Declining Rural Recruitment

The decollectivization policies that were a centerpiece of the early post-Mao reforms also had a negative impact on party recruitment. Once agricultural production changed from the commune system back to individual farming, farmers lived and worked separately and made production decisions on their own. Under those conditions, they were less reliant on the local party organization and had less incentive to join the party. The rural grass roots party organizations had much less control over farmers and agricultural production and consequently were less able to organize party activities.[48] In 1994, the CCP announced that half of its rural party branches had become inactive, a shocking admission of the decay of the party's most basic organizations.

In the countryside, there is a wide-spread belief that the burdens of membership outweigh the advantages. Rural youth are reluctant to join the party because they are worried they will have to attend meetings, obey strict discipline and have limits on their range of actions. Peasants believe that there is no point in applying if they are not well educated because they will be unable to become cadres.[49] As a result, most of those applying for membership in rural areas

---

[46] *"Nantong shi yi liuzhong moshi guanli liudong dangyuan,"* (Nantong City Uses Six Methods to Manage Mobile Party Members), *Dangjian wenhui* (Luoyang) (November 1997), p. 21.

[47] *Renmin ribao*, February 28, 1994, p. 5, in FBIS, March 24, 1994, pp. 22–23.

[48] Liu Kaishou, *"Nongcun jiceng dang zuzhi jianshe mianlin de xin qingkuang he xin wenti"* (New Conditions and New Problems for Building Rural Grass Roots Party Organizations), *Tansuo: Zhe-she ban* (Chongqing) (March 1999), pp. 21–23, 27.

[49] *Zhenli de zhuiqiu* (Beijing), June 11, 1995, pp. 15–18, in FBIS, September 8, 1995, pp. 23–7; *"Nongmin rudang yaoqiu danhua xianxiang toushi"* (Examination of the Phenomenon of the Peasants' Weakened Demand to Enter the Party) *Renmin ribao*, March 31, 1989, p. 5.

are already basic level cadres. Even those with education are often reluctant to apply because they are afraid of being ridiculed.

As a result of these concerns, the rate of party recruitment has been declining. An investigation of almost 10,000 party members in almost 300 village branches in Rudong county revealed that less than one-quarter of them had been recruited in the post-Mao era, and the pace had declined, from 392 per year in 1977–8, to 145 per year in 1979–84, and to 128 per year in 1985–9.[50] In Liaoning, 14 percent of villages had not recruited new members in the five years before 1988, and by 1994 5.8 percent of villages had still not recruited new members in the previous five years. In 9 percent of Tianjin's rural villages, no recruitment took place in the five years prior to 1994. A report from Guizhou said that roughly 20 percent of party branches had not recruited new members in a long, but unspecified, time.[51] In Hunan's rural areas, the average age of party members in most villages is 55, and approximately 60 percent joined during the Cultural Revolution years. Only 20 percent have a high school or better education.[52] In other areas, new recruits are middle-aged, in part because the most talented and ambitious youth leave the village to seek employment elsewhere and are not available for recruitment.[53]

The weakness of party organizations in the rural areas is due not only to problems in recruitment but also economic and social changes brought about by the party's reform policies. The rapid development of TVEs and other rural enterprises with multiple modes of ownership has outpaced the party's ability to build grass roots party organizations. The mobility of party members who join the "floating population" in search of better jobs away from home make it difficult for their original party organizations to monitor their behavior and ensure that they remain active in party life. Party organizations in many rural areas have been unable to cope with these new challenges, but others have experimented with new forms of party building. For example, the party committee in Shaoxing, Zhejiang created a variety of party branches, including united party branches for two or more villages (usually the result of a prosperous village

---

[50] Chen Baoheng and Qian Yushen, *"Nongcun gaige yu xingzheng cun dang de jianshe"* (Rural Reform and Party Building in Administrative Villages), *Nantong xuekan* (April 1991), pp. 9–15.

[51] *Liaoning ribao*, January 12, 1995, in FBIS, February 13, 1995, p. 84; Zheng Yusheng, *"Dui shichang jingji tiaojian xia cunji dang zuzhi jianshe de wudian"*; Huang Jun, *"Kaichuang nongcun dangjian gongzuo xin jumian"* (Initiate a New Phase in Rural Party Building Work), *Lilun yu dangdai* (Guiyang) (July 1994), pp. 20–21.

[52] Huang Youtai and Zhou Yuping, *"Nongcun dang de jianshe yu shehui wending"* (Party Building and Social Stability in the Countryside), *Huxiang luntan* (Changsha) (June 1999), pp. 48–49.

[53] *"Guanyu Shanghai shi Chuanshe xian nongcun jiceng dang zuzhi jianshe zhuangkuang de diaocha"* (An Investigation of Basic Level Party Organization Building in the Rural Areas of Shanghai's Chuanshe County), *Dangzheng luntan* (Shanghai) (November 1988), pp. 38–42.

annexing a less developed village), for a village and a nearby urban neighborhood, or for a village and a TVE, with the TVE manager also serving as branch secretary; party branches for mobile party members who had migrated into Shaoxing; and party branches for specific industries.[54] Shanghai has also allowed united party branches that encompass a large TVE and its original village. This most often happens when a TVE has expanded beyond its original village to the point where the party members in the TVE outnumber the other party members in the village. In those cases, united party branches have been created with the TVE enjoying the largest share of power within the branch. When this happens, the TVE has effectively incorporated its village.[55]

Given the increasing prevalence of the economic logic of the marketplace, it is not surprising that economic solutions have been proposed to handle the problem of declining party recruitment. The argument goes like this: because party members are also citizens, they are affected by the reality of the market economy. The party should therefore offer economic incentives to its members to match the opportunities offered elsewhere in the economy and society. For instance, party members should be given material rewards for exhibiting the advanced conduct expected of them, and they should enjoy special rights, such as receiving higher pensions and being able to get their children into the army, schools, or jobs. These privileges are well known to be available to cadres, but not to rank-and-file members. Because members at the grass-roots level complain that they give more than they receive from the party, these types of incentives would make membership more attractive.[56] In one Fujian village, the local party branch spent 600,000 yuan to send village cadres and party members to universities for study in order to give village leaders advanced degrees. Another Fujian town bought insurance policies for its cadres as protection against bodily harm suffered on the job. Some had been beaten or even killed when implementing unpopular policies. The insurance policies would encourage them to faithfully carry out unpopular policies by guaranteeing support for their families in the

---

[54] "*Nongcun jiceng dang zuzhi shezhi de tansuo yu wanshan*" (Exploration and Perfection of Building Grass Roots Party Organizations in the Countryside), *Zuzhi renshixue yanjiu* (Lanzhou) (January 1999), pp 45–48.

[55] Zhang Mingchu, "*Xin qingkuang, xin bianhua, xin qushi: Shanghai diqu nongcun dang zhibu zuzhi shezhi de diaocha*" (New Conditions, New Changes, and New Trends: A Survey of Grass Roots Party Branches in Shanghai's Countryside), *Dangzheng luntan* (Shanghai) (February 1999); Zhang Mingchu, "*Xiandaihua yu nongcun dang zhibu shezhi de xin bianhua*" (Modernization and New Changes in Party Branches in the Countryside), *Shanghai dangshi yanjiu* (Supplement) (1999), pp. 143–146.

[56] Xiang San and Yang Junfa, "*Guanyu zai shehui zhuyi chuji jieduan baochi dang de xianjinxing de sikao*" (Thoughts on Preserving the Advanced Nature of the Party during the Primary Stage of Socialism), *Shehui kexue zhanxian* (Changchun) (February 1999), pp. 222–226.

case of accidents.[57] These proposals to provide financial incentives to party members to carry out their expected tasks clearly irked some in the party. A *People's Daily* article recalling Chen Yun's views on party building mentioned his disapproval of such schemes. "In my opinion, those who want to be paid for attending training classes or meetings can never become Communists."[58] The logic of the marketplace ran counter to traditional party building and party life.

The CCP is also hampered not only by low recruitment but also by weak organization in the countryside. The State Council reported in 1992 that 60 percent of rural party cells were weak and disorganized, and an additional 30 percent had collapsed altogether. According to a classified report issued by the central committee of the CCP, up to 75 percent of rural organizations were in "a state of collapse."[59] Into this political vacuum have stepped other organizations. Wang Zhen, one of the most conservative of the revolutionary elders (now deceased), complained that the party was losing control of the countryside to reactionary forces, both traditional clans and triads and also newly established Christian churches. He claimed that churches regularly attracted hundreds and even thousands to their services but the party could not even get its own members to attend meetings despite offering to pay them one yuan (!). Party leaders had to ask church leaders to announce party activities and encourage their parishioners to attend.[60] According to Hebei provincial party secretary Cheng Weigao, weak grass roots organizations in some rural areas led to the "rampage of evil forces and even the control of a few villages by degenerate elements, bad elements, and some reactionary forces. In others, the party's grass roots exist only in form and they enjoy no prestige among the masses."[61] In Hunan's Dingcheng and Hanshou districts, over 90 percent of clan leaders were reportedly party members. According to *Legal Daily* (*Fazhi ribao*), clans and triads had supplanted party committees in some areas and as a result crime had spread unchecked.[62] Clans were said to also control "a very large portion" of private enterprises and township and village collective enterprises, allowing

---

[57] You Longbo, "*Xin shiqi Fujian yanhai nongcun xianjin dang zhibu jianshe de chenggong jingyan*" (The Successful Experiences of Building Party Branches in the Coastal Villages of Fujian), *Zhonggong Fujian shengwei dangxiao xuebao* (July 1999), pp. 53–56.

[58] "Do a Good Job in 'Three Stresses' Education, Step Up Party Building – Studying Comrade Chen Yun's Idea on Building of Party Work Style and Clean Government in the New Period," *Renmin ribao*, April 13, 1999, p. 9, in FBIS, April 21, 1999.

[59] Cited in Pei Minxin, "'Creeping Democratization' in China," *Journal of Democracy*, vol. 6, no. 4 (October 1995), p. 73.

[60] *South China Morning Post*, March 12, 1991, pp. 1, 9, in FBIS, March 12, 1991, pp. 32–33.

[61] *Hebei ribao*, June 21, 1995, pp. 1–2, in FBIS, July 7, 1995, p. 58.

[62] *South China Morning Post*, April 28, 1995, p. 7, in FBIS, April 28, 1995, pp. 14–15; *Agence France Presse*, May 3, 1994, in FBIS, May 3, 1994, pp. 21–22.

them to dominate both the local economy and the local government.[63] They also actively protect their villages from economic competition, often eliciting local party and police organs in their efforts. These critiques are echoed by some of China's leading dissident intellectuals, who blame the rise of evil forces in the countryside on the government's loosened control over rural society.[64]

Both the problems of weak party organization and the rise of "feudal" influences are concentrated in the poorest of rural areas, areas where the economic reforms have had the least impact and where the party has few tangible incentives available to maintain the loyalty of local organizations and party members.[65] In fact, the introduction of elections in rural areas in the 1980s may itself have weakened the party's authority. In some western and central areas (i.e., the less economically developed), winners of village elections are often from traditional clans and churches. As a result, the party "must rely on consultations between local party and government organs and local forces to exercise rule over the rural areas."[66] According to Kevin O'Brien's investigation of village elections, township officials and village cadres "argue, with some evidence, that elections may enhance participation and autonomy only for dominant lineages and that other lineages will be effectively disenfranchised."[67] A nationwide survey revealed that clans influenced outcomes in 40 percent of village level elections.[68]

LOCAL EXPERIMENTS IN PARTY BUILDING

Recognizing the weakness of party building during the reform era, a variety of alternatives to traditional party building have been proposed and experimented with. Some have been mentioned above. In this section, innovations in Shenzhen and Xishan will be described.

---

[63] According to "semi-official reports," cited in Pei, "Creeping Democratization," p. 73.

[64] He Qinglian, *Xiandaihua de xianjing: dangdai Zhongguo de jingji shehui wenti* (*The Trap of Modernization: Economic and Social Problems in Contemporary China*) (Beijing: Jinri Zhongguo chubanshe, 1998), especially chapter 8.

[65] *"Guanyu Shanghai shi Chuanshe xian nongcun jiceng dang zuzhi jianshe zhuangkuang de diaocha"* (An Investigation of Basic Level Party Organization Building in the Rural Areas of Shanghai's Chuanshe County), a report by the party building investigation team of Shanghai's municipal party school system, *Dangzheng luntan* (Shanghai) (November 1988), pp. 38–42; Zhong Zhushang, *"Nongcun jiceng dang zuzhi xianzhuang tanxi"* (Examination of Current Conditions in Rural Basic Level Party Organizations), *Liaowang yuekan*, January 1990, pp. 12–14; *South China Morning Post*, April 28, 1995, p. 7, in FBIS, April 28, 1995, pp. 14–15.

[66] *South China Morning Post*, April 28, 1995, p. 7, in FBIS, April 28, 1995, pp. 14–15; *Lienhopao* (Hong Kong), July 18, 1995, p. 8, in FBIS, August 23, 1995, p. 20.

[67] Kevin J. O'Brien, "Implementing Political Reform in China's Villages," *Australian Journal of Chinese Affairs*, no. 32 (July 1994), pp. 52, 56.

[68] Cited in Daniel Kelliher, "The Chinese Debate over Self-Government," *China Journal*, no. 37 (January 1997), p. 79.

## Shenzhen

The problem of adapting the party's grass roots organizations to the changing economic and social environment is probably nowhere greater than in the special economic zone Shenzhen. It has one of the most marketized economies in the country, and in fact was created to experiment with different market-oriented policies and practices when the rest of country was still part of the planned economy. A report from the Shenzhen party committee acknowledged many of the challenges it faced during the city's development. With resources now allocated by the market instead of economic plans made by party officials, what is the role of party organizations in state owned enterprises? With private enterprises operating with modern management practices (which do not include organs for political oversight), should party organizations be established in private enterprises, and if so, what should they do? With the rural economy in Shenzhen organized around joint stock companies, which make production and investment decisions on behalf of the village and in which villagers are stock holders, what is the role of village party committees? With the market economy requiring the free flow of labor, how can the party organize and monitor its mobile members?

Party building in Shenzhen's private sector got off to a slow start for several reasons. First, the local party leadership itself was hesitant to build party organizations within non-state owned enterprises, both because its role was small and uncertain initially and because the center had not issued clear guidelines on the party's role in the private sector. Second, mobile party members who migrated to Shenzhen from other areas did not want to transfer their membership and organizational relations to their new workplaces. In 1995, there were over 1000 mobile party members in Shenzhen's private enterprises, but only 236 had transferred their organizational registration to Shenzhen. Some did not want to go to the trouble of transferring their affiliation, because they frequently changed jobs. Others had a weak identification with the party, and did not want to be active in party life or restricted by party discipline. In other cases, the party organizations themselves did not want to be troubled with new members who were not long-term workers. Even where party organizations were established, they had a hard time being active. One party branch had over ninety members scattered across twenty enterprises. Although the branch held monthly meetings, no one attended or paid their requisite dues.[69]

---

[69] Lu Ruifeng, Zhong Yinteng, Xu Libin, et al. "*Shenzhen shi siying qiye dangde jianshe wenti yu duice*" (Problems and Countermeasures in Party Building in Shenzhen's Private Enterprises), *Tequ lilun yu shixian* (Shenzhen) (December 1995), pp. 35–37.

As in other areas, Shenzhen has experimented with new forms of party organizations. The city's Private Enterprise Association, for instance, has jurisdiction over party members and organizations in the private enterprises. This is part of the party's corporatist strategy of adaptation that will be explained in more detail in Chapter 3. In some villages, the party committee and the village's joint stock company fall under the same party branch, with a unified party organization but separate administrative organizations; in others, the village committee and the company have merged into a single party branch with a unified administrative organization. Unlike in Shaoxing and Shanghai (described earlier in this chapter), however, Shenzhen's goal is to separate these village committees and companies with both the committees and the companies having separate party organizations.[70]

Shenzhen has also experimented with ways of organizing its mobile party members. In July 1999, Shenzhen had about 5100 mobile party members (4.3 percent of party members in the city), including those in joint ventures and private enterprises which did not have party organizations and party members who formerly worked for SOEs but either quit to find jobs in the non-state sector or were laid off and were unemployed. The city's conventional way of dealing with mobile party members is called "collective management by responsible branches" (*guikou guanli*). Those working in joint ventures are supposed to be affiliated with the party organization within the enterprise, but as noted earlier in this chapter the vast majority of joint ventures do not have party branches within them. Those in private enterprises are affiliated with the private enterprise party branch in the chamber of commerce. Those who are self-employed (i.e., *getihu*) are affiliated with the city's Self-Employed Laborers' Association (SELA) branch. Professionals such as lawyers and accountants are affiliated with the party branches in their respective professional associations. Others are affiliated with party branches in their neighborhoods. The main problem with this approach is that the party branches to which mobile party members are supposed to be affiliated see these new members as a burden. The branches are expected to collect dues, organize activities, and be responsible for the behavior of mobile party members, but they often neglect these duties. To address this problem, Shenzhen has experimented with a new scheme in which the mobile party members establish their own party branches in their neighborhoods. A branch in the Xin'an neighborhood consisted of twenty-two members, including private entrepreneurs, technical staff from a joint venture,

[70] "*Jiji tansuo shehui zhuyi shichang jingji tiaojian xia dang de lingdao shixian xingshi*" (Exploring the Realization of the Party's Leadership under the Conditions of the Socialist Market Economy), *Tequ lilun yu shixian* (Shenzhen) (August 1999), pp. 13–17.

and the principal of a private school.[71] This type of innovation derives from the changing environment in China, in which the *danwei* is no longer the sole source of a person's economic, social, and political needs.[72] But neighborhood based branches specifically for mobile party members who are employed elsewhere and may have little interaction with one another are unlikely to lead them to an active party life or to improve the party's capacity to monitor their behavior and influence their thinking.

## *Xishan*

A study of party building in southern Jiangsu's Xishan city noted the tension between the ideological concerns of the party's recruitment policies and the practical need to build grass roots party organizations.[73] With the decline of the party's control over rural areas and the ever-growing importance of private firms in promoting economic development, the cooperation of private entrepreneurs was necessary for successful party building in the private sector. But because private entrepreneurs themselves were officially banned from joining the party, party building in private enterprises was exceedingly slow. Although one of Xishan's suburban towns, Luoshe, was known as a national model for party building, only 6 of its 256 newly privatized firms had a party branch. Another dilemma Xishan faced was whether to allow party branch secretaries to retain their posts after they went into business. There had been a policy that entrepreneurs should not hold leading posts in the party while they were in business, although they were able to retain their party membership. However, because of their indispensable role fostering economic development, in practice it proved difficult to exclude them from holding leadership posts in their party branches. Of the 526 villages under Xishan's jurisdiction, more than 60 had private entrepreneurs as party branch secretaries. The contradictions between policy and reality led to other types of local countermeasures. Some entrepreneurs delayed changing the ownership of their enterprise from collective to private until after their application for party membership was approved. Once they joined the party, they could immediately privatize their enterprise. Some party branches allowed the secretary to keep his post by allowing his

---

[71] *"Liudong dangyuan shequ guanli wenti tansuo"* (Exploring District Management of Mobile Party Members), *Tequ lilun yu shixian* (Shenzhen) (July 1999), pp. 13–16.

[72] Xiaobo Lü and Elizabeth J. Perry, eds., *Danwei: The Changing Chinese Workplace in Historical and Comparative Perspective* (Armonk, NY: M. E. Sharpe, 1997).

[73] For a vivid description of the growing prosperity of southern Jiangsu (Sunan), see Cheng Li, *Rediscovering China: Dynamics and Dilemmas of Reform* (Lanham, MD: Rowman and Littlefield, 1997), especially pp. 75–92.

enterprise to be held in the name of his wife.[74] These were creative ways to stay in technical compliance with the party's recruitment policies, but at the same time these countermeasures subverted the intentions of the policies.

A subsequent study of Xishan by the central party school found that changing ownership patterns had complicated party recruitment. As the city's township and village enterprises (TVEs) changed their original collective ownership system to other modes, including private ownership and joint-stock companies, their party organizations lost their vibrancy. Young people no longer required party membership to pursue their goals of a better life. That was still one option, of course, but they could also simply open their own business or migrate to larger cities in search of work. As a result, fewer young people were interested in joining the party. Moreover, once the TVEs were no longer collectively owned, many of their managers became categorized as private entrepreneurs and therefore technically unqualified to join the party due to the ban imposed in 1989. As we will see in Chapter 4, many private entrepreneurs nevertheless were recruited into the party in violation of central policy, but Xishan's experience also shows that the ban at a minimum put limits on the numbers of entrepreneurs who could join the party. Although other Xishan entrepreneurs wanted to join the party, the reclassification of their enterprises as privately owned complicated their relations with the party and prevented their gaining admission.

Because the party was not able to recruit effectively among young people and entrepreneurs, Xishan faced two problems. First, its party members were aging. Almost half of them were over fifty-five years old. According to the central party school's report, because their older members were not able to keep pace with new developments, this put local party organizations in an awkward position: they were reluctant to solicit the opinions of older party members, but could not entirely ignore them because as veteran party members, they had the right to participate in decisions affecting their community. Second, the range of people who were available for recruitment was narrowing. In particular, competent enterprise managers who were previously targeted for recruitment had become disqualified once they became private entrepreneurs. The authors of this report from the central party school advocated that talented people from non-state owned enterprises be eligible to join the party as long as they were otherwise politically qualified. They argued that people from the non-state sectors would bring needed vitality into the party and also aid in the construction of party

---

[74] Wang Changjiang and Jin Peixing, "*Dui feigong youzhi jingji zhong 'youxiu fenzi' de zhengce xuyao diaocha*" (An Examination of the Policy Requirements towards 'Outstanding Elements' in the Non-State Owned Enterprises), *Lilun qianyan* (Beijing), no. 21 (1998), pp. 20–22.

organizations within their enterprises. At the same time, they also suggested that the older party members be given honorary titles as a face-saving way to relieve them of some of their main responsibilities.[75] This report shows the rationale for lifting the ban and that support for doing so was present long before Jiang Zemin proposed doing so in July 2001.

## SUMMARY

More than two decades of economic reform have brought undeniable material benefits to many in China, but also new challenges for the CCP. The logic of the marketplace itself runs contrary to traditional expectations of proper party member behavior. Party members have difficulty maintaining party principles while operating in the market economy. They now have a diversity of roles: party members, but also enterprise managers, board directors, and in general participants in the market economy. Their obligations as party members often come into conflict with the opportunities in the market. For example, while the party encourages them to live simple and frugal lives, the market encourages them to live a lifestyle appropriate for their level of income.

The necessities of economic reform have also brought unpleasant side effects for many of those who constitute the party's traditional base. The many workers who have been laid off in the course of SOE reform no longer buy into the argument that they are the masters of the country or that the party represents their interests.[76] A growing number of farmers resent the tax burdens imposed on them by local party and government officials and other forms of mistreatment. This has led to increased incidences of local protests and organized appeals to higher levels for redress.[77] In both the cities and the countryside, it is the non-state sector that is the primary source of jobs for laid off workers and surplus rural labor. However, the party has had little success recruiting from within these enterprises or in building party organizations within them. In short, the traditional base of the party has eroded, but the most promising new source of recruitment and party building has not been successfully exploited, both because

---

[75] Liang Yanhui and Yuan Yidao, *"Xiangzhen qiye zhuanzhi hou dang de jianshe xin bianhua"* (New Changes in Party Building in Township and Village Enterprises That Have Changed Their Ownership Modes), *Zhongguo dangzheng ganbu luntan* (Beijing) (February 1999), pp. 32–33.

[76] Timothy B. Weston, "China's Labor Woes: Will Workers Crash the Party?" in Timothy B. Weston and Lionel M. Jensen, eds., *China beyond the Headlines* (Lanham MD: Rowman and Littlefield, 2000), pp. 245–272.

[77] See Lianjiang Li and Kevin J. O'Brien, "Villagers and Popular Resistance in Contemporary China," *Modern China*, vol. 22, no. 1 (January 1996), pp. 28–61; Thomas Bernstein, "Farmer Discontent and Regime Responses," in Merle Goldman and Roderick MacFarquhar, eds., *The Paradox of China's Post-Mao Reforms* (Cambridge: Harvard University Press, 1999), pp. 197–219.

of the inner party debates on the propriety of party building and recruitment in the non-state sectors and the reduced incentives for many to join the party.

These examples of decay in traditional party building reflect both the unintended consequences of reform and the conflict between the needs of the party and the logic of the market. Some local party officials argue that party organs should not be present in the non-state sectors of the economy specifically because they tend to retard growth and frighten off potential investors. From the perspective of the party, however, its organizational interests are being undermined by the deterioration of its support among its traditional base and its weak presence in the new sectors of the economy. As its capacity to monitor compliance with its policies, enforce norms of behavior, and mobilize society on behalf of regime goals deteriorates, the Leninist attributes of the CCP and its viability as the ruling party are also undermined. As Huntington noted, the strength of an authoritarian regime depends in large part on the strength of its party; as the party weakens, so too does the regime it governs.[78] While noting the positive trends of economic reform, we should not lose sight of the negative consequences for the CCP and the implications for the political system as a whole.

Although economic reforms have led to the decline in traditional party building, the party has not stood still and let the economy go by. To partially substitute for party building, and to develop closer ties to the dynamic non-state sectors, the party has devised a two-pronged strategy of creating new institutional links and co-opting the newly emerging economic elites. The elements of this strategy and its implications for China's political system will be examined in the following chapters.

---

[78] Huntington, "Social and Institutional Dynamics of One-Party Systems," p. 9.

# 3

# *New Institutional Links*

Social organizations should abide by the Constitution, laws, regulations, and the state's policy. They are not allowed to oppose the basic principles defined by the Constitution; endanger the state's unification and safety and national unity; damage the state's interests, public interests of society, and legal rights and benefits of other organizations and citizens; and go against social ethics and habit.[1]

T HE CCP's decision at the Third Plenum in December 1978 to abandon class struggle and to pursue economic modernization announced the beginning of the post-Mao reform era and the onset of the CCP's adaptation. These reforms led to profound changes in China's economy and society and consequently its politics. But it also set up a debate within the CCP between those who sought to protect party traditions and preserve their own positions on the one hand, and those who sought the party's adaptation to facilitate economic change, on the other. Although the end of class struggle and the onset of economic reform required the CCP to adopt new ways of organizing itself and interacting with society, many party stalwarts argued that these changes were undermining the party's ability to maintain order in China's political system. This desire to maintain party control while opening up the economy and society has bedeviled the CCP throughout the post-Mao era. While it has not succumbed to the inherent tension between these two seemingly incompatible goals, as many have predicted over the years, the question remains: will these changes lead to the CCP's rejuvenation, or to its eventual disintegration?

Organizations have two main strategies for coping with environmental change: creation of new links with other organizations and co-optation of new

---

[1] Article 4, "Social Organizations Registration and Management Regulations," *Xinhua*, November 5, 1998, in FBIS, November 6, 1998.

personnel. The first strategy is the topic of this chapter; the CCP's strategy of co-optation will be covered in the next chapter. This chapter will begin by describing how Leninist parties and other complex organizations create links with other organizations to gain access to more information and to better integrate themselves with their environment, and also will describe the inherent risks in doing so. It will then assess the CCP's corporatist strategy of allowing, within certain limits, new professional and social organizations to form and the implications of this strategy for promoting political change. Finally, it will look more carefully at the evolving relationship between entrepreneurs and local officials, beginning with a brief historical overview and then focusing in more detail on the political influence of business associations in the post-Mao reform era. This chapter will show that China's private entrepreneurs and their business associations are developing a propensity to assert their interests and to use their business associations to pursue individual and collective goods. However, they see themselves as partners, not adversaries, of the state. Moreover, in the areas that are most economically developed and where privatization has advanced the furthest, the views of entrepreneurs have converged with those of local party and government officials regarding the roles and policy influence of business associations. This harmony of views may vindicate the party's strategy of inclusion, but it is not consistent with the expectations of other scholars and many policy makers who expect China's growing class of entrepreneurs to play a leading role in promoting political change.

THEORETICAL AND POLITICAL RATIONALES FOR
NEW INSTITUTIONAL LINKS

When an organization creates links with other organizations in its environment, it helps facilitate adaptation. These links with other organizations allow information (and potentially influence) to flow between the organizations, elicit support for the organization, and may enhance its legitimacy.[2] Similarly, as a Leninist party enters the period of adaptation (or what Ken Jowitt calls inclusion), it substitutes the manipulation of symbols with the manipulation of organizations.[3] In other words, the party relies less on coercion and propaganda to control society and develops links with other organizations, either new ones that it sanctions or old ones it revives, such as united front organizations, labor

---

[2] Jeffrey Pfeffer and Gerald R. Salancik, *The External Control of Organizations: A Resource Dependence Perspective* (New York: Harper and Row, 1978), pp. 143–147.

[3] Ken Jowitt, "Inclusion," in *New World Disorder* (Berkeley: University of California Press, 1992), pp. 101–102; originally published as "Inclusion and Mobilization in European Leninist Regimes," *World Politics*, vol. 28, no. 1 (October 1975), pp. 69–97.

unions, or professional associations. These corporate groups allow the party to organize interests emerging in the course of reform. Links between the party and the organizations allow both the articulation of those interests and the preservation of the party's role as the arbiter of competing interests.[4] In China, the state has created a dense web of economic and social organizations in order to channel interest articulation, regularize the flow of information between the state and key groups in society, replace direct state controls over the economy and society with at least partial social regulation, and screen out unwanted groups. Thus, official recognition of social organizations serves the dual purpose of incorporating interests and viewpoints the state finds acceptable and repressing those it finds unacceptable or threatening.[5]

Establishing links with other organizations carries potential risks. As March and Olsen note, an organization that previously enjoyed extreme autonomy (as is the case for most Leninist parties prior to adaptation) may be "unable to cope with a world in which it does not have arbitrary control."[6] Moreover, creating links with other organizations may strengthen those organizations at the expense of the party. These organizations may develop an identity separate from the party and eventually seek to represent the interests of their members and resist acting as agents of the party. What begins with the party's manipulation of organizations may lead to those organizations' manipulation of the party. Such an arrangement is incompatible with a Leninist political system, which is designed to change society, not to be changed by it.

For one-party authoritarian regimes and complex organizations, the period of adaptation may be open-ended as the regime or organization makes repeated adjustments to its ever-changing environment. For Leninist parties, however, there is a tension between policies of inclusion and the party's mobilizational needs. Jowitt's original model of inclusion for Leninist parties implied it was a long-term and presumably open-ended strategy of survival, but later suggested it was simply the phase preceding the "Leninist extinction" because the liberalization that accompanied inclusion weakened the foundations of Leninist parties in Eastern Europe and the Soviet Union.[7] China's leaders have been wary of making a similar mistake, and have tried to limit the extent of inclusion

---

[4] Samuel P. Huntington, "Social and Institutional Dynamics of One-Party Systems," in Samuel P. Huntington and Clement H. Moore, eds., *Authoritarian Politics in Modern Society: The Dynamics of Established One-Party Systems* (New York: Basic Books, 1970), pp. 34–36.

[5] See Gordon White, Jude Howell, and Shang Xiaoyuan, *In Search of Civil Society: Market Reform and Social Change in Contemporary China* (Oxford: Oxford University Press, 1996).

[6] James G. March and Johan P. Olsen, *Rediscovering Institutions: The Organizational Basis for Politics* (New York: The Free Press, 1989), p. 47.

[7] Jowitt, "The Leninist Extinction," in *New World Disorder*, pp. 249–283.

in order to achieve "reform without liberalization,"[8] but have had a difficult time balancing the two elements of this dichotomy. As the CCP adopted economic modernization as its key task, it confronted precisely the same mobilizational challenges that are inherent to the period of inclusion for Leninist parties identified by Jowitt: increased social heterogeneity as the working classes developed a clearer identity independent of the state;[9] increased occupational and geographic mobility, which challenged the party's ability to monitor and control society;[10] the displacement of the traditional "revolutionary" classes by new elites with professional and technical skills;[11] the cynicism of youth, in particular the changing attitudes toward the party.[12] But the biggest challenge concerns the party's own identity. How can it reconcile its co-optation of wealthy businessmen and the promotion of entrepreneurial skills with its traditional status as a vanguard party representing the interests of workers, peasants, and soldiers? How can the party balance its desire to integrate with society to promote economic modernization with its desire to maintain its monopoly on legitimate political organization and its ability to mobilize society on behalf of political and social goals?

## THE CORPORATIST LOGIC OF PARTY ADAPTATION IN CHINA

A key element of party adaptation concerns organizational arrangements. The party may rejuvenate united front groups, or create new organizations to incorporate new groups into the political system. Recent scholarship on China has found extensive evidence of this type of inclusion and has defined it as corporatism.[13] The concept of corporatism is a familiar one in comparative politics,

---

[8] This phrase was coined by Kevin O'Brien; see his *Reform without Liberalization: China's National People's Congress and the Politics of Institutional Change* (New York: Cambridge University Press, 1990), esp. pp. 6–8 and 174–178.

[9] Andrew G. Walder, "Industrial Workers: Some Observations on the 1980s," in Arthur Lewis Rosenbaum, ed., *State and Society in China: The Consequences of Reform* (Boulder: Westview Press, 1992).

[10] Dorothy J. Solinger, "China's Urban Transients in the Transition from Socialism and the Collapse of the Communist 'Urban Public Goods Regime'," *Comparative Politics*, vol. 27, no. 2 (January 1995), pp. 127–146.

[11] See the discussion in Chapter 2, and also Cheng Li, *China's Leaders: The New Generation* (Lanham, MD: Rowman and Littlefield, 2001) and Hans Hendrischke, "Expertocracy and Professionalism," in David S. G. Goodman and Beverly Hooper, eds., *China's Quiet Revolution: New Interactions Between State and Society* (New York: St. Martin's Press, 1994).

[12] Stanley Rosen, "The Chinese Communist Party and Chinese Society: Popular Attitudes toward Party Membership and the Party's Image," *Australian Journal of Chinese Affairs*, no. 24 (July 1990), pp. 51–92.

[13] Margaret M. Pearson, "The Janus Face of Business Associations in China: Socialist Corporatism in Foreign Enterprises," *Australian Journal of Chinese Affairs*, no. 31 (January 1994),

and describes a system of interest representation in which interests are vertically organized into peak associations to limit and institutionalize the participation of key groups in the policy process.[14] Corporatist arrangements may be dominated by the state in an authoritarian political system, a variant known as state corporatism, or they may provide greater autonomy and influence for the groups themselves in a more pluralist setting, a variant known as societal corporatism.

The emerging corporatist elements in China's political system provide a rationale for the more harmonious relations between state and society in the reform era. The corporatist model points out that the state and society relationship is based on achieving consensus and common goals, not a zero-sum struggle for power. As Douglas Chalmers notes, "Corporatism has much in common with socialism's understanding of society after the end of class conflict." A harmony of interests is possible without the total transformation of society.[15] Similarly, Alfred Stepan identified the universal appeal of corporatism to elites facing "a perceived threat of fragmentation" and who reject both the liberal ideals of individualism and checks and balances and the Marxist ideals of class conflict "because they are seen as legitimizing conflict."[16]

Corporatist structures are consequently emerging in China as a substitute for coercion, propaganda, and central planning to maintain party hegemony. As Jonathan Unger and Anita Chan argue, corporatism is "a mechanism through which the state's grip could be lessened" but not released altogether. "The more the economy decentralizes, the more corporatist associations get established as substitute control mechanisms."[17] This is a perfect illustration of the logic of inclusion: because the CCP is no longer able to manipulate the nation with symbols and propaganda, it therefore tries to manipulate the organizations through which society interacts with the state.

---

pp. 25–46; Jonathan Unger and Anita Chan, "Corporatism in China: A Developmental State in an East Asian Context," in Barrett L. McCormick and Jonathan Unger, eds., *China after Socialism: In the Footsteps of Eastern Europe or East Asia* (Armonk, NY: M. E. Sharpe, 1996); Anita Chan, "Revolution or Corporatism? Workers In Search of a Solution," in Goodman and Hooper, eds., *China's Quiet Revolution;* White, Howell, and Shang, *In Search of Civil Society;* Jonathan Unger, "'Bridges': Private Business, the Chinese Government and the Rise of New Associations," *China Quarterly,* no. 147 (September 1996), pp. 795–819; Christopher Earle Nevitt, "Private Business Associations in China: Evidence of Civil Society or Local State Power," *China Journal,* no. 36 (July 1997), pp. 25–43.

[14] Philippe C. Schmitter, "Still the Century of Corporatism?" in Schmitter and Gerhard Lehmbruch, eds., *Trends Towards Corporatist Intermediation* (Beverly Hills, CA: Sage, 1979).

[15] Douglas A. Chalmers, "Corporatism and Comparative Politics," in Howard J. Wiarda, ed., *New Directions in Comparative Politics* (Boulder: Westview Press, 1985), p. 62.

[16] Alfred C. Stepan, *The State and Society: Peru in Comparative Perspective* (Princeton: Princeton University Press, 1978), p. 58.

[17] Unger and Chan, "Corporatism in China," pp. 105, 107.

The "Regulations on the Registration and Management of Social Organizations," issued in draft form in 1989 and finalized in 1998, established the corporatist strategy of the CCP. Neither the state nor the social organizations use corporatist terminology for describing the links between them. But as Philippe Schmitter pointed out, corporatist structures may exist even in the absence of an awareness of corporatism in the state's doctrine. The regulations reveal familiar elements of corporatism: every organization must register with the government and be sponsored by a state organizational unit. The state's sponsoring unit is responsible for its daily affairs, which can include providing officers and a budget. Social organizations have a representational monopoly, at least at their level. In any jurisdiction, there can be only one organization for each profession, activity, or interest. When more than one exist, the state requires them to merge or to disband. Some local social organizations belong to peak organizations, but others have limited horizontal or vertical links to other similar organizations. This representational monopoly is one of the weaker aspects of the corporatist strategy in China. For instance, in the burgeoning software industry, there is a growing multiplicity of organizations, many with overlapping memberships and areas of interest and activity. And while they must continue to have a state sponsor, they use this embeddedness in the state to work on behalf of their members.[18]

While drawing attention to the evolving corporatist structures, some scholars also allude to other unintended consequences of economic reform. For instance, Unger and Chan assert that "Yet at the very same time that these new corporatist structures get erected and firmed up by the Chinese state, forces are simultaneously at work that undermine and weaken the central state's power over them."[19] They believe that at least some of China's groups operating in the current state corporatist mold are "shifting gradually but perceptibly in a 'societal-corporatist' direction," in which organized groups will assert the interests of the people they nominally represent.[20] Gordon White, Jude Howell, and Shang Xiaoyuan also repeatedly allude to the potential of civic associations evolving from a corporatist logic to constitute a civil society, with a dense mix

---

[18] Scott Kennedy, *In the Company of Markets: The Transformation of China's Political Economy*, Ph.D. dissertation (George Washington University, 2001), chapter four.

[19] Unger and Chan, "Corporatism in China," p. 107.

[20] Unger and Chan, "Corporatism in China," p. 129. Unger and Chan make the same point in their separate writings; see for instance Unger, "'Bridges': Private Business, the Chinese Government and the Rise of New Associations," and Chan, "Revolution or Corporatism?" Not all advocates of corporatism are so optimistic. Pearson notes "the absence of a compulsion to resolve the tension between autonomy and state dominance"; see "Janus Face of Business Associations," p. 446.

of organizations largely autonomous from constraints imposed by local officials, but still embedded in the state.[21] In a study of local trade unions, Yunqiu Zhang argues they are moving from state corporatism to social representation, a precursor to civil society. Oddly enough, Zhang claims state corporatism best describes the Maoist system, whereas most people hold that Mao's China more closely approximated a "totalistic" logic, if not outright totalitarianism. Zhang does not claim that a civil society already exists in China, but does "find the concept useful in identifying trends in social change as well as in characterizing particular changes in state-society relations in the reform years."[22]

This points to a more provocative question: are corporatist arrangements compatible with a Leninist system? Or will the emergence and evolution of corporatism lead to the decay of Leninist institutions? To answer these questions, it is necessary to explore the implications of the corporatist model.

Most studies that explore the relationship between the state and social organizations begin by trying to determine if the organizations are simply agents of the state or if they are the agents of their members. In other words, how much autonomy do these new social organizations enjoy? The issue of autonomy is a key factor in understanding whether the state's corporatist strategy is working, or if a civil society may be emerging. But most studies conclude that social organizations have a dual role: they simultaneously represent the interests of the state and their own members, although the balance between these roles varies considerably, depending on the organization, the attitude of local officials, the issue involved, and the broader political context. The issue of autonomy is therefore something of a red herring: as is true in many developing countries, particularly in Asia, these organizations want to be autonomous enough to have some leeway in their activities, but embedded enough to be effective. The leaders and members of these organizations see no inconsistency in this arrangement: both elements are necessary for organizations to be successful.

While many Western scholars see the two functions of state control and organizational autonomy to be in conflict, in China they are not. Margaret Pearson refers to the "Janus faced quality" of business associations in China. She notes that as far back as the late Qing, throughout the Republican period, and in the present, guilds and business associations were not truly autonomous. Instead, both state dominance and autonomy characterize the role of the associations.

---

[21] White, Howell, and Shang, *In Search of Civil Society*. This is the mirror image of Peter Evans' notion of "embedded autonomy": Here it is the civil associations that seek connections with the state in order to be effective.

[22] Yunqiu Zhang, "From State Corporatism to Social Representation: Local Trade Unions in the Reform Years," in Timothy Brook and B. Michael Frolic, eds., *Civil Society in China* (Armonk, NY: M. E. Sharpe, 1997), p. 125.

Similarly, Unger's study of business associations found varying degrees of state control and autonomy of the associations, depending on the membership of the organization, whether membership was voluntary or compulsory, whether the association fell under the jurisdiction of the CCP or the government, the level of local economic development, and other factors. White, Howell, and Shang's study of associational life began by looking for signs of autonomy but reached the conclusion that social organizations of all kinds are characterized by the dualism of state control and autonomy.

What explains the variation in the level of state control and autonomy? One factor is the types of resources controlled by the association. Vivienne Shue studied associations in the countryside and found that the degree of autonomy was related to their control of usually financial resources but sometimes technical resources.[23] A more common argument concerns the perspective of local officials. Jonathan Unger hypothesized that "the interests of middle and local level officials will ... prove to be among the most important determinants of an association's performance and viability."[24] In smaller cities and towns, for instance, private entrepreneurs are not looked down upon as they are in larger cities, especially Beijing. As a result, they enjoy a certain social standing and closer ties with officials. Unger's finding echoes that of White, Howell and Shang, who also conclude the attitude of local officials is perhaps the most important factor in the growth and effectiveness of social organizations.[25] Yijiang Ding also surmised that it may be the attitude of officials, more than the nature of the organization, that determines whether it is the agent of the state or society.[26] Christopher Nevitt found that it was the career strategies of officials that determined their attitudes toward the organizations, and therefore the degree of state control over them. Those who pursued a "ladder of advancement" strategy saw their main task as controlling smaller entrepreneurs, rather than representing or serving them. Those who pursued a "big fish in a small pond" strategy developed closer ties with large-scale entrepreneurs and insulated them and their local associations from higher level state organizations.

How useful is corporatism for understanding Chinese politics? In his critique of the interest group model of Soviet politics, William Odom listed three criteria for evaluating a model: it must capture the core elements of the political system;

---

[23] Vivienne Shue, "State Power and Social Organization in China," in Joel S. Migdal, Atul Kohli, and Vivienne Shue, eds., *State Power and Social Forces: Domination and Transformation in the Third World* (Cambridge: Cambridge University Press, 1994).

[24] Unger, "'Bridges,'" p. 817.

[25] White, Howell, and Shang, *In Search of Civil Society*, p. 181.

[26] Yijiang Ding, "Corporatism and Civil Society in China: An Overview of the Debate in Recent Years," *China Information*, vol. 12, no. 4 (Spring 1998), p. 57.

it must be comparative in nature; and it must account for change.[27] According to Odom, the interest group model failed on two accounts: first, it focused most of its attention on peripheral elements of the system (institutional pluralism) and second, it therefore misinterpreted signs of political decay for political development. The advocates of the corporatist model in China are not so ambitious in their claims for political change, but generally limit themselves to analysis of the evolving institutional arrangements that govern China's political economy. Still, they do include allusions of political transformation that deserve greater scrutiny. Like the proponents of the Soviet interest group model, advocates of Chinese corporatism may be misleading us in terms of the expected future course of Chinese politics.

Is China a corporatist system? Most scholars do not argue that China has a full-blown corporatist system, only that there are corporatist elements emerging in the course of economic reform. Corporatism is an ideal type; it does not define a political system, but corporatist elements are present in a variety of contexts. Democratic countries such as Britain and the Netherlands, bureaucratic authoritarian countries such as Brazil and Argentina, military regimes such as Peru and South Korea, one-party regimes such as Mexico and Taiwan, and communist countries such as Poland, the Soviet Union, and most recently China have been described as corporatist. The corporatist model does capture core elements of China's political system, especially concerning its political economy. The state has created or licensed associations for independent entrepreneurs, owners of private enterprises, enterprises with foreign investment, organized labor, Catholic and Protestant churches, writers, scientists, and other functional interests. These associations are non-competitive and when two or more exist the state forces them to merge or one or more to disband. Membership is compulsory; e.g., members in business associations are often enrolled when they receive their business license. The leaders of these associations are often officials from the party or government offices responsible for regulating or managing them, and association offices are often in government compounds.

These corporatist elements have very much in common with the key aspects of a Leninist system. A Leninist system is based on the ruling party's monopoly on legitimate political organization. The state may create mass organizations to link state and society, and these organizations are typically staffed and budgeted

---

[27] William G. Odom, "Soviet Politics and After: Old and New Concepts," *World Politics*, vol. 45, no. 1 (October 1992), pp. 66–98. Odom borrowed these criteria from Huntington's "Paradigms of American Politics: Beyond the One, the Two, and the Many," *Political Science Quarterly*, vol. 89, no. 1 (March 1974), p. 7.

in large part by the state. A Leninist party also prevents the spontaneous formation of new organizations, especially where an official one already exists, and
the presence of organizations outside of its control is a challenge to its authority.
During periods of transformation and consolidation, the state uses these organizations as "transmission belts" to send authoritative decisions to lower levels
of the organizations. The state grants leaders of these organizations a degree of
leeway to manage their organizations and the people they nominally represent,
but prevents interests and preferences from working their way back up through
the organization to influence state policy. During the period of inclusion, these
same organizations become channels for interest representation so that these
interests can be incorporated into the state. As the party loses its ability to
monitor the activities of these organizations and sanction the behavior of their
members, and society more generally, the stability of the Leninist system itself
is also weakened.[28] This points up the contradictions in the competing goals of
inclusion and mobilization for a Leninist party.

To portray the potential evolution of corporatism, advocates of the corporatist
model in China highlight examples of leaders who change from being agents of
the state to becoming advocates for their associations. But the corporatist model
considers the state as a "'naturally' divided entity" with different interests de-
rived from its relations with economic and professional groups. According to
Chalmers, "One cannot talk of state interests as opposed to those of society
when the state is in fact made up of ties with interests in society."[29] Interest
representation is not the defining difference between state and societal corporatism. Rather, the power relationship between the state and corporate groups
distinguishes the two sub-types, and that relationship is dependent on whether
the political system is authoritarian or pluralistic in nature. Unger found that the
federation for large-scale business "is still too tightly bound to the party-state
in its structure and staffing" to be described as societal corporatist although it
was "gravitating" in that direction due to "a growing desire even on the part of
some of its minders for it to play such a societal corporatist role."[30] The desire
for increased autonomy for organized interests undoubtedly continues to exist

[28] Andrew Walder describes the "institutional pillars" of communist systems in "The Decline of
Communist Power: Elements of a Theory of Institutional Change," *Theory and Society*, vol. 23,
no. 2 (April 1994), pp. 297–323, and "The Quiet Revolution from Within: Economic Reform as
a Source of Political Decline," in Walder, ed., *The Waning of the Communist State: Economic
Origins of Political Decline in China and Hungary* (Berkeley: University of California Press,
1995).
[29] Chalmers, "Corporatism and Comparative Politics," pp. 67–68.
[30] Unger, "'Bridges,'" p. 818.

in China, but those wishes are not compatible with the CCP's desire to preserve its power.

Despite its policies of inclusion, the central fact of China's political system remains that it is ruled by a Leninist party. The party enjoys and protects its monopoly on political organization. In his case study of Xiaoshan city, Gordon White found that only the most politically inconsequential of social organizations (sports, arts and culture, retired teachers, and female factory managers) were autonomous, in that there was no overlapping of personnel with the sponsoring government bureau and no financial subsidies.[31] At the same time, bottom-up demands for new and autonomous social organizations (for labor, entrepreneurs, students, etc.) were rejected and repressed. Unger and Chan argue that some of the key demands during the 1989 protests involved gaining state approval for autonomous unions for students and workers in Beijing. "To the extent that they were demanding a *structural* change in the political system, it was to effect a shift to a societal corporatism in which they could choose their own leadership and set their own agendas."[32] But the CCP's rejection of this demand and its violent repression of protestors shows that Leninism, not corporatism, still defines China's political system. Beginning in 1998, the CCP has repeatedly suppressed efforts to create an opposition party, showing that a Leninist logic still prevails in China. If the party's monopoly is undermined, we will witness not simply an incremental and gradual evolution from state to societal corporatism, but increased disintegration of the communist system itself.

Corporatist trends are nevertheless effecting several key factors of China's political system. An important variation on corporatism as practiced in China is that corporatist groups are usually sanctioned and controlled by local party and government authorities and not always vertically organized into peak associations whose primary interaction is with the central state. This has exacerbated the decentralization of political and economic authority. Just as corporate associations no longer act as transmission belts, local governments do not act as loyal agents of the center.[33] This is a potential sign of disintegration, not just for the CCP but the political system as a whole. According to Ding, local associations put pressure on local officials to resist central directives and emphasize

---

[31] White, "Prospects for Civil Society."
[32] Unger and Chan, "Corporatism in China," p. 112; emphasis in original.
[33] See Jia Hao and Lin Zhimin, eds., *Changing Central-Local Relations in China* (Boulder: Westview, 1994); and Wang Shaoguang, "The Rise of the Regions: Fiscal Reform and the Decline of Central State Capacity in China," in Walder, ed., *Waning of the Communist State*; for a contrary view, see Yasheng Huang, *Inflation and Investment Controls in China: The Political Economy of Central-Local Relations during the Reform Era* (New York: Cambridge University Press, 1996).

local interests over central ones. "Grass roots pressure may be as responsible as local state interests for the tension between different levels of government and the fragmentation of the overall corporatist system."[34] Relatedly, as a result of these newly created institutional links, the party's traditional concern with party building as a means of linking state and society and monitoring compliance with party policy has atrophied, as explained in Chapter 2.

The second criterion for a model is that it allow comparisons to be drawn with other countries, and the corporatist model is clearly comparative in nature. But because corporatism is present in so many contexts, it is important to clearly identify the subtypes of the concept so that comparisons are drawn with the right countries. Both state and societal corporatism are monopolistic forms of group politics and therefore are structurally similar. Yet their origins and dynamics are fundamentally different. State corporatism is generally associated with authoritarian regimes, whereas societal corporatism is "more an evolution – perhaps a corruption – of liberalism."[35] Societal corporatism is not compatible with a Leninist system because the former requires the types of autonomous and politically active groups that the latter refuses to tolerate. The notion of state corporatism is less threatening to the regime: instead of autonomy, corporate groups are embedded in the state, where they can be manipulated, their leaders replaced, and their finances controlled. Leninist parties seek to prevent autonomous groups, and for good reason. The Eastern European experience shows that the rise of civil society has a significant – and in some cases decisive – impact on the collapse of communism.[36]

The third criterion of a model's utility is its ability to account for change, and this is where the corporatist model as applied to China most falls short. The depiction of a gradual and incremental evolution from state to societal corporatism is not consistent with the wider literature. According to Philippe Schmitter, state corporatism is unlikely to transform itself continuously toward societal corporatism; instead, it must "degenerate into openly conflictual, multifaceted, uncontrolled interest politics – pluralism in other words."[37] This is exactly what Leninism is designed to prevent. We should not expect that the transition from state to societal corporatism will occur amidst regime continuity.

---

[34] Ding, "Corporatism and Civil Society in China," p. 59.

[35] Chalmers, "Corporatism and Comparative Politics," p. 60; see also Schmitter, "Still the Century of Corporatism?" pp. 22–25.

[36] Timothy Garton Ash, *The Uses of Adversity: Essays on the Fate of Central Europe* (New York: Vintage, 1990); Marcia A. Wiegle and Jim Butterfield, "Civil Society in Reforming Communist Regimes: The Logic of Emergence," *Comparative Politics*, vol. 25, no. 1 (October 1992), pp. 1–24; Vladimir Tismaneanu, *Reinventing Politics: Eastern Europe from Stalin to Havel* (New York: The Free Press, 1992).

[37] Schmitter, "Still the Century of Corporatism?" p. 41.

The incremental transformation depicted by the advocates of the corporatist model is based not only on faulty logic but also problematic analogies. Unger and Chan suggest that Japan, South Korea, and Taiwan all made smooth transitions from state to societal corporatism and conclude that a similar transformation in China is possible. But in all three cases the transition from state to societal corporatism was epiphenomenal to changes taking place in the larger political system. In each case, societal corporatism was the consequence of democratization, but the modes of democratization were fundamentally different in each country. Despite the near ubiquity of corporatism in all sorts of political systems, we should be wary of drawing comparisons across different types of political systems. Unger and Chan further suggest that as political liberalization continues in China, "it is far more likely to involve such incremental shifts into societal corporatism rather than the introduction of any form of political democracy." But societal corporatism and democracy are not independent of one another. The emergence of societal corporatism was the consequence of democratization elsewhere in East Asia, not an alternative to it. In other countries, societal corporatism developed in an already pluralist setting. The combination of societal corporatism and rule by a Leninist party would therefore not likely be a stable one.

Corporatism may survive the transition from communism in China, but communism is unlikely to survive the transition to corporatism. Chan cites the relegalization of Solidarity in spring 1989 as a possible model for increased autonomy of China's labor organizations.[38] But within a few months of this step, the communist government in Poland negotiated its way out of existence. This example of "socialist societal corporatism" existed only for the short period of time between the relegalization of Solidarity in April 1989 and the appointment of the first non-communist prime minister, Solidarity adviser Tadeusz Mazowiecki, in September 1989.[39] This is a poor precedent, either for theory building or for party policy.

A more promising approach may be to apply Stepan's typology of inclusionary and exclusionary poles within state corporatism. The distinction between the two poles concerns whether the state incorporates "salient" groups or suppresses them through coercion. A regime can shift between exclusionary and inclusionary policies over time, and even practice them simultaneously. For instance, the CCP has allowed the All-China Federation of Trade Unions in recent years to advocate strongly the interest of labor in the policy and legislative process, but also imprisoned those who advocate the formation of independent

---

[38] Chan, "Revolution or Corporatism?" p. 83.
[39] Tismaneanu, *Reinventing Politics*, pp. 192–194.

trade unions. Stepan's typology may account for trends that scholars are find-ing without stretching the concept of societal corporatism beyond recognition. Both inclusionary and exclusionary forms of state corporatism are intended to "restrict the autonomy of groups they encapsulate," and are understood as variants of authoritarianism. Even inclusive policies within state corporatism are not similar to the kind of pluralism associated with societal corporatism.[40] The notion of exclusionary and inclusionary poles also fits well the CCP's strat-egy of incorporating certain individuals, groups, and interests into the political system while continuing to exclude others. It is willing to co-opt successful entrepreneurs into the party, in part to help promote the goal of economic mod-ernization and in part to prevent these entrepreneurs from becoming a potential source of opposition outside the state. At the same time, it continues to exclude and in many cases persecute those who challenge the CCP's priorities with ex-plicitly political goals. The impact of the CCP's selective policies of inclusion will be examined in the next chapter.

Corporatist features are clearly emerging in China as a substitute for the CCP's more totalitarian impulse to control state and society in the Maoist years. But the ultimate political implications of this trend are still uncertain. Whereas some scholars see the promise of societal corporatism coming into view, others see signs of political disintegration. The creation of corporatist organizations to link state and society was part of the CCP's strategy of inclusion and it remains dedicated to preventing the rise of autonomous organizations. Before societal corporatism replaces Leninism as the defining feature of China's political sys-tem, the party would have to abandon its monopoly on political organization. This is a fundamental change that the CCP has steadfastly opposed. If the party's control over key organizations erodes to such an extent that state corporatism begins to transform into societal corporatism, the real story will not be about the rise of corporatism but more fundamental political change in China.

### CHINA'S ENTREPRENEURS AND THEIR ASSOCIATIONS

The gradual and limited liberalization of China's political system in the post-Mao era created renewed interest in notions of civil society. A vibrant debate began among scholars about whether a civil society was emerging as a conse-quence of the *gaige kaifang* (reform and opening) policies, whether these trends had antecedents in the late imperial and Republican eras, and even about the use-fulness of the concept for understanding state-society relations in contemporary

---

[40] Stepan, *State and Society*, pp. 73–81; quote is on p. 74n.

China.[41] The potential for civil society in the 1980s looked quite fragile after seeming to be snuffed out at the time of the Tiananmen massacre in 1989. But the gradual and limited liberalization of China's political system has been accompanied by an increase in organizational activities. Associations of all kinds, from professional groups to hobby clubs, have blossomed all over the country.[42] Business associations have received particular attention because they have the resources – the means to create economic growth – that the state requires, and because of the special contributions entrepreneurs have made to political change in other countries.

Private entrepreneurs and their associations in the pre-1949 era have also received a great deal of attention from historians and political scientists. Businessmen became increasingly well organized from the late Qing forward, sometimes as extensions of the state, other times as autonomous bodies representing local interests to the state. In contrast to the traditional assessment of the Qing state as anti-business, more recent scholarship has shown a cooperative relationship between progressive officials and businessmen, especially at the local level. Government policy toward business from the late Qing onward has been complex and often contradictory, providing ample evidence for competing claims that the state repressed, neglected, colluded with, or promoted commerce.[43]

Local guilds, trade associations, and chambers of commerce had several main functions: regulatory, such as setting standards and weights, regulating new entrants into a given trade, establishing contractual obligations, and providing credit; social, such as local worship and philanthropy; and representative, conveying not only the views of their own members but also a wider array of local opinion to local and higher level officials.[44] These guilds and associations

---

[41] Martin King Whyte, "Urban China: A Civil Society in the Making?" in Arthur Lewis Rosenbaum, ed., *State and Society in China: The Consequences of Reform* (Boulder: Westview Press, 1992); "Symposium: 'Public Sphere'/'Civil Society' In China?," *Modern China*, vol. 19, no. 2 (April 1993), with contributions from Frederic Wakeman, Jr., William T. Rowe, Mary Backus Rankin, Richard Madsen, Heath B. Chamberlain, and Philip C.C. Huang; Jeffrey N. Wasserstrom and Elizabeth J. Perry, eds., *Popular Protest and Political Culture in Modern China* (Boulder: Westview Press, 1994); Timothy Brook and B. Michael Frolic, eds., *Civil Society in China* (Armonk, NY: M. E. Sharpe, 1997).

[42] Minxin Pei, "Chinese Civic Associations: An Empirical Analysis," *Modern China*, vol. 24, no. 3 (July 1998), pp. 285–318; Tony Saich, "Negotiating the State: The Development of Social Organizations in China," *China Quarterly*, no. 161 (March 2000), pp. 124–141.

[43] William T. Rowe, *Hankow: Commerce and Society in a Chinese City, 1796–1889* (Stanford: Stanford University Press, 1984).

[44] Rowe, *Hankow*; Joseph Fewsmith, *Party, State, and Local Elites in Republican China: Merchant Organizations and Politics in Shanghai, 1890–1930* (Honolulu: University of Hawaii Press, 1985); David Strand, *Rickshaw Beijing: City People and Politics in the 1920s* (Berkeley: University of California Press, 1989).

were primarily local in nature, but over time they began to create inter-guild linkages to better assert their interests and influence. The Qing government, believing chambers of commerce to be "cost-effective instruments for extending administrative reach," built an empire-wide network of chambers of commerce to encourage merchants' identity with the state and allow greater influence over economic affairs.[45] As the guilds and chambers of commerce became better organized and more closely embedded in the state, they got involved in all aspects of municipal affairs, from road construction to establishing police forces and local courts.

The representative function of guilds and chambers of commerce proved to be the most controversial, creating conflict between merchants and the state and also within the merchant groups themselves. Many merchants were politically progressive and sought a more influential role in public affairs. Most chambers of commerce actively supported the 1911 revolution, the May 4th movement, and the May 30th movement, but there were sharp disagreements within local chambers about whether they should play a militant or more conciliatory role. The political influence of chambers of commerce rose and fell with the stability of the government: in times of instability, chambers of commerce played an active role in providing government services and mediating between contending political elites (as in the late Qing and warlord eras). But once the stability of the state was restored, the new leaders restricted the political activities and influence of merchants.

The Nationalist government tried to organize local merchants for its own purposes, as had the Qing. Their goal was to create "a politically conscious merchant community that could be mobilized for the goals of the party-state."[46] But once Chiang Kai-shek and other government leaders were able to gain dominance over those in the party bureaucracy, this effort was abandoned. Chiang and his supporters sided with the conservative economic elites over the more militant merchants. This ushered in a more coercive, less cooperative relationship between government and business. In the latter years of the Nanking decade (1927–37), the government "gained control of business and banking organizations, seized the banking industry, and usurped the leadership of the commercial and industrial sectors."[47] Government policy emphasized exploiting capitalists, especially in Shanghai, to squeeze additional revenue for military operations, rather than collaboration between government and business to

---

[45] Strand, *Rickshaw Beijing*, p. 101.
[46] Fewsmith, *Party, State, and Local Elites in Republican China*, p. 137.
[47] Parks M. Coble, Jr., *The Shanghai Capitalists and the Nationalist Government 1927–1937* (Cambridge: Harvard University Press, 1980).

promote national development. The Nationalist government in Nanking sharply restricted the autonomy and scope of activities of business elites and their organizations.

When the CCP came to power in 1949, they followed a united front strategy of cooperating with a wide range of non-communist groups. Private entrepreneurs were designated the "national bourgeoisie" to distinguish them from the "bureaucratic capitalists" who had links to the old Nationalist government and whose property was confiscated by the new regime. In the early years of the PRC, these national bourgeoisie were treated with respect and given positions in the coalition government. But this policy of collaboration was short-lived. In 1952, the CCP launched the Five Anti campaign against alleged economic crimes and tax evasion by large scale entrepreneurs. In 1953, the government announced a new "general line for the transition to socialism" that called for the eventual socialization of industry and commerce. By 1956, the private sector was eliminated and all significant industrial and commercial assets taken over by the state, with some compensation given to their former owners.[48] Small scale private trade in the rural areas was also abolished during the mid-1950s.[49] For the remainder of the Maoist era (1949–76), the state controlled all significant aspects of industry and commerce in China.

As the post-Mao reform era unfolded, the private sector began to reemerge, initially comprising street vendors and very small scale enterprises, and later expanding to include much larger industrial and commercial operations.[50] With the expansion in the size and scope of the private sector came business associations established and staffed by state officials. These associations were designed to allow state influence over the growing private sector through direct organizational links with private enterprises.

Scholars have noted two particular features about business associations and individual entrepreneurs in contemporary China, both of which are related to the scholarly debate about the implications of civil society and corporatism in China. First, different associations have varying degrees of autonomy and influence, based largely on the types and amount of resources they control. Associations made up of large-scale manufacturing enterprises have more clout than those made up of individual vendors. Consequently, the more influential

---

[48] Frederick C. Teiwes, "Establishment and Consolidation of the New Regime," in Roderick MacFarquhar, ed., *The Politics of China: The Eras of Mao and Deng*, 2nd ed. (New York: Cambridge University Press, 1997).

[49] Dorothy J. Solinger, *Chinese Business under Socialism: The Politics of Domestic Commerce in Contemporary China* (Berkeley: University of California Press, 1984).

[50] Susan Young, *Private Business and Economic Reform in China* (Armonk, NY: M. E. Sharpe, 1995).

associations may be developing an identity of their own that will lead them to represent the interests of their members rather than to be loyal agents of the state.[51] Second, although businessmen have a keen awareness of their business interests, interviews with individual businessmen indicate they are reluctant to get involved in politics, either by supporting other societal groups pushing for political reform or by using their associations for collective political action.[52] At best, they may be part of what Yanqi Tong calls the "non-critical realm" of civil society, essentially businessmen, professionals and other similar occupations who do not pose a direct challenge to the regime, and may even be welcomed by it. The emergence of this realm as an autonomous element of civil society may have important implications for subsequent political change, but will not lead directly to democratization without the cooperation of the "critical realm" of dissidents and political activists.[53] Taken together, these two insights suggest that China's entrepreneurs are developing a clearer notion of their individual and group interests, but they are unwilling – at least at present – to be advocates of political change.

Most of these studies are based on intensive work in one location, and sometimes in one economic sector.[54] To assess the generalizability of the above findings, I conducted a survey and interview project targeting the owners and operators of large and medium scale private enterprises and the local party and government officials with whom they interact (see the Appendix to this chapter for details on the design and content of the survey). This is not a random sample of China's population, and was not intended to be. The respondents represent the economic and political elites in their communities. In all, 524 private entrepreneurs and 230 local party and government officials participated in the survey. Although the generalizability of the survey data may be limited because of its size and the type of respondents in the sample, it holds important insights for the themes of this study. The following analysis is based on data collected from this survey.

---

[51] Nevitt, "Private Business Associations in China"; Unger, "'Bridges'"; Shue, "State Power and Social Organization in China."

[52] David L. Wank, "Private Business, Bureaucracy, and Political Alliance in a Chinese City," *Australian Journal of Chinese Affairs*, no. 33 (January 1995), pp. 55–71; Margaret M. Pearson, *China's New Business Elite: The Political Consequences of Economic Reform* (Berkeley: University of California Press, 1997); and Pearson, "China's Emerging Business Class: Democracy's Harbinger," *Current History*, vol. 97, no. 620 (September 1998), pp. 268–272.

[53] Yanqi Tong, "State, Society, and Political Change in China and Hungary," *Comparative Politics*, vol. 26, no. 3 (April 1994), pp. 333–353; see also Baogang He, *The Democratic Implications of Civil Society in China* (New York: St. Martin's Press, 1997).

[54] White, Howell, and Shang, *In Search of Civil Society*.

Table 3.1 *Membership in Business Associations* (percentages)

| Business association | Poor counties | Rich counties | Total |
|---|---|---|---|
| SELA | 33.0 | 10.0 | 22.5 |
| PEA | 12.8 | 31.9 | 21.5 |
| ICF | 19.8 | 22.7 | 21.1 |
| Other | 1.8 | 7.9 | 4.6 |
| None | 32.6 | 27.5 | 30.3 |

THE POLITICAL INFLUENCE OF BUSINESS ASSOCIATIONS

Most of the private entrepreneurs in this study belonged to one or more business associations, and the distribution of membership varied significantly depending on the level of development among the eight counties studied (see Table 3.1). When private entrepreneurs belonged to more than one business association, they were asked which one they most closely identified with, and the analysis below is based on this distinction.

A brief word about each of the main associations will set the stage. Although there has been an explosion of industry-specific business groups, the main ones are the catch-all associations that are organized by the scale of the enterprise rather than the industrial sector. In a classic state corporatist arrangement, they were organized by the state to provide a means to integrate the state with these organizations, and their heads generally serve simultaneously as party or government officials. The Self-Employed Laborers' Association (SELA, *geti laodongzhe xiehui*) is aimed at small-scale operations with small numbers of workers and low sales volumes. As a consequence of this, previous research has found SELA to have the least amount of prestige and influence.[55] The Private Enterprises' Association (PEA, *siying qiye xiehui*) encompasses slightly larger enterprises and was created at the urging of private entrepreneurs who did not want to be confused with *getihu*. The Industrial and Commercial Federation (ICF, *gongshang lian*) includes the largest and most prestigious enterprises, and is therefore found to have the greatest clout. Whereas ICF members were evenly split between prosperous and poor counties, PEA members were concentrated in the prosperous counties and SELA members in the poor ones. Although SELA and PEA are products of the post-Mao era, the ICF has its origins in the 1950s united front strategy of including capitalists in the policy deliberations of the state. Its status is equivalent to one of the eight so-called democratic parties, holdovers of the pre-1949 period that exist to perpetuate the myth of the

[55] Nevitt, "Private Business Associations in China"; Unger, "Bridges."

74

CCP's united front strategy. Each of the business associations is headquartered in Beijing with local branches throughout China.

How do local party and government officials view the business associations in their communities? In the major metropolitan areas, such as Beijing and Tianjin, Unger and Nevitt report that officials have a patronizing attitude toward entrepreneurs and their associations. In other areas, the relationship between officials and entrepreneurs is more symbiotic, and officials may be more tolerant of collective action on behalf of business interests. The officials surveyed as part of my study were roughly evenly split between those who thought the most important role of the business associations was to ensure party leadership over the private sector (47.8 percent) and those who thought the associations should represent the views of their own members (42.4 percent; the remainder gave a variety of other responses). In fact, in the more developed counties, local officials were exactly evenly split (45.6 percent apiece), but in the less developed counties a slight majority felt that party leadership was more important relative to representing the interests of businessmen (50.9 versus 40.5 percent). Ironically, village level officials were most likely to see the primary role of business associations as ensuring party leadership: 57.5 percent of all village officials, and 70.8 percent of those in poorer counties, felt this way. However, regardless of what officials feel is the most important role of these associations, over 75 percent believe they are effective means of party leadership over local private enterprises. Again, village officials were more likely to strongly agree on this question (52.3 percent, compared to 38.9 percent of county level leading officials, 21.2 percent of county level bureau officials, and 35.1 percent of township officials). Local officials ranked the importance of the private sector for creating prosperity behind the state sector but ahead of the çollective sector (this was true for cadres at all levels, except township officials who gave equal importance to both state-owned and private enterprises). As the private sector has emerged as an essential component to local prosperity, so too has the need for organizational links with that sector.

Members of all business associations show a strong identification with their associations (see Table 3.2). The vast majority of businessmen believe that business associations represent the interests of their members. Similar proportions of business association members believe that their business association shares their personal views. Cadres have similar views on these two questions, and a difference of means test shows no significant difference between the two groups. One surprising finding is that even entrepreneurs who do not belong to any business association believe that the associations represent their members, and even share their own views. This may allow for increased opportunities for collective action in the future.

Table 3.2 *Views toward Business Associations* (percentages)

Q1: Business associations are able to represent the interests of their members.

| Business association | Strongly agree | Agree | Disagree | Strongly disagree |
|---|---|---|---|---|
| SELA | 24.3 | 55.9 | 15.3 | 4.5 |
| PEA | 33.3 | 55.9 | 10.8 | 0.0 |
| ICF | 30.1 | 55.3 | 12.6 | 1.9 |
| Other | 38.1 | 52.4 | 4.8 | 4.8 |
| None | 22.5 | 54.1 | 18.0 | 5.4 |
| *All entrepreneurs* | 28.3 | 54.2 | 14.1 | 3.4 |
| *Officials* | 27.0 | 50.9 | 17.6 | 4.5 |

Q2: Under most circumstances, the business association and I share the same viewpoint on the affairs of enterprises.

| Business association | Strongly agree | Agree | Disagree | Strongly disagree |
|---|---|---|---|---|
| SELA | 22.9 | 56.0 | 17.4 | 3.7 |
| PEA | 25.2 | 62.1 | 11.7 | 1.0 |
| ICF | 23.8 | 61.4 | 14.9 | 0.0 |
| Other | 28.6 | 66.7 | 4.8 | 0.0 |
| None | 14.0 | 61.7 | 18.7 | 5.6 |
| *All entrepreneurs* | 21.5 | 60.4 | 15.7 | 2.4 |

*Note:* Due to rounding, rows may not sum to 100.

Table 3.3 *Business Associations and the Government's Views* (percentages)

Q: On most matters, the business associations represent the government's views.

| Business association | Strongly agree | Agree | Disagree | Strongly disagree |
|---|---|---|---|---|
| SELA | 24.1 | 23.2 | 35.2 | 17.6 |
| PEA | 30.7 | 31.7 | 30.7 | 6.9 |
| ICF | 15.2 | 37.4 | 38.4 | 9.1 |
| Other | 28.6 | 33.3 | 38.1 | 0.0 |
| None | 8.5 | 47.2 | 33.0 | 11.3 |
| *All entrepreneurs* | 20.5 | 34.3 | 33.7 | 11.5 |
| *Officials* | 11.0 | 51.4 | 29.4 | 8.3 |

*Note:* Due to rounding, rows may not sum to 100.

But before we get too excited about the relationship between associations and entrepreneurs, we should first look at whether businessmen believe the associations represent the government's views. As seen in Table 3.3, a slight majority of businessmen also believe the associations represent the government's position. Given findings by previous studies, we would expect to find that

76

private entrepreneurs belonging to the SELA would be more likely to agree that their business association represented the interests of the government over their own, and that private entrepreneurs in less developed areas would have the same viewpoint. But neither of these predictions is supported by the survey data. Only 47.2 percent of SELA members believed their business association represented the government; in contrast over 78 percent believed SELA represented the interests of its members and the personal views of the respondent. A slight majority of ICF members believed the ICF – the largest and generally regarded as the most influential business association – represented the government. The PEA and other local business associations had the highest percentage of members who believed their associations represented the government's perspective. In short, there was no simple linear relationship between the reputations for independence and influence of a business association and the views of its members regarding whether it represented the views of the government.

The level of economic development and privatization strongly influenced the beliefs of entrepreneurs among the respondents. Those in the four counties with prosperous economies and high levels of privatization were much more likely to agree that their business association represented the government's viewpoint: 71.9 percent as opposed to only 41.6 percent in the four less prosperous counties. A difference of means test was highly significant ($t = 6.55$, $p(t) = .0000$). This apparently paradoxical finding fits the findings of other studies from China, and even elsewhere in East Asia, of a close partnership between government and business, rather than the adversarial relationship more familiar in the U.S.[56] In the areas where the economy as a whole and the private economy in particular is more prosperous, the government-business relationship in China may also be more developed and the belief in shared interests more pronounced.

Ironically, the views of local party and government officials did not vary according to the level of economic development. On average, 62.4 percent of officials agreed that business associations represented the government. Whether through better socialization, better knowledge, or a different perspective on the roles of government and businessmen, officials consistently shared similar views on whether business associations represented the government's

---

[56] Marc Blecher, "Development State, Entrepreneurial State: The Political Economy of Socialist Reform in Xinju Municipality and Guanghan County," in Gordon White, ed., *The Chinese State in the Era of Economic Reform: The Road to Crisis* (Armonk, NY: M. E. Sharpe, 1991); Jean C. Oi, "Fiscal Reforms and the Economic Foundations of Local State Corporatism,"*World Politics*, vol. 45, no. 1 (October 1992), pp. 99–126; Nan Lin, "Local Market Socialism: Local Corporatism in Action in Rural China," *Theory and Society*, vol. 24, no. 3 (June 1995), pp. 301–354; for the cases of Korea and Taiwan, see Karl J. Fields, *Enterprise and the State in Korea and Taiwan* (Ithaca: Cornell University Press, 1995).

perspective. Businessmen, however, had rather different views depending on the level of development of their counties. As seen above, in the most prosperous counties, an even larger share of entrepreneurs than party and government officials agreed that the business associations represented the government's viewpoint.

Although business associations may not simply be agents of the state, neither are they completely autonomous. This delicate balance between autonomy and embeddedness is the key to government-business relations and successful economic development in a variety of developing countries, and is similar to how other studies have found individuals in China view their relationship with the state.[57] Changes in that balance may indicate the changing potential for political change. However, the evidence here suggests that the perceived harmony of interests between the state and business associations *rises* with economic development. If private entrepreneurs are expected to be agents of political change, we would expect the views of private entrepreneurs and officials to be diverging in the most prosperous areas. That is not what these survey data reveal, however. Instead, we may find that economic development will accentuate the convergence of views between government and business, at least in the short run. This convergence is not the result of changes in the views officials brought on by the experience of economic development or the pressure of businessmen, but instead is the result of changes in the views of the businessmen themselves.

One clear test of the efficacy of business associations is whether they can help solve the practical problems of their members. Interviews by other scholars found that many businessmen did not hold their associations in high regard or find them of much use in solving business related problems.[58] However, most businessmen surveyed in this project reported they have used their business association to try to resolve their problems (see Table 3.4). These problems most commonly related to economic and financial matters (such as getting loans on time and payment of taxes), disputes between businesses, or general problems, such as getting permits or having goods inspected for export. In previous studies, Unger and Nevitt reported that the SELA

[57] Peter Evans, *Embedded Autonomy: States and Industrial Transformation* (Princeton: Princeton University Press, 1995); Andrew J. Nathan, *Chinese Democracy* (Berkeley: University of California Press, 1985); Kevin J. O'Brien, "Chinese People's Congresses and Legislative Embeddedness: Understanding Early Organizational Development," *Comparative Political Studies*, vol. 27, no. 1 (April 1994), pp. 80–107.

[58] Kristen Parris, "The Rise of Private Business Interests," in Merle Goldman and Roderick MacFarquhar, eds., *The Paradox of China's Post-Mao Reforms* (Cambridge: Harvard University Press, 1999); Scott Kennedy, *In the Company of Markets: The Transformation of China's Political Economy*, Ph.D. dissertation (George Washington University, 2001).

Table 3.4 *The Helpfulness of Business Associations to Their Members*
(percentages)

Q1: When you encounter problems, have you ever gone through your business
association to solve them?

| Business association | Yes | No |
|---|---|---|
| SELA | 58.5 | 41.5 |
| PEA | 69.6 | 30.4 |
| ICF | 44.9 | 55.1 |
| Other | 57.9 | 42.1 |
| None | 32.2 | 67.8 |
| *All entrepreneurs* | 51.0 | 49.0 |

Q2: How helpful was the business association in solving your problem?

| Business association | Very helpful | A little helpful | Not very helpful | Not helpful at all |
|---|---|---|---|---|
| SELA | 30.7 | 56.5 | 9.7 | 3.2 |
| PEA | 34.3 | 53.7 | 11.9 | 0.0 |
| ICF | 26.2 | 66.7 | 4.8 | 2.4 |
| Other | 20.0 | 80.0 | 0.0 | 0.0 |
| None | 10.3 | 69.2 | 12.8 | 7.7 |
| *All entrepreneurs* | 26.8 | 60.9 | 9.6 | 2.7 |

Q3: If you encounter a problem again, will you ask the business association
to help you solve it?

| Business association | Yes | No |
|---|---|---|
| SELA | 84.8 | 15.2 |
| PEA | 85.9 | 14.1 |
| ICF | 79.2 | 20.8 |
| Other | 88.2 | 11.8 |
| None | 68.5 | 31.5 |
| *All entrepreneurs* | 79.7 | 20.3 |

is the weakest of the associations. Although a majority of SELA members interviewed in my project reported they had sought help from it, the percentage was
smaller than for the PEA (58.9 versus 69.6). However, only 45.8 percent of ICF
members had sought the association's help. There appears to be no direct correlation between the perceived clout of a business association and the willingness
of its members to seek its help. However, in the most developed areas, a different
picture emerges. In these counties, 69.8 percent of SELA members sought its
help (compared to 55.4 percent in the less developed counties), but only 42.9 percent of ICF members (compared to 46.9 percent in the less developed counties).

There appears to be two stories running in parallel here. First, ICF members have other resources to draw upon to solve their problems and do not need to rely on their business association. The fact that roughly the same percentage sought ICF help in prosperous and poor areas supports this claim. SELA members have less resources to draw upon than ICF members, and in particular do not have close ties with influential officials. For example, 44.5 percent of SELA members reported that gaining the support of the local government was a severe or very severe problem (compared to 28.3 percent for PEA members and 26.9 percent for ICF members).[59] When personal ties are so difficult, relying on their association may be the only option for SELA members.

The second story explaining the helpfulness of the SELA concerns the local context of the association's activities. In areas with developed economies, SELA may have a greater role to play because the private sector as a whole is more developed and officials are more inclined to lend their help.[60] This claim is supported by responses to a follow-up question. In the developed areas, 43.8 percent said SELA had been very helpful in solving their problems, but in poorer areas only 26.1 percent said it had been very helpful. SELA's reputation for effectiveness seems higher in the more developed areas. As a result, SELA members in the more developed counties were more likely to seek the association's help and more likely to be very satisfied with its help than were SELA members in less developed counties. The effectiveness of SELA in developed areas likely encourages its members to seek its help, but this finding is not consistent with previous scholarship, based largely on Beijing and Tianjin. My survey only includes relatively large-scale private entrepreneurs. Other SELA members who operate smaller operations may not be so fortunate. Further work is needed in other locations with varying degrees of development and privatization to clarify how the local level of development affects the degree to which business associations are able to provide tangible help to their members.

While noting the variations in the data, it is important not to lose sight of a more fundamental point. The members of these business associations are learning to turn to them to solve their problems, and the overwhelming majority of businessmen have found the associations to be effective. This indicates strong confidence that the business associations can act on behalf of their members, specifically by intervening to resolve their business problems. This experience will make them more likely to turn to the business associations again in the future

---

[59] It should be no surprise that entrepreneurs who were party members were less likely to report problems with their dealings with local government officials than were non-members.

[60] The percentage of PEA members who sought its help dropped slightly in the more developed areas, from 72.7 to 67.7. I am afraid I do not have a simple story for this discrepancy.

Table 3.5 *The Policy Influence of Business Associations* (percentages)

Q: The business association can influence the local implementation of policies.

| Business association | Strongly agree | Agree | Disagree | Strongly disagree |
|---|---|---|---|---|
| SELA | 27.3 | 43.6 | 20.9 | 8.2 |
| PEA | 25.0 | 40.0 | 25.0 | 10.0 |
| ICF | 17.4 | 49.0 | 23.5 | 10.2 |
| Other | 23.8 | 38.1 | 33.3 | 4.8 |
| None | 15.1 | 55.7 | 22.6 | 6.6 |
| *All entrepreneurs* | 21.5 | 46.8 | 23.3 | 8.4 |
| *Officials* | 5.5 | 19.6 | 48.0 | 26.9 |

and will encourage others to do likewise. While business associations will not totally replace clientelism as a means for getting things done (as seen in the small numbers of ICF members who sought its help), it does add another option to their repertoire of problem solving techniques. Developing a reputation for "delivering the goods" is the best way for business associations to demonstrate their value to private entrepreneurs, and to elicit greater support from them.

Can business associations influence the local implementation of policy? That is a more important measure of their potential for acting as agents of change, and therefore a potentially more contentious matter in a political system that has limited interaction between the state and organized groups outside the state. On this crucial issue, businessmen and officials express markedly different views: over two-thirds – 68.4 percent – of businessmen believe that the associations *can* influence policy implementation (ironically, SELA members are the most optimistic), but three-quarters – 74.9 percent – of officials believe that business associations *cannot* influence policy (see Table 3.5). On this issue, the difference between the businessmen and officials is a difference of kind, not of degree, and shows the potential for future conflict. If the associations and their members believe they can influence policy, they are more inclined to try; and if they believe they can influence implementation of policy, it is a small step to try to influence the actual making of policy.

Do all private entrepreneurs believe their business associations can influence the implementation of policy? In the less developed areas, roughly three-quarters of private entrepreneurs believe they can, and this optimism holds across all business associations, and even among those who do not belong to one. In the more developed counties, however, private entrepreneurs have a less optimistic – and one might say more realistic – perception of business association influence over policy. Nevertheless, a clear majority – 61.2 percent – of

81

private entrepreneurs in prosperous counties believe business associations can influence policy, and there is a positive relationship between the perceived clout of a business association and the degree to which its members believe it can influence policy implementation, with SELA lowest and ICF highest (ironically, those who do not belong to any association are the most optimistic on this point).

In follow-up interviews, entrepreneurs were asked for examples of how business associations had influenced the local implementation of policy. Their answers were vague, indicating they had confidence in the association's ability to influence policy but did not have concrete evidence to support their confidence.

A multivariate analysis shows that cadre status, party membership among entrepreneurs ("red capitalists"), and the level of development all influence attitudes toward the policy influence of business associations, but in a negative fashion: Cadres, red capitalists, and those in better developed counties are less optimistic than others. This would support part of the logic of co-optation: party members among entrepreneurs seem less likely to agree that business associations can influence local policy implementation, and therefore less likely to be agents of change (or troublemakers, from the perspective of local officials!). None of the business associations alone are significant independent variables for explaining views on the policy impact of the business associations.

Taken together, these data indicate that businessmen view business associations as appropriate means of representing their views, solving their problems, and influencing the local implementation of policy. These three factors, especially the last, are positive indicators of an emerging sense of collective identity among entrepreneurs, and this shared identity may in fact lead to a concept of citizenship.[61] The organization of interests is seen as legitimate by both businessmen and officials, and therefore creates the potential for those organizations to engage in collective action on behalf of those shared interests. These business associations may have been created by the state as part of its strategy of adaptation and incorporation of new elites, but if they serve the interests of its members as much as – if not more than – the interests of the state, the foundation of a civil society will be enhanced.

However, one of the more surprising findings in these data is that local prosperity has a major impact on the views of entrepreneurs toward the influence

---

[61] For a general introduction to the concept of citizenship, see Martin Bulmer and Anthony M. Rees, eds., *Citizenship Today: The Contemporary Relevance of T.H. Marshall* (London: UCL Press, 1996) and Ronald Beiner, ed., *Theorizing Citizenship* (Albany: SUNY Press, 1995). For its application to China, see Kristen Parris, "Private Entrepreneurs as Citizens: From Leninism to Corporatism," *China Information*, vol. 10, nos. 3/4 (Winter 1995/Spring 1996), and Merle Goldman and Elizabeth J. Perry, eds., *Changing Meanings of Citizenship in Modern China* (Cambridge: Harvard University Press, 2002).

of their business associations, but not in the ways expected by those who anticipate entrepreneurs will become agents of political change in China. In fact, the impact of development is clearer and more consistent than differences between the associations themselves or between party members and non-members among the entrepreneurs. The views of officials, on the other hand, are remarkably constant regardless of the level of development. Unger's study of business associations in Beijing hinted at the potential impact of the local level of development, and his supposition is borne out by the survey data presented here. This finding suggests a cautionary note: Economic development is clearly having a major impact on the views of entrepreneurs, but instead of leading them to assert a more independent role for themselves and their associations, they are moving closer to the views of local party and government officials and away from entrepreneurs in the less prosperous areas. In the more developed areas, the views of private entrepreneurs and officials regarding the roles of business associations are converging, and the expectation of business associations' influence over policy implementation is also lower than elsewhere. These findings suggest increased embeddedness, not greater autonomy, which the literatures on citizenship and civil society identify as a necessary factor for political progress. If this relationship is generalizable to other areas of China, then the notion that entrepreneurs will be agents of change needs to be reconsidered. The entrepreneurs surveyed here, at least, do not seem inclined to play that role. It also questions the argument that business associations are moving in a societal corporatist direction, if in fact they are not trying to assert their autonomy.

SUMMARY

In order to adapt itself to the new environment in which market forces have steadily supplanted central planning and limited political liberalization has replaced policies of class struggle, the CCP has created new institutional arrangements to link state and society. The corporatist approach helps uncover important changes in China's political economy that may have profound implications for its political system.

Some of the claims made for the potential impact of corporatism in China may be quite misleading, however. As a model of state–society relations in other countries, the corporatist approach is not used to explain the dynamics of political change. Just the opposite: corporatist strategies are more often designed by states to structure and sharply limit the avenues of interest mediation in order to prevent societal demands for political change. Corporatism can be particularly useful if we keep in mind Stepan's distinction between exclusionary and inclusionary poles within state corporatism. The CCP's corporatist strategy is

designed to include certain new groups into the political arena, particularly entrepreneurs and those with scientific and technical expertise, while at the same
time excluding participation by others. If the CCP's corporatist strategy fails,
it will not be because state corporatist arrangements gradually evolved into
societal corporatism. If societal corporatism arises in China, it will be the consequence, not the cause, of political change. Those who predict that societal corporatism will gradually emerge in China do not give sufficient emphasis to the
central fact of China's political system – the continued rule of a Leninist party.
The corporatist approach also does not give adequate attention to the experience
of other Leninist parties for whom political change was tumultuous, not gradual.

The evidence provided in this chapter suggests that the CCP's corporatist
strategy of creating new institutional links with key groups in China's new
economic and social environment may be successful, at least in the short run.
The strategy was designed to allow the party to continue to play a leading
role in the private economy. The CCP substituted new organizational links
for the traditional Maoist methods of maintaining the state's domination – a
centrally planned economy and "totalistic" ambitions of penetrating society.
This is a key element of policies of inclusion, which both political scientists
and organizational theorists identify as facilitating adaptation. Local party and
government officials seem satisfied that the business associations successfully
provide party leadership over the private sector, while also acknowledging that
the associations are able to represent the interests of their members as well as
the government's viewpoint.

China's entrepreneurs show an evolving concept of organized interests
and are willing to use the business associations for collective and individual
purposes to address business concerns. However, they believe that their associations represent both their interests and the viewpoint of the government. While
they are not demanding civil, political, or social rights that would clearly mark
themselves as citizens, they do exhibit an awareness of their shared interests
and potential for collective action that may set the stage for a more explicit
concept of citizenship to emerge. This is an important trend, even if it does not
have immediate and direct implications for China's potential democratization.

China's entrepreneurs are not yet seeking an autonomous status with which
they can challenge the state. In fact, in the areas that are most economically
developed and where privatization has advanced the furthest, the views of entrepreneurs are more supportive of the state's leadership than is the case in less
prosperous areas. This is in sharp contrast to theories of citizenship and civil
society based on the Western experience, even though it is in keeping with the
experience of other East Asian countries and China's own past. Instead of seeking an officially recognized and protected autonomy, they seek to be embedded

in the state, and the state in turn has created the institutional means for linking itself with private business interests. For those who expect entrepreneurs to be agents of political change in China, the evidence so far – based upon the data presented here and in previous research by other scholars – does not lend much support. While they already exhibit a strong belief in the efficacy of their business associations and their ability to influence policy that may one day lead them to play a more assertive role, they are not yet ready to play that role.

Not only do the business associations play a dual role of representing both the state's and the members' interests, the entrepreneurs themselves see the government-business relationship as a symbiotic one. As the next chapter will show, private entrepreneurs also believe they have the types of skills and experience that the party needs. This is the second aspect of inclusion: co-opting new members into the organization. While creating new institutional links may create the risk of being influenced by outside forces whose interests may not be fully in line with those of the organization, co-optation brings those influences directly into the organization, thus potentially creating a second and more direct cause of adaptation.

# *Appendix*

## *Survey Design and Implementation*

The survey data used throughout this book were collected in fall 1997 and spring 1999. In all, eight counties were selected as survey sites: two each in Zhejiang, Shandong, Hebei, and Hunan. The sites were selected to include a mix of areas with varying levels of economic development and privatization. The survey was conducted in three counties in fall 1997, and the other five counties in spring 1999. Because of the terms under which the survey was conducted, the identities of the individual respondents as well as the counties themselves must remain anonymous.

The survey targeted two specific groups: the owners and operators of large and medium scale private enterprises (those with reported annual sales of over 1 million RMB) and the local party and government officials with either general executive responsibilities or particular authority over the private economy.

The design of the questionnaire and the sample and the actual implementation of the survey itself were done in coordination with the Research Center for Contemporary China (RCCC) of Peking University. A series of meetings were held in the summer of 1997 to develop a set of specific questions that would be both relevant to the theoretical issues of the project and also appropriate to the political and economic context in China. A survey team from the RCCC visited each county in advance of the survey work to seek the permission of local officials and plan the practical details of implementation.

In each county, entrepreneurs were selected from three townships and towns where the private economy was relatively developed for that particular county. In one county, four townships and towns were selected in order to get the desired number of entrepreneurs. Although the private economy was very well developed in this county, its enterprises were relatively small scale and therefore did not fit the sample design. The name lists of relatively large-scale enterprises provided by the Industry and Commerce Bureau were used to create a sampling pool with the first 100 names from the lists of two townships/towns and the first 150 names of the list of a third township/town. Using a random start, fixed interval system, a sample of 20 enterprises was chosen from the first 2 townships/towns, and a sample of 30 from the other.

In each county, 29 specific officials were targeted: 17 county-level party and government cadres, including the party and government leaders and those in charge of the relevant political, economic, and united front departments; 6 cadres from the townships and towns (*xiangzhen*) where the enterprises in the sample were located; and 6 village-level cadres.

Separate questionnaires were used for these two groups, but most questions were asked of both. At the suggestion of local officials, the questionnaires were self-administered under the supervision of the survey team, instead of individual face to face interviews with a member of the survey team recording the responses. In each county, the county, township/town, and village-level officials gathered in separate meetings to fill out the questionnaires. They received the questionnaire, filled it out, and returned it in the same room. During this process, a member of the survey team was present at all times to pass out the questionnaires, explain the requirements of the survey, answer questions from the respondents, and collect the filled out questionnaires. This was done to protect the integrity of the survey.

The entrepreneurs selected for the sample were invited by the county officials to attend meetings to fill out the questionnaire. The office that took charge of the implementation of the survey varied: in different counties, the main work was done by either the organization department, the propaganda department, the county party committee's work office, or the industrial and commercial bureau of the government. In one county, the Private Entrepreneurs' Association provided enthusiastic support, mobilizing private entrepreneurs to attend the group meetings and even providing subsidies to those who filled out questionnaires. At each meeting, members of the survey team checked the identity of the respondents. In some cases, entrepreneurs sent staff members or family members in their place. When this happened, the survey team did not allow the entrepreneurs' representatives to fill out the questionnaire, but had township officials deliver the questionnaire to the entrepreneur and return it once it was completed either that same day or the next. At the meetings where most entrepreneurs filled out their questionnaires, a member of the survey team was present at all times to supervise and monitor the survey.

In the counties where the private economy was not well developed, the guidelines for selecting the sample had to be relaxed for several reasons. First, local procedures for registering enterprises were not always uniform. The local industrial and commercial bureaus did not always clearly distinguish between *geti* and private enterprises (the formal bureaucratic distinction is based primarily on the number of workers employed, but this was not always followed in practice). Second, where the local economies, and the private sector in particular, were not well developed, there were few enterprises with annual revenues of over one million yuan. Yet another reason was the wariness of entrepreneurs themselves, who were afraid of being asked to pay more taxes and therefore underreported the number of workers and enterprise profits. For these reasons, larger samples were drawn in these counties in order to reach the target of seventy respondents. Additional efforts were made to contact the entrepreneurs who did not attend the group meetings. Members of the survey team went to individual enterprises in order to have them fill out the questionnaire. Members of the survey team checked each questionnaire filled out at group meetings or after direct contacts; those that did not have the proper status, had too few workers, or for other reasons were invalid were not included in the final dataset.

In the end, the dataset from this survey consists of the responses of 524 private entrepreneurs and 230 local party and government officials. This is not a random sample of China's population, and was not intended to be. While the results may not be generalizable to the population as a whole, or even to the full range of private entrepreneurs in China, the respondents do represent the economic and political elites in their communities and are therefore of most relevance for the questions asked in this study.

# 4

# *The Politics of Co-optation*

If we allow private entrepreneurs [to join the party], it would create
serious conceptual chaos within the party, and destroy the unified
foundation of the political thought of the party that is now united,
and destroy the baseline of what the party is able to accommodate
in terms of its advanced class nature. . . . The party name, the party
constitution, and the party platform all would have to be changed.[1]

The practical experience of our party shows that the structure of the
party membership is related to and to a certain degree influences
the party's character. However, it is not the decisive factor affecting
the party's character.[2]

WITH the beginning of the reform era, the CCP not only created new
organizations to link itself with the changing economic and social environment, it also undertook a determined and extensive effort to recruit new
members with new sets of skills into the party. This was a direct consequence of
the party's decision to switch its key task from promoting class struggle during
the Mao years to promoting economic modernization in the post-Mao era. The
change in goals necessitated a change in criteria for recruiting new members
and appointing new personnel to key posts in the party and government at all
levels. Party leaders recognized that the kinds of people who joined the party
when waging revolution and class struggle were the focus of the party's agenda
were ill suited to the more pragmatic efforts to develop the economy and raise
standards of living.

---

[1] Lin Yanzhi, "How the Communist Party Should 'Lead' the Capitalist Class," *Shehui kexue
zhanxian* (Social Science Battlefront), June 20, 2001, translated in FBIS, July 14, 2001. This
article, written by a deputy party secretary of the Jilin Provincial Party Committee, was originally published in the May issue of *Zhenli de zhuiqiu*.

[2] *Qiushi*, November 16, 2001, translated in FBIS, November 29, 2001.

The co-optation of new members is a key dimension of the policy of inclusion that allows Leninist parties to adapt, and is also an important factor for promoting organizational change in a variety of organizations. This chapter will begin by describing the logic of co-optation, its intended and unintended consequences, and the controversies it can generate within the organization. Cases of other Leninist parties which were transformed by the co-optation of new members will be compared with the Chinese case to show that who is co-opted has important implications for the kinds of changes that will follow. It will then show how changes in the CCP's recruitment strategies to target intellectuals and entrepreneurs led to sharp criticism by those who felt that co-opting these former "class enemies" into the CCP was undermining the party's integrity and betraying the interests of its traditional base, the workers and farmers. Finally, it will look more closely at party building within the private sector, including party membership among the owners of private enterprises, the recruitment of party members from workers in the private sector, and the creation of party organizations for private entrepreneurs and their workers. It will use survey data to distinguish the characteristics of red capitalists from non-party members among the entrepreneurs. Whereas the previous chapter focused on the external institutional links between the party and the private sector, this chapter will examine the inclusion of entrepreneurs into the party.

## THE POLITICAL LOGIC OF CO-OPTATION

Organizations have two main strategies for coping with environmental change: creating new links with other organizations (discussed in the previous chapter) and co-opting new personnel. These strategies allow the organization to be better integrated with its environment and better informed of changes occurring therein. Co-optation allows the organization to add new skills, experiences, and resources (such as political support) that may enhance its performance and increase its chance of survival. But co-optation can also threaten the organization if these co-opted actors do not share its goals. The organization may receive needed support but as a consequence be diverted from its original mission.[3] Therefore, the co-optation decision may be contested within the organization. Other organizational goals, such as self-preservation and self-replication, can become paramount, limiting the organization's ability to adapt successfully to new challenges. Opponents of adaptation may point to party traditions and

[3] Philip P. Selznick, *TVA and the Grass Roots* (Berkeley: University of California Press, 1949); Jeffrey Pfeffer and Gerald B. Salancik, *The External Control of Organizations: A Resource Dependence Perspective* (New York: Harper and Row, 1978), pp. 164–165.

established norms as more legitimate grounds for resisting change than sheer self-interest.[4]

The experience of authoritarian parties, and Leninist parties in particular, is consistent with this dilemma posed by co-optation. As they abandon class struggle for the sake of economic modernization, these parties typically switch from an exclusionary to an inclusionary, or co-optive, recruitment policy.[5] Organizations co-opt those they depend on, who possess resources they require, or who pose a threat to the organization. In the post-Mao period, the switch from class struggle to economic modernization as the key task of the party has made the party dependent on the technocrats and entrepreneurs who make the economy grow. Former class enemies and counter-revolutionaries are now brought into the party because they have the skills desired by party leaders to accomplish their new policy agenda. This may lead to the rejuvenation of the party, but may also lead to long-term degradation if the interests of these new members conflict with party traditions. As the party tries to adapt by co-opting new members, supporters of party traditions resist "assimilating new actors whose loyalty to the organization (as opposed to its ostensible goals) is in doubt."[6] This is precisely the dilemma posed by admitting technocrats and entrepreneurs into the CCP: They are committed to economic growth, but more orthodox leaders question their support of communism and loyalty to the CCP. Those who are more concerned with self-preservation than adaptation resist the arrival of former enemies into their midst.

But the concerns of defenders of party traditions about the potential threat posed by entrepreneurs are not totally self-interested. Huntington notes that the main threat to an authoritarian regime is the "diversification of the elite resulting from the rise of new groups controlling autonomous sources of economic power, that is, from the development of an independently wealthy business and indus-trial middle class."[7] The creation of autonomous sources of wealth weakens one of what Walder calls "the institutional pillars" of a communist system: state control over the economy, resulting in organized dependence, that is, the depen-dence of society on the state for economic security (jobs, housing, food, etc.)

---

[4] Michael T. Hannan and John Freeman, *Organizational Ecology* (Cambridge: Harvard University Press, 1991), pp. 67–68; Pfeffer and Salancik, *The External Control of Organizations*, p. 82.

[5] Samuel P. Huntington, "Social and Institutional Dynamics of One-Party Systems," in Samuel P. Huntington and Clement H. Moore, eds., *Authoritarian Politics in Modern Society: The Dynamics of Established One-Party Systems* (New York: Basic Books, 1970); Ken Jowitt, "Inclusion," in *New World Disorder* (Berkeley: University of California Press, 1992).

[6] Patrick H. O'Neil, "Revolution from Within: Institutional Analysis, Transitions from Authoritar-ianism, and the Case of Hungary," *World Politics*, vol. 48, no. 4 (July 1996), pp. 579–603, quote from p. 585.

[7] Huntington, "Social and Institutional Dynamics," p. 20.

as well as political protection.[8] As economic reform creates alternative paths toward career mobility and acquisition of wealth (through education and entrepreneurship), dependence on the state is reduced, and the power of the state and its ruling party is similarly diminished. Thus, the fears of party conservatives are not totally self-serving or illusory.

Despite the inherent risks and the controversies it engendered, the CCP embarked on a strategy of co-optation in order to facilitate its goal of economic modernization and to help reconcile the state with society after the vagaries of the late Maoist era. To assess the likely implications of this strategy for the fate of the party, it is best to first examine the impact of co-optation on other Leninist parties, and then to compare those results with the Chinese case.

### COMPARING THE POLITICAL IMPLICATIONS OF CO-OPTATION IN CHINA, HUNGARY, AND TAIWAN

What are the political consequences of these policies of co-optation? Will they lead to rejuvenation of the party by drawing in new elites, or will they undermine the foundations of the Leninist system in China? Scholars have generally seen the inclusion of new elites into the party as a positive development. According to Hong Yung Lee, the presence of technocrats in the party and government bureaucracies better balances "the political needs of the Leninist party and the structural prerequisites of economic development."[9] Similarly, Kristen Parris sees entrepreneurs as a "force for change within the party rank and file."[10] While co-optive parties tend to be more adaptable than those with exclusive recruitment policies, *who* is being co-opted has important implications for *how* the party adapts. To show why this is so, it is best to distinguish different types of elites.

Yanqi Tong makes a useful distinction between a civil society organized to regulate the supply of goods and services (a "non-critical realm" that does not pose a direct challenge to the regime, and may even be welcomed by it) and a political society designed to "influence state decisions or to obtain a share

---

[8] Andrew G. Walder, "The Decline of Communist Power: Elements of a Theory of Institutional Change," *Theory and Society*, vol. 23, no. 2 (April 1994), pp. 297–323, and "The Quiet Revolution from Within: Economic Reform as a Source of Political Decline," in Walder, ed., *The Waning of the Communist State: Economic Origins of Political Decline in China and Hungary* (Berkeley: University of California Press, 1995).

[9] Hong Yung Lee, *From Revolutionary Cadres to Party Technocrats in Socialist China* (Berkeley: University of California Press, 1991), p. 2. Lee believes that markets and Leninism are incompatible, leading eventually to an authoritarian developmental state in China.

[10] Kristen Parris, "Local Initiative and National Reform: The Wenzhou Model of Development," *China Quarterly*, no. 134 (June 1993), p. 261.

of state power" (a "critical realm" which does threaten the regime's monopoly on power and therefore becomes the target of repression). The success of the critical realm depends on the existence and support of the non-critical realm. They are complementary, though not equal, and "the development of non-critical and critical realms often represent different stages in the emergence of an autonomous civil society and, in the process, of political change."[11]

In a Leninist system, the presence of this "non-critical realm" is the result of political liberalization, not its cause. Party leaders, who need allies in their inner-party battles and who need social organizations to take over social and economic self-regulatory functions as the state liberalizes its control over society, support the emergence of this realm of civil society. The rise of a "critical realm," in contrast, is the product of its own leaders, and is rarely welcomed by the regime, even by party reformers. The non-critical realm of civil society reinforces the regime's decision to liberalize (reduced state interference in the economy and the daily lives of the citizenry) but it is the critical realm of political society that pressures the regime to democratize (public involvement in the selection of state leaders and accountability over their actions).

The implications of this distinction between critical and non-critical realms are best seen by comparing the experience of Leninist parties in Hungary, Taiwan, and China.

In Hungary, the policy of co-optation focused on the critical intelligentsia. Leaders of the Hungarian Socialist Workers' Party decided in the early 1960s to co-opt non-manual workers into the party, including not only clerical and managerial staff but also young intelligentsia. Other Eastern European communist parties responded to demands for political reform by purging party ranks of intellectuals and thereby creating an external social opposition. The Hungarian party instead eliminated the potential threat of external dissent by drawing critical intelligentsia into the party. In so doing, "the party [in Hungary] both perpetuated its rule and created the means of its eventual downfall."[12] At the central level, intellectuals were channeled into government positions, leaving party loyalists in control of all key party posts. In rural areas, however, conservative party secretaries with extensive patronage networks shut intellectuals out of influential positions.

---

[11] Yanqi Tong, "State, Society, and Political Change in China and Hungary," *Comparative Politics*, vol. 26, no. 3 (April 1994), p. 334. Gordon White and his collaborators make a similar point regarding the separate but potentially reinforcing market and political dynamics of China's emerging civil society; see Gordon White, Jude Howell, and Shang Xiaoyuan, *In Search of Civil Society: Market Reform and Social Change in Contemporary China* (Oxford: Oxford University Press, 1996), especially pp. 7–10.

[12] O'Neil, "Revolution from Within," p. 587.

Frustrated by the lack of upward mobility and by their exclusion from decision making arenas, local intellectuals therefore organized informal networks which in the 1980s became the basis for the "party reform circles." These party reform circles took shape as political circles outside the party were growing and as the reformist coalition in the party elite, which had forced hard-liner Janos Kadar's resignation as party chief in 1988, was itself splitting, creating more space for political activity.[13] In May 1989, the party reform circles held their first national conference, attended by 440 delegates representing over 10,000 members of 110 reform circles.[14] In alliance with central party reformers, the reform circles achieved the dissolution of the Socialist Workers' Party and its reformation as the Hungarian Socialist Party in October 1989. Originally formed as an anti-establishment movement against the official party structure, however, the circles refused to institutionalize themselves and quickly lost the initiative to older party leaders. The circles themselves broke up shortly after the creation of the Socialist Party. Although they contributed immeasurably to the transformation of the Hungarian party and the democratization of the Hungarian political system, reform circle members were unable to benefit from the changes they brought about.

Co-optation was also a major factor in the transformation of the Kuomintang (KMT), the ruling party in Taiwan.[15] In the early 1970s, the central leaders of the KMT, principally Chiang Ching-kuo and Li Huan, sponsored the Taiwanization policy, which brought large numbers of youth with political ambitions into the party. The policy had two main goals. First, Taiwanization was designed to change the reputation of the KMT. Before Taiwanization, all key positions were held by émigrés from the mainland; beginning in the early 1970s, the KMT gradually shed its mainlander reputation and came to represent a broader spectrum of Taiwan's society. Second, Taiwanization was intended to improve the effectiveness of the ruling party by attracting young people of talent rather than simply those with political connections. Most new members were recruited when they were still in college, and some were given scholarships for foreign graduate study, mostly in the United States, where they were exposed to the workings of a democratic political system. The KMT co-opted these educated youth in order to channel their political ambitions into the KMT and preempt their joining the opposition. The KMT also used the promise of elected office to attract these young elites. With opposition parties banned, an official nomination

---

[13] Tong, "State, Society, and Political Change," pp. 346–347.

[14] O'Neil, "Revolution from Within," p. 594.

[15] Bruce J. Dickson, *Democratization in China and Taiwan: The Adaptability of Leninist Parties* (Oxford and New York: Oxford University Press, 1997), pp. 122–130.

by the KMT virtually guaranteed electoral victory. At the same time that it co-opted some youth, it continued to repress the political opposition that was excluded from the party and made it difficult for them to compete in elections.

Many of those who played key roles in the transformation of the KMT and the gradual democratization of Taiwan's political system during the 1980s were recruited under the Taiwanization program of the 1970s. The centrally sponsored policy of co-optation known as Taiwanization led to the adaptation of the political system in several ways. First, young elites with political ambitions created pressure within the KMT for democratization. They sought more open, competitive elections to advance their careers. Second, their experience in the United States and other foreign countries exposed them to more liberal political systems, further fueling their desire for democratization. These internal pressures in combination with the growing support for democratization outside the party eventually led to the democratic breakthrough of 1986–7. Third, Taiwanization also led to a basic change in the key task of the KMT: from achieving reunification with the mainland to the economic and political development of Taiwan itself.[16]

In Hungary and Taiwan, the ruling parties reduced the potential threat of external dissent by co-opting critical intelligentsia and politically ambitious youth, i.e., those from the critical realm of political society, into the party. In contrast, the CCP continues to exclude critical intelligentsia from the political system in general and the party in particular. Instead, it targets experts and entrepreneurs from the non-critical realm of civil society. The ultimate consequences of the CCP's policy of inclusion is not yet clear; indeed, in Hungary and Taiwan there were lengthy gaps between the initial co-optation and the subsequent political effects. But there is little reason to assume that technocrats and entrepreneurs will make similar demands on the CCP that critical intelligentsia did in Hungary and Taiwan. Technocrats and entrepreneurs may indeed prove to be a force for change within the CCP, but more time – and more research – is needed to determine what types of change they will promote.

As members of the non-critical realm, technocrats and entrepreneurs could play a supporting role in the course of political change. Some have argued that technocrats are more likely to favor democratization than the revolutionaries they replaced; others have argued that technocracy will only lead to a more efficient form of authoritarianism.[17] For my purposes, the key point is

---

[16] Ibid., pp. 204–216.

[17] Cheng Li and Lynn White, "Elite Transformation and Modern Change in Mainland China and Taiwan: Empirical Data and the Theory of Technocracy," *China Quarterly*, no. 121 (March 1990), pp. 1–35; Hans Hendrischke, "Expertocracy and Professionalism," in David S. G. Goodman and

that technocrats belong to the non-critical realm. They are primarily concerned with promoting economic growth and to that end limiting the influence of ideology in policy making. But technocrats may also be essential allies of democrats. A key element of Hungary's democratization was the informal alliance of technocrats who desired less party interference in the economy, party reformers who wanted to be rid of conservatives, and democrats outside the party.[18] But in China, "bureaucratic technocrats are not enthusiastic about political democratization."[19] Moreover, most technocrats were trained in China, the former Soviet Union, or Eastern Europe. Unlike KMT elites, many of whom received college degrees in the United States and other Western countries, CCP technocrats lack exposure to alternative political values and institutional arrangements.[20] Cheng Li notes that leaders of the upcoming "fourth generation" typically were educated in China's own schools, especially engineering schools, and lack the broader perspectives that education abroad or in the social sciences can offer.[21] However, younger technocrats have been acquiring more exposure to the West, and in the future may be more open to adaptation.

Could entrepreneurs be allies of democrats in China? The evidence so far has been mixed. Margaret Pearson argues that they are not likely to initiate demands for systemic change but could be "available to lend support if others take the lead in pressuring for economic and political change."[22] During the 1989 demonstrations, Wan Runnan's Stone Group in Beijing provided ample and visible support for student demonstrators, but elsewhere in China entrepreneurs withheld their support. In Xiamen, one of the special economic zones in southern China, David Wank found that entrepreneurs disapproved of students' demands for rapid reform, preferring state-sponsored reform to bottom-up pressures that could result in instability.[23] Entrepreneurs may favor liberalization in order to promote economic growth, but there is little evidence that these same people favor democratization. The growing alignment between local political and economic

---

Beverly Hooper, eds., *China's Quiet Revolution: New Interactions between State and Society* (New York: St. Martin's, 1994).

[18] Tong, "State, Society, and Political Change," p. 347.

[19] Hong Yung Lee, "China's New Bureaucracy," in Arthur Lewis Rosenbaum, ed., *State and Society in China: The Consequences of Reform* (Boulder: Westview, 1992), p. 71.

[20] Dickson, *Democratization in China and Taiwan*, pp. 134–135.

[21] Cheng Li, *China's Leaders: The New Generation* (Lanham, MD: Rowman and Littlefield, 2001), especially chapter three.

[22] Margaret M. Pearson, "The Janus Face of Business Associations in China: Socialist Corporatism in Foreign Enterprises," *Australian Journal of Chinese Affairs*, no. 31 (January 1994), pp. 25–46; and "China's Emerging Business Class: Democracy's Harbinger?" *Current History*, vol. 97, no. 9 (September 1998), pp. 268–272.

[23] David L. Wank, "Private Business, Bureaucracy, and Political Alliance in a Chinese City," *Australian Journal of Chinese Affairs*, no. 33 (January 1995), pp. 63–65.

elites may in fact reinforce the status quo because both sets of actors benefit from its preservation. As shown in Chapter 3, higher levels of economic development seem to accentuate the notion of shared interests between local officials and private entrepreneurs. As a consequence, the party retains its monopoly over political participation and takes credit for the economic growth created by the entrepreneurs. Entrepreneurs may be unwilling to risk the certain benefits of the existing system, despite its many irrationalities, for the uncertainties of an alternative arrangement. Indeed, Jonathan Unger and Anita Chan note that entrepreneurs and even intellectuals who belong to the Chinese People's Political Consultative Conference "support further economic and political reforms – but they are usually *not* pro-democracy."[24]

The reforms in Hungary and Taiwan also had an element of indigenization that is wholly lacking in China. In Hungary, the communist party was seen as the creation of the Soviet Union, especially after the repression of the 1956 uprising, and therefore lacked domestic legitimacy. The party used its policy of co-optation and tolerance of pluralism within the party to soften its image as an alien force and to legitimize its rule.[25] In Taiwan, the policy of co-optation was motivated by a desire to change the KMT's image as an unwanted occupying force. The very name of the program, Taiwanization (in Chinese, *bentuhua*, literally indigenization) announces its goal. In so doing, the KMT tried to sink roots in local society, not just to control it, but also to appear more responsive to it. The CCP lacks these motivations for adaptation. One of its primary bases of legitimacy is its victory in the Chinese civil war. It is not motivated by the search for domestic sources of legitimacy nor by the type of ethnic conflict that prompted Taiwanization.

Technocrats and entrepreneurs have had an important impact on the progress of reform and the performance of the CCP. They have been strong supporters of liberalization and have contributed to the rapid pace of economic growth. But their overt support for liberalization must be distinguished from their muted support for democratization. As the comparisons with Hungary and Taiwan show, co-optation enhances the adaptability of Leninist parties, but not all co-opted elites favor the same types of adaptation. China's technocrats and entrepreneurs, drawn from the non-critical realm of civil society, are unlikely

---

[24] Jonathan Unger and Anita Chan, "Corporatism in China: A Developmental State in an East Asian Context," in Barrett L. McCormick and Jonathan Unger, eds., *China after Socialism: In the Footsteps of Eastern Europe or East Asia?* (Armonk, NY: M. E. Sharpe, 1995), p. 111; emphasis in original.

[25] John Ishiyama, "Communist Parties in Transition: Structures, Leaders, and Processes of Democratization in Eastern Europe," *Comparative Politics*, vol. 27, no. 3 (January 1995), pp. 158–159.

to initiate democratizing reforms, although they may prove to be indispensable allies of those who do favor such reforms.

## THE DEBATE OVER CO-OPTING ENTREPRENEURS IN CHINA

Beginning in the mid-1980s, entrepreneurs were co-opted into the party in large numbers. The State Industrial and Commercial Administrative and Management Bureau reported that 15 percent of owners of private firms were party members as of 1988.[26] A 1989 survey of private (*siying*) entrepreneurs in Wenzhou found that 31.7 percent were party members, of whom two-thirds had at least a senior high-school education and 17 percent were former state cadres. In addition, one-quarter of members in Wenzhou's People Run Business Association (*minying gonghui*) were party members.[27] Surveys in the mid-1990s showed that 15 to 20 percent of private entrepreneurs belonged to the CCP, but their sampling designs make these figures suspect.[28]

The presence of newly wealthy entrepreneurs in the party irritated some party veterans, who felt their contributions to the revolution were being betrayed by the party's new commitment to economic growth. This is reminiscent of the frustration felt by revolutionary veterans in the early 1950s, when the CCP switched from waging war to running the government and had to recruit new people with new kinds of skills to perform new tasks. Then as now, those who had committed many years of loyal service to the party were displeased with the sudden emphasis on expertise and the reliance upon new personnel who had not demonstrated their commitment to the party's ultimate goals. The recruitment of entrepreneurs into the party in the 1980s was also a very potent symbol of the adoption of market oriented policies and decline of communist ideology in post-Mao China. Fearing that bourgeois influences were spreading into the party, the CCP banned the new recruitment of private entrepreneurs into the party in August 1989, following the crackdown on demonstrators in Tiananmen Square and elsewhere around the country; entrepreneurs already in the party could no

---

[26] Reported in *Jingji cankao*, 4 November 1988, in FBIS, 7 December 1988, p. 36.

[27] Parris, "Local Initiative and National Reform," pp. 259, 261.

[28] According to a survey of 1171 private firms in 83 counties spread across 12 provinces and provincial level cities, 13.1 percent of private entrepreneurs belonged to the CCP in 1993, 17.1 percent in 1995, and 16.6 percent in 1996. However, local officials were apparently allowed to handpick the people they interviewed as part of these surveys, rather than select a more representative sample. See *Zhongguo siying jingji nianjian, 1996* (China's Private Economy Yearbook, 1996) (Beijing: Zhongguo gongshang lianhe chubanshe, 1996), p. 162, and *Zhongguo siying qiye fazhan baogao (1978–1998)* (Report on the Development of China's Private Enterprises, 1978–1998) (Beijing: Shehui kexue wenxian chubanshe, 1999), p. 164.

longer hold official positions.[29] Party leaders were angered by the support given to student demonstrators by entrepreneurs, most prominently Wan Runnan of Beijing's Stone Corporation. In September 1995, the organization department repeated that the party would not admit private entrepreneurs "because they are capitalists bent on exploiting the labor force."[30] In April 1999, the deputy director of the CCP's central organization department, Yu Yunyao, reiterated that local departments must adhere to the rule that private entrepreneurs are not allowed to join the party, even though some local officials were in favor of lifting or at least modifying the ban.[31]

Criticism of this trend has been especially prominent in the journals representing the party's orthodox positions, such as *Zhenli de zhuiqiu* (The Pursuit of Truth). These journals publish exposé-style articles that criticize the practice of recruiting entrepreneurs into the party and appointing them to official positions (which violates official party policy) and the policy of encouraging party members to take the lead in getting rich (*daitou zhifu*). These articles argue that the presence of wealthy people in the CCP contradicts the allegedly proletarian nature of the party, creating confusion regarding the party's identity and policies.[32] One of the party's ideological journals, *Zhongliu* (Mainstream) reported that up to half of new party members in the towns and rural districts of coastal China were private entrepreneurs, and that many party cells were headed by entrepreneurs. It warned that "Private businessmen cannot accept the party's principles and policies. . . . They only want to join the party to influence the adoption and implementation of local policies. They hope to enroll more private businessmen into the party to strengthen their own role."[33]

Leftists in the party decried the dangers inherent in the rise of the private sector, while paying lip service to the correctness of the policy itself. One widely circulated report known as the "10,000 character statement" (*wanyan shu*) received a good deal of media attention in 1996, in part because of suspicions that it was written to reflect Deng Liqun's thinking on the matter. Deng Liqun, a former secretary to Liu Shaoqi, is a leading voice of Leninist orthodoxy and

---

[29] This was first reported in *South China Morning Post*, 29 August 1989, in FBIS, 29 August 1989, and later confirmed in *Zhenli de zhuiqiu*, 11 November 1994, in FBIS, 12 January 1995.

[30] Organization and Personnel News of the central organization department, as reported in *Zhongguo xinwenshe*, September 6, 1995, in FBIS, September 6, 1995.

[31] See his talk on party construction while on an inspection tour of Fujian in *Fujian dangjian* (Party Construction in Fujian), April 1999, pp. 8–10.

[32] See, for instance, "*Lun dangyuan daitou zhifu yu dailing qunzhong gongtong zhifu*," *Zhenli de zhuiqiu* (July 1998), pp. 13–20; "Has a New Capitalist Class Been Formed in Our Country at Present?" *Zhenli de zhuiqiu* (May 2001), in FBIS, July 3, 2001.

[33] Jasper Becker, "Capitalists Infiltrating Party, Article Warns," *South China Morning Post*, July 14, 2000.

one of the few remaining conservative party elders (ironically, conservative and leftist are synonymous in the context of Chinese politics). As such, his views carry more weight than the small number of his supporters would otherwise warrant. The report noted the rapid rise in the private sector, and in return the decline of the state sector, which accelerated in the 1990s. The increase in private wealth led to increases in corruption, decadent lifestyles, and a fascination for all things foreign, especially symbols of the United States, leading the author of the report to conclude that such people "are likely to betray the interests of the motherland and directly undermine China's security." More worrying to the party's leftists were the growing numbers of private entrepreneurs who were serving in official posts, such as people's congresses and people's political consultative conferences, and were being elected to leading posts at the grass roots level, including party branch secretaries. This was not illusory: according to a report on the development of the private sector, over 5400 entrepreneurs belonged to peoples' congresses at the county level or higher, and over 8500 belonged to political consultative conferences at the county level or higher.[34] Private entrepreneurs were alleged to have broader political ambitions that posed a threat to the party. Already they had established newspapers and business associations to assert their viewpoints. But the real threat to the party came from the budding alliance between entrepreneurs and "bourgeois liberals." Entrepreneurs were allegedly subsidizing the research and publications of intellectuals (this accusation was presumably based on the actions of Wan Runnan, head of the Stone Group who fled China in 1989 due to his outspoken support of the Tiananmen demonstrations). This alliance between the critical and noncritical realms of civil society would then set the stage for challenging the CCP's continued rule in China. "Once the conditions are mature, they will 'completely destroy' the communist party with the backing of the international bourgeoisie and openly use bourgeois dictatorship to replace proletarian dictatorship." In short, class struggle was alive and well, despite the party's decision in 1978 to abandon class struggle as the focus of the party's work for the sake of economic development. "If our party cannot correctly understand and handle classes and class struggle, we may not be able to hold on to state power."[35]

Even though the report's identification of the negative and largely unintended consequences of economic reform was largely accurate, its interpretation of the implications of those trends was highly debatable. It put a more sinister spin on efforts by foreign countries that hoped to use increased trade and privatization

---

[34] See *Zhongguo siying giye fazhon baogao, 1978–1998*, p. 109.
[35] *Yazhou zhoukan* (September 14, 1996), pp. 22–28, in *Summary of World Broadcasts* (September 16, 1996), pp. S1/1–9.

to bring about a civil society, the rule of law, and eventually a change of regime. Cao Siyuan, one of China's leading liberal economists and advocates of political reform, denounced the report's message and conclusions in an article originally published in an internally circulated party journal but later banned from being reprinted.[36] He accused them of rejecting the entirety of the post-Mao policies of reform and opening and risking another Cultural Revolution by calling for the renewed emphasis on class struggle. Others turned the leftists' argument around and warned of the political dangers of *not* recruiting them into the party: as the numbers of private entrepreneurs grew, they were developing an economic force and social influence and could turn into a dissident force if the party did not ally with them.[37] Although all sides in the debate acknowledged the rise of private entrepreneurs, there was sharp disagreement on the implications for the party and what it should do in response.

The rationale for banning the new recruitment of private entrepreneurs into the CCP was straightforward, and in large part understandable. Private entrepreneurs have been officially labeled (and during the Maoist years were persecuted) as exploiters of the working class, not members of it. Since the CCP presents itself as the vanguard of the working class and the champion of its interests, allowing exploiters of labor to join the party would be inconsistent with the party's original mission and detrimental to its integrity. This reasoning is sound ideologically, but increasingly problematic politically. As the party shifted its work from class struggle to economic modernization, it came to rely more and more heavily on the private sector to achieve its economic goals. The private sector has been the primary source of economic growth, new jobs, new investment, and technological innovation throughout the reform era. As a result, the party's attitude toward the private sector has evolved from initial tight restrictions in the 1980s to permitting its growth (especially after Deng's "southern tour" of 1992) and eventually promoting it by the end of the 1990s. In October 2000, the CCP went even further, announcing that "the healthy development of the self-employed and privately-owned businesses . . . [will be] supported, encouraged, and guided."[38] No longer seen as pariahs in China's still nominally communist system, private entrepreneurs had become partners in the party's efforts to modernize the economy and improve living standards. Advocates of

---

[36] His article was later published in the Hong Kong newspaper *Ming Pao*, August 16, 1996; a translation is available in *Summary of World Broadcasts* (September 3, 1996).

[37] Lu Ruifeng, Zong Yinteng, Xu Libin, et al, "*Shenzhen shi siying qiye dang de jianshe wenti yu duice*" (Problems and Counter-Measures in Party Building in Shenzhen's Private Enterprises), *Tequ lilun yu shixian* (Shenzhen) (December 1995), pp. 37–39.

[38] This new policy was announced in the communiqué of Fifth Plenum of the 15th Central Committee of the CCP; see *Xinhua*, October 11, 2000.

co-opting entrepreneurs into the party argued they were succeeding by dint of their own expertise and by following the party's policies of reform and opening and should not be "punished" for their success by being excluded from the party. These advocates also noted the specious logic of banning entrepreneurs but not large shareholders in non-state owned enterprises or compelling party members to quit the party once they open their own businesses. A leading cadre in Shanghai's organization department reported that in the high tech companies located in Shanghai, 47 percent of employees held university and graduate degrees, and many of them were shareholders in their firms. Although there was no uniform policy on whether the party should admit large shareholders, there was no explicit restriction on doing so. His underlying message was that given their talents, the party would suffer an immeasurable loss if it excluded them.[39]

Despite this evolving policy climate, the ban on recruiting entrepreneurs into the CCP remained in place. Beginning in 2000, however, party leaders struggled to find an ideological basis for allowing entrepreneurs into the party. The campaign to promote the "three represents" theory of the party's role became a vehicle for changing either the definition of the working class or the CCP's vanguard status to justify the inclusion of entrepreneurs. Instead of simply representing the interests of China's workers and farmers, this new theory asserts that the party should represent the developmental needs of the advanced social productive forces, the promotion of advanced culture, and the fundamental interests of the greatest majority of the people. This is a very expansive definition of the party's role, much wider than simply representing China's proletariat. It was reminiscent of Nikita Khrushchev's announcement in 1961 that the Soviet Union had become an "all people's state," not simply a dictatorship of the proletariat. Nearly overlooked when it was first outlined by Jiang Zemin in February 2000, and described in more detail by him in May, the "three represents" theory later became the focus of intense efforts by party theorists and the media to define a new role for the party. It also was harshly criticized by party conservatives for betraying the party's traditions and promoting the interests of capital at the expense of labor.[40] This in fact has been the leitmotif of the entire post-Mao reform efforts but it has not been enshrined in party doctrine so explicitly.

[39] Zhou Heling, "*Dangqian jiceng dang zuzhi he dangyuan duiwu jianshe de jige wenti*" (Several Problems Regarding Grass Roots Party Organizations and Party Members), *Dangzheng luntan* (Shanghai) (April 2000), pp. 4–7.

[40] For Jiang's original statements on the topic, see *Xinhua*, February 25, 2000, in FBIS, February 29, 2000 and *Xinhua*, May 15, 2000, in FBIS, May 16, 2000. For an excellent introduction to the theory and the controversy it triggered, see Susan V. Lawrence, "Three Cheers for the Party," *Far Eastern Economic Review* (October 26, 2000).

Additional indications of the more supportive attitude of the party toward entrepreneurs also emerged in recent years. Party schools at the central and local levels began to offer special classes and programs for private businessmen. For instance in April 2000, the central party school held a course on the market economy for around seventy entrepreneurs from Wenzhou, a city known as a pioneer in privatization. This was reportedly the first course of its kind sponsored by the central party school. Local party schools in the coastal provinces have held similar courses.[41] The central party school now reportedly offers short-term classes on a routine basis for private entrepreneurs. Although they are required to attend political education sessions, the main focus of these classes includes Western business practices and adjusting to China's entry into the World Trade Organization. They are seen as a prelude to the CCP formally opening its doors to private entrepreneurs.[42]

According to a press account from the Japanese media, Jiang Zemin acknowledged in January 2001 that the party was considering lifting the ban on entrepreneurs, perhaps to prevent them from aligning themselves with the pro-democracy political activists.[43] As noted above, this is precisely one of the motivations behind co-optation: to preempt a potential challenge or threat outside the organization. The opposition to entrepreneurs in the party also demonstrates part of the logic of co-optation: Those who want to uphold the original goals of the organization resist the inclusion of these potential enemies into the organization.

Finally, Jiang Zemin publicly recommended lifting the ban on entrepreneurs in his July 1, 2001 speech marking the 80th anniversary of the founding of the CCP. In reviewing the consequences of the reform and opening policies, he noted that private entrepreneurs, free lance professionals, scientific and technical personnel employed by Chinese and foreign firms, and other new social groups had emerged. "Most of these people in the new social strata have contributed to the development of productive forces and . . . are working for building socialism with Chinese characteristics." While claiming that the workers, farmers, intellectuals, servicemen, and cadres would remain the "basic components and backbone of the party," Jiang claimed the party also needed "to accept those outstanding elements from other sectors of the society."[44]

---

41 *Xinhua*, July 1, 2000, in FBIS, July 3, 2000.
42 *South China Morning Post*, December 4, 2001, in FBIS, December 4, 2001. Sources cited in the article give different reasons for these classes at the central party school. They could reflect the new consensus on the propriety of admitting entrepreneurs into the party; they could also reflect the party school's desire to make more money by offering practical classes.
43 Kyodo News International, January 15, 2001.
44 Jiang's speech was carried by *Xinhua*, July 1, 2001, in FBIS, July 1, 2001. See also John Pomfret, "China Allows Its Capitalists To Join Party: Communists Recognize Rise of Private Business,"

The party's orthodox leftists immediately rebuked the proposal in a series of open letters. Not only did they challenge the ideological propriety of admitting capitalists into a communist party, they also attacked the personal leadership style of Jiang Zemin. They accused him of violating party discipline by making such a significant recommendation without getting formal approval from the party's central committee, or Politburo. They even compared him to Mikhail Gorbachev and Lee Teng-hui, leaders who are widely criticized in China for betraying their parties' interests.[45] Jiang Zemin responded to these attacks by ordering *Zhenli de zhuiqiu* and *Zhongliu* to cease publication. The party also initiated an extensive media campaign extolling the virtues of Jiang's "three represents" theory and the party's ability to be the vanguard of the whole country, not just the working class. All this was done to prepare the party and the country for the upcoming 16th Party Congress, where it was expected that private entrepreneurs would be among the people chosen as delegates and the party constitution would be revised to permit them and other "new social strata" to join the party.

Despite continued opposition from leftists, the CCP reportedly planned to admit 200,000 entrepreneurs as new party members before the 16th Party Congress scheduled for the fall 2002. Over 100,000 private entrepreneurs reportedly applied to join the party in the weeks immediately after Jiang's speech and the party's central organization department ordered localities to immediately implement Jiang's recommendation.[46] Jiang also reportedly directed that the CCP designate ten provinces as experimental sites for admitting entrepreneurs into the party. Among the provinces on Jiang's list was Jilin, where deputy party secretary Lin Yanzhi has been an outspoken representative of the orthodox leftist perspective regarding entrepreneurs in the party.[47]

Local leaders began to fall in line behind the new policy. Zhang Dejiang, party secretary of Zhejiang, presided over a meeting of his provincial party committee's theoretical study group which advocated supporting Jiang's recommendation. This was particularly noteworthy because in April 2000 he published an article in *Dangjian yanjiu* (Studies in Party Building) saying "it must be crystal clear that private entrepreneurs cannot join the party." Even though they were contributing to the development of the country by following the party's own policies, they were still capitalists and the nature of the party would be

*Washington Post*, July 2, 2001; Craig S. Smith, "China's Leader Urges Opening Communist Party to Capitalists," *New York Times*, July 2, 2001.

[45] A text of the letter identified with Deng Liqun was translated by FBIS, August 2, 2001.
[46] *Ming Pao*, July 23, 2001 (Internet version), in FBIS, July 24, 2001.
[47] *Sing Tao Jih Pao*, August 18, 2001, in FBIS, August 18, 2001.

blurred if they were allowed to join. Once in the party, they could also cause great problems for the party by using their economic resources to build their own power base and take control of local party and government organizations.[48] This was the orthodox position when he published the article (which was excerpted by *Zhenli de zhuiqiu* in May 2001 under the title "Private Entrepreneurs Must Not Be Allowed to Enter the Party"[49]), but with the shift in policy, he and other local leaders had to change their tune.

Even before the ban was lifted, however, local party committees found ways to circumvent it. Some local party committees classified private enterprises as collective or joint-stock enterprises, thereby allowing them to recruit their leaders while remaining in technical compliance with the central ban.[50] The head of the organization department in an unspecified city in Shandong defended the practice of recruiting entrepreneurs, who have proven their innovativeness, administrative skills, and ability to produce wealth, which he claimed are the main criteria for party membership. "While maintaining party member standards, active recruitment into the party of outstanding people from among the owners of private enterprises can highlight the timeliness of the socialist market economy, and can make full use of the role of party members as vanguards and models in leading the masses along the path of common prosperity." Shenzhen even created special party branches for entrepreneurs who join the party.[51] These actions are consistent with the overall emphasis on economic modernization: rather than be bound by ideological propriety, local party committees are seeking to maintain their influence by co-opting successful entrepreneurs into the party. These trends were repeatedly criticized by the center. Orthodox leaders contended that the ability to innovate, manage, and create wealth cannot substitute for the political standards also required of party members. In September 1995, Yu Yunyao, deputy director of the CCP's organization department, said

---

[48] Zhang Dejiang, *"Jiaqiang feigong youzhi qiye dang jianshe gongzuo xu yanjiu jiejue de jige wenti"* (Several Questions about Party Construction in Non-State Owned Enterprises that Require Study and Solution), *Dangjian yanjiu* (Beijing) (April 2000), pp. 13–16.

[49] Translated in FBIS, July 3, 2001.

[50] Interviews in Zhejiang, summer 1997. Classifying private enterprises as collectives (known as "red hat" enterprises) is not done solely, or even primarily, to allow party recruitment; rather it is done for the mutual benefit of entrepreneurs and local officials. See Kristen Parris, "Private Entrepreneurs as Citizens: From Leninism to Corporatism," *China Information*, 10 (Winter 1995/Spring 1996), pp. 1–28; Parris, "The Rise of Private Business Interests," in Merle Goldman and Roderick MacFarquhar, eds., *The Paradox of China's Post-Mao Reforms* (Cambridge: Harvard University Press, 1999).

[51] Quoted in *Zhenli de zhuiqiu*, 11 November 1994, in FBIS, 12 January 1995, pp. 24–25; the article went on to criticize this viewpoint. The information about Shenzhen is in *Zhongguo xinwenshe*, June 8, 1994, in FBIS, June 9, 1994, p. 51.

even debating the advantages and disadvantages of recruiting entrepreneurs was irresponsible.[52]

Why was the ban on private entrepreneurs so ineffective, even though it had been in force for over ten years before Jiang recommended it be lifted in 2001? Recruiting entrepreneurs into the party is advantageous for both local officials and entrepreneurs. For officials, it allows them to co-opt potential opposition, to establish links with the private sector and promote growth, and to create personal ties to wealthy and successful entrepreneurs. Local party committees may seek connection with local economic elites to share in the fruits of their success and identify themselves with the people who are bringing prosperity to the local community. Entrepreneurs are willing to provide capital to build roads, schools, and hospitals and provide jobs, things local party committees are often unable to do because the center provides less capital for local investment. Local entrepreneurs have the resources the local party needs. Relatedly, party committees may co-opt local economic elites in order to have some influence over their community investments and to share in the public acclaim generated from them (see Chapter 5). On a more personal level, as more and more party officials are getting involved in business operations, they have built close ties with private entrepreneurs and support their admission into the party.[53]

Why do entrepreneurs want to get into the CCP? Some seek to join the party to gain access to some of the resources still controlled by the party, such as personnel decisions, financial policies, and the distribution of material resources, including loans. Moreover, the desire to be "within the system" is stronger than the desire for autonomy in China, where autonomy from the state often means weakness in the political system. As elsewhere in Asia, China's entrepreneurs are partners with the state, not adversaries of it, as described in Chapter 3. By joining the party, and especially by taking an active role in local party affairs, entrepreneurs may gain better protection from economic competitors and easier access to material resources and financial and tax benefits than would be the case if they were outside the party. There is a strong belief that CCP members have advantages in business. Party membership gives them easier access to loans, official discretion, and protection from competition and unfair policy implementation. At the same time, being co-opted also means that they can avoid the negative consequences of autonomy: party committees

---

[52] *Zhongguo xinwenshe*, 6 September 1995, in FBIS, 8 September 1995, p. 16.
[53] See the discussion of motives in *Zhenli de zhuiqiu*, November 11, 1994, in FBIS, January 12, 1995, pp. 25–26. Party cadres are also willing to be co-opted *by* local entrepreneurs, a trend generally known as corruption. In Wang Zhen's speech on the rise of "feudal" influences in rural areas, he also noted how local entrepreneurs hire party cadres as consultants. See *South China Morning Post*, March 12, 1991, pp. 1, 9, in FBIS, March 12, 1991, pp. 32–33.

may deny the above benefits to entrepreneurs who remain aloof. Even if party membership does not provide much in the way of positive discernible benefits, it may allow entrepreneurs to avoid the interference of party and government organizations into their business affairs.

In short, the relationship between the party and entrepreneurs is a symbiotic one, with different benefits accruing to each side. Local and individual interests outweighed the negligible risk of punishment for violating the formal ban. In fact, the state constitution was revised in spring 1999 to protect the rights of the private sector. In this context, because it is the CCP that approves all constitutional and policy changes, cooperation between local officials and private entrepreneurs is sure to grow.

## THE CCP AND PRIVATE ENTREPRENEURS

Despite the controversies described above, the CCP has forged a close relationship with the private sector in China, forged in several different ways reminiscent of Jowitt's concept of "inclusion" for post-revolutionary Leninist regimes and for how complex organizations more generally adapt to their changing external environment. First, as described in the previous chapter, it has created organizations to link the state with the private sector, with the intention of thereby being able to control it, but also setting up the potential for having influence run in both directions between the state and society.

The second way the CCP has been connected to the private sector has been to encourage party members to plunge into the sea of private enterprise, a step widely known as *xiahai*, thereby leading by example (what I will refer to as "*xiahai* entrepreneurs" below). Deng Xiaoping's axiom "to get rich is glorious" was met with skepticism by many of his fellow leaders, who feared backsliding from the traditional goals of the party and a return to capitalism, and by many in society, who feared a reversal of policy, so common in the Maoist era, would expose them to retribution if they too enthusiastically embraced Deng's call. Throughout the 1980s and early 1990s, the CCP wavered on whether to restrict or encourage its members' private business operations, but after 1992 the party has generally been supportive of such activities.

A third means of linking the party and the private sector is recruiting businessmen into the CCP. Among the respondents in my survey, one-third of the entrepreneurs who were party members had been co-opted into the party after they went into business. The practice is widespread: Every county in the sample had co-opted members, and in two counties the majority of party members had been co-opted. Officials showed little support for the ban: less then 25 percent of all cadres agreed or strongly agreed that entrepreneurs should not be allowed

Table 4.1 *Party Membership among the Business*
*Associations* (percentages)

| Business association | Co-opted entrepreneurs | *Xiahai* entrepreneurs | Non-CCP entrepreneurs |
| --- | --- | --- | --- |
| SELA | 9.9 | 17.1 | 73.0 |
| PEA | 14.8 | 23.2 | 62.0 |
| ICF | 16.8 | 34.7 | 48.5 |
| Other | 19.1 | 38.1 | 42.9 |
| None | 12.0 | 22.7 | 65.3 |
| TOTAL | 13.4 | 24.6 | 61.9 |

*Note:* Due to rounding, rows may not sum to 100.

to join the party. The support for the ban declined at lower levels: 27. 4 percent of county officials, 21.6 percent of township officials, but only 10.4 percent of village officials supported the ban.

According to earlier reports, roughly one-fifth of private entrepreneurs are party members.[54] Of the entrepreneurs surveyed in this project, 40.4 percent confessed to being party members, which is much higher than the national average. As noted above, approximately two-thirds of these party members were *xiahai* entrepreneurs and slightly more than one-third were co-opted entrepreneurs. This large proportion of party members among the entrepreneurs in my survey is to be expected because they operate large enterprises, both in terms of workers and revenue. Among smaller scale enterprises, it is likely that the proportion would be smaller.[55] There was tremendous variation across the counties in the proportion of entrepreneurs who were party members, ranging from 22 percent to 78 percent. Following the logic of co-optation, we would expect that the CCP would target the largest, most successful entrepreneurs for recruitment, and in fact, the business association most identified with that type of entrepreneur, the ICF, also has the largest share of co-opted members. In a more general sense, the higher the prestige of a business association, the more likely its members are to be party members, either as co-opted or *xiahai* entrepreneurs (see Table 4.1).

Membership in a particular business association is not a significant factor in explaining party membership among entrepreneurs, however, when other individual attributes are also taken into account. A multivariate analysis reveals the distinctive characteristics of *xiahai* entrepreneurs and co-opted entrepreneurs

[54] See note 26.
[55] According to a nationwide representative sample organized by Andrew Walder, 2.6 percent of those classified as *getihu* and 14.8 percent of private entrepreneurs were party members. I would like to thank him for sharing his data with me.

Table 4.2 *Attributes of CCP Members among Private Entrepreneurs* (multinomial regression; numbers in parentheses are standard errors)

|  | Xiahai entrepreneurs | Co-opted entrepreneurs |
|---|---|---|
| Age | .114**** | .007 |
|  | (.022) | (.029) |
| Gender | −.191 | .090 |
|  | (.639) | (.637) |
| Level of education | .826*** | .824**** |
|  | (.162) | (.181) |
| Family income | −.032 | .037 |
|  | (.095) | (.102) |
| Level of development | .275 | .544 |
|  | (.321) | (.385) |
| Years in business | .067* | .121*** |
|  | (.040) | .045 |
| *Getihu* background | −.521* | .885** |
|  | (.298) | (.406) |
| Revenue | .000 | −.000 |
|  | (.000) | (.000) |
| Years in county | .064**** | .060*** |
|  | (.017) | (.022) |
| SELA | .091 | −.091 |
|  | (.415) | (.471) |
| PEA | .144 | −.259 |
|  | (.393) | (.482) |
| ICF | .632* | .669 |
|  | (.381) | (.442) |
| Constant | −9.431**** | −8.182**** |
|  | (1.508) | (1.634) |

*Notes:* The comparison group is private entrepreneurs who are not party members.
N = 408; LR $\chi^2(24)$ = 170.14; $p(\chi^2)$ = .0000;
Log likelihood = −289.090; Pseudo $R^2$ = .227
* $p < .1$; ** $p < .05$; *** $p < .01$; **** $p < .001$

relative to non-party members (see Table 4.2). *Xiahai* entrepreneurs are typically older, better educated, and have resided longer in their counties than non-party members. Each of these variables is highly significant ($p < .001$). *Xiahai* entrepreneurs are also less likely to come from a *getihu* background, have been in business for fewer years, and are more likely to be ICF members than non-CCP members, but the coefficients for these variables are less significant ($p < .1$). Gender, family income, and enterprise revenue were not significant variables, in part because of the nature of the sample: the vast majority of business surveyed were men, and they were drawn from the largest firms. A broader sample incorporating smaller scale enterprises might yield different results, but the focus of this study was on the entrepreneurs who could easily be considered part of the local economic elite.

The characteristics of co-opted entrepreneurs are slightly different from both *xiahai* entrepreneurs and non-CCP members. Like *xiahai* entrepreneurs, co-opted entrepreneurs are better educated than non-CCP members, but there is no significant difference in the ages of co-opted and non-CCP entrepreneurs. Similarly, basic indicators of enterprise success, such as revenue or family income of the entrepreneur, also do not help predict which entrepreneurs are targeted for co-optation. Instead, three other variables are significant predictors of co-optation: the longer an enterprise has been in business, the longer the entrepreneur has lived in that county, and if the entrepreneur comes from a *getihu* background, the more likely he or she will be co-opted. All three of these variables concern social standing: The first two show that they have been established in the community for a longer period of time and therefore are more likely to be seen as part of both the economic and social elite. These are the kinds of people the CCP would be most inclined to co-opt. In fact, when the variables for how long the entrepreneur has been in business and has lived in the county are left out of the equation, the age of the entrepreneur and the level of development of the county become statistically significant variables. This indicates the importance of social ties over simply socioeconomic factors in explaining the logic of co-optation. The positive impact of *getihu* status on the likelihood of co-optation is more surprising, however. Although the *getihu* label was previously seen as a stigma, apparently some were able to gain acceptance through their business success.[56] Ironically, their *getihu* backgrounds distinguish them from both *xiahai* entrepreneurs and non-members: 80.6 percent of co-opted entrepreneurs, 65.3 percent of non-members, and only 46.7 percent of *xiahai* entrepreneurs reported being *getihu* at the time of the survey or in the past.

In addition to the large number of private entrepreneurs who are party members, still more would like to join the CCP and many of them have already applied. Among the entrepreneurs in my sample, more than one-quarter (26.7 percent) said they wanted to join the party, and about half of them had applied.[57] Local officials were also eager to co-opt more entrepreneurs into the party: about one-quarter of the non-CCP entrepreneurs reported that local

---

[56] For the social stigma originally attached to *getihu*, see Susan Young, "Private Entrepreneurs and Evolutionary Change," in Goodman and Hooper, eds., *China's Quiet Revolution*.

[57] This corresponds to an earlier report that 24.1 percent of private entrepreneurs not already in the CCP wanted to join; see *Zhongguo siying giye fazhan baogao, 1978–1998*, p. 164.

party officials had approached them about joining the party; of these, about two-thirds said they wanted to join the party, and the remainder were not interested. Remember that only 5 percent of the general population are party members. The fact that 40 percent of large and medium scale entrepreneurs are already party members, and that more than 25 percent of the other respondents have been targeted for recruitment and are willing to join the party, is truly astounding. It shows that the party and the private sector are closely entwined: Two-thirds of the entrepreneurs in this survey were either already party members or wanted to be. Even so, the formal ban on co-opting entrepreneurs put limits on the numbers and perhaps the types of private entrepreneurs who could join the party, despite the numerous examples of co-optation. With the ban now lifted, it is likely that an even greater share of entrepreneurs will join the CCP.

Local officials interviewed as part of my survey project gave different explanations for this practice of co-optation. Some denied knowledge of the ban on private entrepreneurs, which is hardly credible given the center's repeated publicity on not allowing entrepreneurs into the party. Others said the entrepreneurs were managers of collective or joint-stock enterprises (*gufen qiye*), so strictly speaking they were not private entrepreneurs and therefore they were complying with the ban. This claim is also not credible, according to the entrepreneurs themselves. Of the entrepreneurs in my sample who had been co-opted into the party, 47.8 percent said their enterprises were officially registered as private (see Table 4.3). Only 4.5 and 22.4 percent said their enterprises were registered as collective or joint-stock enterprises, respectively (another 23.9 percent owned individual enterprises and 1.5 percent operated joint ventures). Remarkably, *none* of the *xiahai* entrepreneurs who went into business after they were already party members had their enterprises registered as collectives.

This distribution of ownership categories is surprising. Previous research in China noted the prevalence of "red-hat" collectives, enterprises that for all

Table 4.3 *Distribution of Party Membership and Enterprise Ownership*
(percentages)

| Ownership category | Co-opted entrepreneurs | *Xiahai* entrepreneurs | Non-CCP entrepreneurs | Total |
|---|---|---|---|---|
| Individual | 23.9 | 15.0 | 26.4 | 23.2 |
| Private | 47.8 | 60.6 | 61.6 | 59.6 |
| Collective | 4.5 | 0.0 | 1.6 | 1.6 |
| Joint-stock | 22.4 | 23.6 | 8.2 | 13.9 |
| Joint venture | 1.5 | 0.8 | 2.2 | 1.8 |

*Note:* Due to rounding, numbers in columns may not sum to 100.

111

Table 4.4 *Do Private Entrepreneurs Belong in the CCP?* (percentages)

Q1: Private entrepreneurs should not join the CCP.

|  | Strongly agree | Agree | Disagree | Strongly Disagree |
|---|---|---|---|---|
| Entrepreneurs | 5.8 | 6.2 | 30.9 | 57.2 |
| Officials | 12.3 | 10.1 | 32.0 | 45.6 |

Q2: Private entrepreneurs provide the skills the party currently needs.

|  | Strongly agree | Agree | Disagree | Strongly Disagree |
|---|---|---|---|---|
| Entrepreneurs: | | | | |
| developed counties | 25.2 | 36.5 | 26.6 | 11.7 |
| less developed counties | 11.3 | 16.8 | 41.6 | 30.3 |
| Officials | 12.0 | 46.2 | 35.6 | 6.2 |

intents and purposes were privately owned and operated but were registered as collective in order to gain official sanction and some degree of protection.[58] By the late 1990s when my survey was conducted, the legality of the private sector was more firmly established, even written into the constitution. Perhaps as a consequence of this, nearly 60 percent of the firms in my survey were officially registered as privately owned. In six of the eight counties in my survey, private enterprises constituted the largest share of the sampled firms. In only one county were joint-stock enterprises the most common and in one other individual enterprises were most common. The joint-stock category is a relatively recent one, and the firms in this category were on average the newest and more often located in the most prosperous counties.

Despite the logic that underlies this strategy of co-optation, officials and private entrepreneurs disagree on some of the implications of private entrepreneurs in the party. A majority of private entrepreneurs strongly disagree that private entrepreneurs should be banned from the party, whereas almost one-quarter of officials agree they should be banned, and the difference of means test is statistically significant ($t = 3.68$, p($t$) $= .0003$; see Table 4.4). On this issue, there is also a difference among private entrepreneurs, with red capitalists strongly

---

[58] Yia-Ling, "Reform from Below: The Private Economy and Local Politics in the Rural Industrialization of Wenzhou," *China Quarterly*, no. 130 (June 1992), pp. 293–316; Parris, "Local Initiative and National Reform"; Chih-jou Jay Chen, "Local Institutions and Property Rights Transformations in Southern Fujian," in Jean C. Oi and Andrew G. Walder, eds., *Property Rights and China's Economic Reforms* (Stanford: Stanford University Press, 1999).

disagreeing with the ban on private entrepreneurs in the party and non-party members simply disagreeing ($t = 2.27, p(t) = .02$). In addition, there is a sharp difference on *why* they should be allowed into the party. Although both officials and private entrepreneurs agree in roughly equal proportions that party members have advantages when it comes to business, private entrepreneurs also believe that the party benefits from what they have to offer. Private entrepreneurs in the developed counties are more likely to agree that they have the type of skills and experiences the party needs, whereas entrepreneurs in the poorer counties feel they have little to offer the party. Ironically, non-party entrepreneurs are *more* likely to agree with this statement than are red capitalists. While many entrepreneurs recognize that they derive benefits from their party membership, they also believe the party stands to gain from their skills, and therefore view their relationship with the party as symbiotic. Under these circumstances, they are unlikely to simply be loyal agents of the party. Local officials also see the relationship as symbiotic: Over 58 percent of them agree or strongly agree that the party needs the skills offered by entrepreneurs, compared to just over 43 percent of all entrepreneurs. Unlike entrepreneurs, the responses of local officials do not vary with the level of local development.

Although the CCP has targeted entrepreneurs with some success, they have been less successful recruiting workers from private enterprises or building party organizations in them. Only 24.7 percent of private entrepreneurs included in my survey reported that workers in their enterprises had been recruited into the party in recent years, and only 18.4 percent said there was a party organization in their enterprise. This fits with reports in the Chinese media of the party's weak organizational presence in the private sector (as described in Chapter 2). Although the share of private enterprises in my sample that had party organizations is remarkably low, it is still higher than the examples given in Chapter 2. This is so for at least two reasons. First, the party has made a higher priority of party building in the private sector in recent years. The examples in Chapter 2 were from the early and mid-1990s, but this survey was done in the late 1990s. However, there was no statistical difference between the entrepreneurs who were surveyed in 1997 and in 1999 regarding recruitment of their workers into the party. On the question of which entrepreneurs had party organizations within their firms, the proportion in 1999 was actually lower than for the entrepreneurs surveyed in 1997, even when holding the size of the firm constant. The passage of time is at best only a partial explanation for the higher incidence of party building in my sample.

The second and more important reason for the relatively large proportion of enterprises with party organizations and party members is due to the nature of the sample itself. The sample used in this survey was not a random sample of all private enterprises, but of the largest and wealthiest. It is reasonable to expect that enterprises with more workers would be more likely to have party organizations in them and their workers recruited into the party. Firms in the sample that had party organizations employed an average of 110 workers, whereas those without party organizations had an average of only 27 workers. Similarly, firms that reported their workers had been recruited into the party had an average of 89 workers, compared to only 27 where no recruitment was reported. Clearly, the larger size of these enterprises made them easier and more visible targets for party building.

The party status of the entrepreneurs themselves was also a significant factor in explaining party building in their enterprises. Red capitalists were more likely to report their enterprises had party organizations and their workers had been recruited into the party than were non-party members. This was true even when the size of the enterprise and the year of the survey were held constant. This supports the argument made by advocates of recruiting private entrepreneurs into the party, reported in Chapter 2, that excluding them also damaged other aspects of traditional party building. With the ban lifted, it is likely that not only more entrepreneurs will join the party but also that the party's organizational presence in their enterprises and recruitment of their workers will also increase.

The party's co-optation strategy is a partial substitute for its traditional party building practices – it is now targeting elites instead of its traditional focus on workers and peasants – but the absence of party life inside the private sector presents a challenge to the party's ability to monitor what goes on there. The transition from socialism is weakening the party's traditional means of monitoring trends in society. The co-optation strategy is a partial substitute for the deeper penetration of the state into society that characterized the Maoist era, but whether it will suffice is not yet clear.

CONCLUSION

The logic of inclusion offers a useful framework for analyzing the CCP's policies of co-opting new elites and forging links with non-party organizations, as well as understanding the problems that have arisen as a consequence. Although inclusion seems to be a natural phase in the evolution of Leninist parties, the tension between inclusion and mobilization also indicates why adaptation is so difficult, and why the transformation of Leninist parties is so rare. While co-optation and the creation of organizational links seem necessary to promote economic modernization, neither is sufficient to guarantee the party's survival. Instead of leading to rejuvenation, inclusion may contribute to a Leninist party's disintegration.

The co-optation of new elites is a classic strategy of adaptation for Leninist parties and for organizations in general, but it is a risky strategy. As the case of the CCP shows, co-opted elites may not support or even sympathize with party traditions – indeed, the technocrats and entrepreneurs who are now being courted were previously targeted as class enemies. Even though the newly co-opted technocrats and entrepreneurs are unlikely to initiate pressures for democratizing reforms, they may be powerful allies if others inside and outside the party do so. The attention given to co-opting new elites and promoting economic reforms has also led to deterioration of traditional party building, leaving the party less able to mobilize and control society and its own members at a time of increasing political, economic, and social change.

The ultimate test of what impact the co-optation of private entrepreneurs into the CCP will have on the party itself, and ultimately on China's political system, requires an examination of their basic political beliefs and patterns of political behavior. Will they serve as "agents of change" either within the CCP or as an external force, or will they be a conservative force that upholds the political status quo? That is the subject of the next chapter.

# 5

# The Political Beliefs and Behaviors
# of China's Red Capitalists

Since China adopted the policy of reform and opening up, the com-
position of China's social strata has changed to some extent. There
are, among others, entrepreneurs and technical personnel . . . [M]ost
of these people in the new social strata have contributed to the
development of productive forces and other undertakings in a socialist society through honest labor and work or lawful business
operation. . . . They are also working for building socialism with
Chinese characteristics.

> Jiang Zemin, "Speech at the Meeting Celebrating the 80th
> Anniversary of the Founding of the Communist Party of China,"
> *Xinhua*, July 1, 2001.

If [private entrepreneurs] are allowed into the party, some of them
may even use their economic strength to stage-manage grass-roots
level elections and control grass-roots organizations. This will have
serious political ramifications.

> Zhang Dejiang, "Private Entrepreneurs Must Not Be Allowed
> to Enter the Party," *Zhenli de zhuiqiu* (May 11, 2001), in FBIS,
> July 3, 2001.

WILL the emergence and growth of private entrepreneurs lead to the
transformation of China's political system? This is the hope of many
observers of Chinese politics, and also the fear of the remaining leftists within
the CCP. The former group wants to encourage the continuation of privatization
in China, expecting that privatization will lead to the formation of a civil society
which in turn will lead to eventual democratization. Advocates of increased
trade with China and the integration of China into the international economic
system often make such claims. The latter group, in contrast, wants to curtail
the size of the private sector, prevent entrepreneurs from joining the CCP, and

restrict existing members from going into business. They are fighting a losing battle, but they continue to fight.

The eventual impact of privatization on China's political system is still uncertain, but previous research and the experiences of China's entrepreneurs provide grounds for assessing their potential to be agents of change. As will be shown below, they are playing increasingly active public roles, as seen both in their donations to community construction and welfare projects and in their willingness to be candidates in village level elections. Beyond knowing what roles they are playing in their communities, we would also like to know what values they hold and what types of policies they prefer. If they become politically influential, will they use that influence to promote a liberal democracy with broad political participation, or will they prefer a strong state to maintain political stability and restrict participation?

This chapter will begin by examining the civic and political behavior of private entrepreneurs in China, with particular attention to which entrepreneurs make charitable donations and run as candidates in local elections. Next, the political beliefs and policy preferences of both entrepreneurs and local officials will be compared. Finally, based on this examination, we will consider whether the evidence supports several hypotheses regarding their potential to promote political change, and of what kind.

### CIVIC ROLES OF PRIVATE ENTREPRENEURS

One of the important public roles that private entrepreneurs can play is contributing to community charitable and construction projects. This type of role is not overtly political, since these contributions do not challenge the state, and is one example of how the "non-critical" sphere of civil society can be publicly active.[1] Previous reports show that China's private entrepreneurs commonly make donations to the local community, but the motivations for these donations are not clear. Some attribute this behavior to be a result of official pressure, especially in those areas where the local government does not itself have the financial means to build new schools, better roads, or other similar projects. Others argue that it is a "payback" to the local community for the sudden prosperity of the new entrepreneurial class; i.e., businessmen give back to the community to preempt societal dissatisfaction with them and their businesses. A third possibility is that private entrepreneurs feel a sense of civic responsibility, separate from tacit or overt pressure from state or society.

---

[1] See Yanqi Tong, "State, Society, and Political Change in China and Hungary," *Comparative Politics*, vol. 26, no. 3 (April 1994), pp. 333–353, and discussion in chapter four.

Table 5.1 *Community Contributions by Private
Entrepreneurs* (percentages)

|  | Total |
| --- | --- |
| Schools | 54.6 |
| Roads, bridges, dams, wharfs, etc. | 42.6 |
| Social welfare projects | 42.4 |
| Help students with financial hardships | 29.8 |
| Local holidays or other celebrations | 26.5 |
| Hospitals and medical facilities | 4.6 |
| Temples | 9.9 |
| Parks | 3.5 |
| None | 10.1 |

The civic activities of China's private entrepreneurs have precedents in the pre-1949 era. Beginning in the late Qing, guilds performed civic duties, such as building canals and roads, firefighting, and town planning, to compensate for the orthodox Confucian view of merchants as selfish and illegitimate. However, these civic duties were collective goods from which they also benefited. This was not exactly philanthropy, even though the local community gained from the efforts organized by the guilds.[2]

According to the respondents in my survey, private entrepreneurs have contributed to a variety of community projects, the most common being local construction and social welfare projects (see Table 5.1). A comparison of the business associations reveals that members of the ICF – the oldest business association and comprised of the largest entrepreneurs – donate at a higher than average rate on most categories, and that entrepreneurs who do not belong to a business association donate at a lower than average rate on many issues. There is no discernible pattern in the regional variation of civic contributions; although donations for roads and temples are more common in poorer counties and those for parks more common in more developed counties, the overall rate of contributions is generally consistent.

[2] William T. Rowe, *Hankow: Commerce and Society in a Chinese City, 1796–1889* (Stanford: Stanford University Press, 1984); Joseph Fewsmith, *Party, State, and Local Elites in Republican China: Merchant Organizations and Politics in Shanghai, 1890–1930* (Honolulu: University of Hawaii Press, 1985); Mary Backus Rankin, *Elite Activism and Political Transformation in China: Zhejiang Province, 1865–1911* (Stanford: Stanford University Press, 1986); David Strand, *Rickshaw Beijing: City People and Politics in the 1920s* (Berkeley: University of California Press, 1989).

Table 5.2 *Determinants of Community*
*Contributions by Entrepreneurs* (ordered
probit estimates; numbers in parentheses are
standard errors)

| | |
|---|---|
| CCP | .061 |
| | (.125) |
| Age | −.006 |
| | (.008) |
| Gender | .163 |
| | (.202) |
| Level of education | .041 |
| | (.057) |
| Level of development | −.281** |
| | (.120) |
| Family income | .090*** |
| | (.033) |
| Years in business | .066**** |
| | (.014) |
| Years in county | .002 |
| | (.006) |
| Enterprise revenue | .000**** |
| | (.000) |
| Private capital | −.004** |
| | (.003) |
| Member of business association | .528**** |
| | (.122) |
| *Getihu* | .060 |
| | (.113) |

*Notes:* N = 393; $\chi^2$ = 91.61; $p(\chi^2)$ = 0.0000
pseudo $R^2$ = 0.0685
* $p < .1$; ** $p < .05$; *** $p < .01$; **** $p < .001$

A multivariate analysis shows several distinctive trends (see Table 5.2).[3] First of all, several measures of enterprise success – years in business, family income, and enterprise revenue – are strongly and positively correlated with an entrepreneur's level of donations. This is not a surprising finding: the more you have, the more you can give. Second, the level of development is negatively correlated with charitable giving. This is more surprising, because we would

---

[3] This multivariate analysis uses an index of charitable donations as the dependent variable. The index was created by summing the types of community projects to which an entrepreneur claimed to have contributed. Because there was no way to independently verify the monetary value of a person's donation, or when it occurred, this index is presented as a substitute measure of charitable giving.

assume more affluent areas would have higher levels of giving. To directly test this hypothesis, we would need a direct measure of the monetary value of charitable donations, but this was not part of my survey. Nevertheless, the fact that fewer entrepreneurs in the more prosperous areas make donations to charitable and community projects suggests that at least part of the explanation for this type of behavior is local need: in poorer counties, local governments tend to have fewer resources of their own and contributions from successful entrepreneurs are more necessary, and quite likely more appreciated, than in other areas. Third, entrepreneurs who did not belong to a business association and those who received most of their investment capital from family and friends had lower levels of charitable giving. This can be seen as an indication of how well connected an entrepreneur is to the community. Members of business associations are better organized, and the business associations may also mobilize their members for charity projects. Those who do not belong to an association, and do not depend on collective or state sources of capital, may not feel as compelled to contribute to community projects. Finally, several socioeconomic factors that are normally important independent variables are not significant on the question of charitable giving: party membership, age, level of education, years living in current county, and *getihu* background are all not statistically significant. These have been key determinants of many types of political behavior, but on this particular index of charitable giving, they do not have a discernible, independent impact.

Why do entrepreneurs make contributions to community projects? On this issue, entrepreneurs and officials show marked differences of opinions (see Table 5.3). The vast majority of entrepreneurs said their donations were entirely voluntary, whereas less than half of the officials agreed. Of those who said pressure played at least some part, the smallest portion of both officials and private entrepreneurs said it was due to state pressure alone, more said it was due to societal pressures alone, and the largest portion of both groups said it was a combination of societal and state pressures. The proportions are noticeably different, but the rank order is the same for both groups.

The large proportion of private entrepreneurs who said their contributions were entirely voluntary – 80.6 percent of the total – deserves more attention. Other reports have suggested that one motivation for charitable donations is to enhance the local reputations of entrepreneurs and protect them from backlashes motivated by the "red eye disease" (jealousy and resentment felt by others). The data from my survey indirectly support that finding, especially since many of the local projects to which entrepreneurs most commonly contribute – schools, social welfare, providing financial aid to needy students – do not directly benefit business operations. Almost 85 percent of entrepreneurs agreed that private entrepreneurs had an obligation to help local poor families. In contrast, only

Table 5.3 *Reasons for Community Contributions by Private Entrepreneurs* (percentages)

Q1: Did you provide contributions to these public welfare projects voluntarily or were you under pressure? (Officials were asked a similar question regarding private entrepreneurs' motivations.)

|                | Entrepreneurs | Officials |
|----------------|---------------|-----------|
| Voluntarily    | 80.6          | 46.4      |
| Under pressure | 1.7           | 1.8       |
| Both           | 17.8          | 51.8      |

Q2: If you were under pressure, what kind of pressure was it? (Officials were asked a similar question regarding private entrepreneurs' motivations.)

| Source of pressure: | Entrepreneurs | Officials |
|---------------------|---------------|-----------|
| Social              | 28.9          | 32.4      |
| State               | 26.5          | 9.5       |
| Both                | 39.8          | 57.1      |
| Other               | 4.8           | 1.0       |

72 percent of officials agreed. On a related question of whether private entrepreneurs had the responsibility to contribute to local public welfare projects, the proportions are almost identical to the previous question: 86.4 percent of private entrepreneurs and 73.5 percent of officials agreed. In both cases, private entrepreneurs felt they had a greater obligation than officials, although for both groups the numbers were quite large.

If private entrepreneurs give local donations to enhance their social standing, then by their own estimates they have been successful. Over 80 percent said their social status had improved in the past year, and slightly more said it had improved since they went into business. More specifically, the higher the entrepreneurs scored on the index of charitable giving, the more likely they were to feel their social status had increased. Local officials may not be the most neutral observers on this questions, but 56.5 percent of them said the social status of private entrepreneurs had clearly improved in recent years, and another 42.6 percent said it had improved somewhat; in other words, over 99 percent of officials felt that the social status of private entrepreneurs was getting better. In contrast, only 41.9 percent of officials felt their own social status had improved in recent years[4] (the wording of these particular questions

---

[4] This is one of the few questions where the level of development influenced cadre responses: in the most developed counties 57.9 percent of cadres felt their social standing had improved, but

asked of entrepreneurs and officials was slightly different, preventing direct comparison, but the differences are still clear).[5]

These data indicate that private entrepreneurs are involved in their community, not just by providing jobs and tax revenue, but also by helping provide collective goods to their communities. In return, their contributions may benefit their own reputations as good citizens. This combination – increasing wealth coupled with increasing social status – confirms the party's logic in co-opting and organizing these new elites in order to cooperate with them, rather than compete with them.

POLITICAL PARTICIPATION BY PRIVATE ENTREPRENEURS

As private entrepreneurs have come to play more prominent roles in the local community, economically as well as socially, they are also gaining new political roles. In addition to their membership and participation in business associations and the CCP, private entrepreneurs are also beginning to assume official positions. A few private entrepreneurs serve, or have served, as members of local people's congresses and political consultative conferences. Among the private entrepreneurs in this sample, 55 (11.3 percent) either have served or are serving in local people's conferences, and 23 (4.8 percent) in local political consultative conferences.[6] The vast majority of them are party members (77.8 percent of private entrepreneurs in people's congress and 60.9 of those in consultative conferences). The CCP obviously carefully screens those who are able to participate in these congresses; for all those, including private entrepreneurs, who want to be politically active in formal institutions, party membership has definite advantages. Only seven private entrepreneurs (1.6 percent) belonged to one of the eight democratic parties (and three of them also belonged to the CCP). Some have speculated that one avenue for private entrepreneurs to become more active in the political arena – aside from their involvement in the CCP – may be through the democratic parties, which have shown renewed signs of life over the past decade. Based on data from these eight counties, there is little evidence of that.

---

only 25.9 percent in poorer counties agreed. This is also one of the few questions where cadres were asked to give an assessment about themselves, as opposed to their views toward business, and the differences are striking.

[5] On a related issue, 93.6 percent of private entrepreneurs but only 20.5 percent of officials felt their material lives had improved in the past year.

[6] A 1997 survey of private entrepreneurs found that 6.4 percent were members of people's congresses at various levels, and 12.7 were members of political consultative conferences at various levels. See *Zhongguo siying qiye fazhan baogao (1978–1998)* (Report on the Development of China's Private Enterprises, 1978–1998) (Beijing: Shehui kexue wenxian chubanshe, 1999), p. 164.

Of greater importance is the participation of private entrepreneurs in village level elections. Anecdotal evidence from around China indicates that private entrepreneurs in some areas have begun running for village chief or for village councils, ostensibly in an attempt to combine their economic power with some measure of political power. In my sample, 81 private entrepreneurs (16.1 percent) had been candidates in village elections, and there was no difference between counties due to level of development. There was, however, considerable variation in the proportion of entrepreneurs who had been candidates, ranging from a low of 3.6 percent to a high of 34.8 percent (both these extremes were in relatively prosperous counties). In 20 of the 25 townships and towns that were part of this survey, private entrepreneurs had run for village chief or village council. Of these candidates, 72.5 percent were party members. Moreover, co-opted entrepreneurs had a higher level of participation in village elections than did other entrepreneurs: 40.6 percent of co-opted entrepreneurs had run for village chief or their village council, as opposed to only 22.8 percent of *xiahai* entrepreneurs, and 7.6 percent of non-members. This again vindicates the party's strategy in co-opting private entrepreneurs: As always, the party wants to keep all political participation under its control, so if private entrepreneurs are going to run for local office, the party would prefer that they also be party members. Otherwise, having large numbers of non-CCP entrepreneurs successfully run for village chief and village council could present a challenge to its control over political positions.

The multivariate model used in Chapter 4 to explain party membership among entrepreneurs was modified to explain which entrepreneurs choose to compete in village elections (see Table 5.4). In addition to the socioeconomic and entrepreneurial-related variables, two others were added: whether respondents had been co-opted into the party, and whether they were *xiahai* entrepreneurs. Party membership, whether gained before or after going into business, is strongly correlated with candidacy, as noted above. Age, or more specifically youth, is also a significant factor. Education is ironically negatively correlated with candidacy, but it is not a statistically significant factor, all else being equal. Less than 10 percent of the entrepreneurs with at least some university education have been candidates, whereas 22.5 percent of those with primary education have run in village elections. Among the goals of village elections has been getting younger people into village posts, which is supported by the data here, but also to get better educated village leaders, which seems not to be the case, at least among these wealthy entrepreneurs. To be fair, though, village elections may be leading to improved education levels of grass-roots officials. Of the entrepreneurs in the sample who have been candidates, 35 percent have junior high education and 42.5 percent have senior high education. Given the

Table 5.4 *Determinants of Electoral Candidacy*
*among Entrepreneurs* (probit regression analysis;
numbers in parentheses are standard errors)

| | |
|---|---|
| Co-opted entrepreneurs | 1.299*** |
| | (.251) |
| *Xiahai* entrepreneurs | 1.247*** |
| | (.245) |
| Age | −.037** |
| | (.017) |
| Gender | .472 |
| | (.387) |
| Level of education | −.152 |
| | (.096) |
| Family income | −.078 |
| | (.060) |
| Level of development | −.347 |
| | (.223) |
| Years in business | .095*** |
| | (.025) |
| Years in county | .018 |
| | (.012) |
| Revenue | −.000 |
| | (.000) |
| SELA | .342 |
| | (.255) |
| PEA | .474 |
| | (.278) |
| ICF | .179 |
| | (.271) |
| Other business associations | .655 |
| | (.421) |
| *Getihu* | .388* |
| | (.207) |
| Constant | −1.426 |
| | (.753) |

*Notes:* $N = 396$; $\chi^2 = 88.11$; $p(\chi^2) = .0000$; pseudo $R^2 = .251$
* $p < .1$; ** $p < .05$; *** $p < .01$.

relatively poor education levels in many of China's villages, this would undoubtedly be an improvement.

To what extent do measures of social standing influence the likelihood an
individual will choose to be a candidate? The longer the entrepreneurs have
been in business, the more likely they have been a candidate. However, another
measure of local roots – how long they have lived in their county – is not a

significant factor in explaining whether they have been a candidate when all other factors are held constant. Those from a *getihu* background, all else being equal, are more likely to have been a candidate than others. As was true for explaining who gets co-opted into the party, a *getihu* background is not an insurmountable handicap in gaining political status for those who become economically successful. In general, learning more about who chooses to compete in village elections and why is an area in need of further research. The data presented here may have important insights regarding which entrepreneurs are inclined to run for village chief, but they do not necessarily reflect general patterns in the population at large.

Private entrepreneurs and officials show very similar attitudes toward this trend of having entrepreneurs run for village positions (see Table 5.5). Both groups are – in principle, at least – in favor of having private entrepreneurs run for village chief, and although officials are more likely to prefer that private entrepreneurs have proper qualifications, very few from either category advocate restrictions on private entrepreneurs running for local office. Should a private entrepreneur be elected who is not already a party member, both private entrepreneurs and officials agree – in large proportions – that he should join the party. But a surprisingly large number of officials responded that private entrepreneurs should not join the CCP, even if they have been elected as village chief. This is understandable, since most of these officials also believed private entrepreneurs do not belong in the CCP at all.

Table 5.5 *Attitudes Toward Participation by Private Entrepreneurs in Local Elections* (percentages)

Q1: In some areas, successful businessmen have run as candidates in elections for village head and village council. What do you think of this trend?

|  | Entrepreneurs | Officials |
|---|---|---|
| Should be encouraged | 37.7 | 25.7 |
| Only if qualified | 58.6 | 72.6 |
| Should be restricted | 3.7 | 1.7 |

Q2: If a private entrepreneur is elected as a village official, but he is not a CCP member, should he join the CCP?

|  | Entrepreneurs | Officials |
|---|---|---|
| Yes | 67.9 | 59.0 |
| Does not matter | 28.4 | 27.5 |
| No | 3.7 | 13.5 |

If the trend of private entrepreneurs running and winning village elections continues, and furthermore if competitive elections move up to higher levels of the political system, as recent indications suggest they might, the CCP may be faced with an awkward dilemma. If private entrepreneurs demonstrate they have the local popular support needed to win elections, the CCP may not be able to refuse their candidacy or disavow their election, especially if they are already party members. Are the beliefs of private entrepreneurs sufficiently different from the local officials with whom they most interact that their incorporation into the political system will necessitate change in that system? To ascertain the likelihood of this scenario, the last section of this chapter will compare the political beliefs of private entrepreneurs and officials.

## COMPARING THE POLITICAL BELIEFS OF PRIVATE ENTREPRENEURS AND LOCAL OFFICIALS

In comparing the views of private entrepreneurs and local officials, a pattern is apparent: although private entrepreneurs and officials have significantly different outlooks on most basic political beliefs, they are rather alike on policy specific issues, such as the pace of reform. Although basic beliefs may differ, this difference alone may not lead to political action by private entrepreneurs so long as their issue-specific opinions conform to those of officials.

### *The Causes and Consequences of Personal Prosperity*

The respondents in my survey, entrepreneurs and officials alike, were asked a series of questions designed to tap basic political beliefs. The first group of questions concerns the causes and consequences of personal prosperity (see Table 5.6). According to Doug Guthrie, *guanxi* is declining in importance for Chinese firms.[7] Personal relationships and connections continue to be important to business in China, but in the same way that relationships are important to business in any country. Relying exclusively on *guanxi* to get things done is increasingly seen as inappropriate and even illegal, because it is often tied to corruption. He argues that the practice of *guanxi* is being replaced by reliance on laws and regulations and competitive pressures within the market.[8] Guthrie's research was based on Shanghai. The data from my survey drawn from eight

---

[7] Doug Guthrie, *Dragon in a Three-Piece Suit: The Emergence of Capitalism in China* (Princeton: Princeton University Press, 1999).

[8] In contrast, David Wank found that entrepreneurs in Xiamen, a special economic zone in Fujian, favored clientelism over government regulations and policies as the preferred way of getting things done. See his "Private Business, Bureaucracy, and Political Alliance in a Chinese City," *Australian Journal of Chinese Affairs*, no. 33 (January 1995), p. 65.

Table 5.6  *Comparing Beliefs on the Causes and Consequences of Economic Success* (percentages)

| | Strongly agree | Agree | Disagree | Strongly disagree |
|---|---|---|---|---|
| Because of *gaige kaifang* policies, anyone with ambition and skill is able to succeed in business. | | | | |
| Private entrepreneurs | 44.8 | 39.2 | 14.0 | 2.1 |
| Officials | 33.5 | 38.3 | 22.0 | 6.2 |
| Enterprise success mainly depends on relationships (*guanxi*) and connections (*menhu*). | | | | |
| Private entrepreneurs | 11.3 | 17.7 | 43.7 | 27.2 |
| Officials | 4.8 | 15.4 | 47.4 | 32.5 |
| The law is an effective means of solving economic disputes. | | | | |
| Private entrepreneurs | 66.7 | 26.7 | 5.3 | 1.4 |
| Officials | 64.6 | 29.3 | 4.4 | 1.8 |
| Rich people should have more influence in policy making than poor people. | | | | |
| Private entrepreneurs | 13.3 | 35.9 | 38.9 | 11.9 |
| Officials | 8.4 | 26.9 | 41.0 | 23.8 |
| What is good for business is good for the local community. | | | | |
| Private entrepreneurs | 39.2 | 42.8 | 15.5 | 2.6 |
| Officials | 15.7 | 44.4 | 35.9 | 4.0 |

different counties of varying levels of development support his finding. As will be seen below, private entrepreneurs and officials downplay the importance of *guanxi* in business and emphasize that personal success is based on ambition and skill, and that the legal system is a reliable means of resolving business disputes.

A multivariate analysis allows us to see more clearly how various personal and political factors shape attitudes toward the causes of business success and other questions (see Appendix for all multivariate tables). When looking at officials and entrepreneurs together, the level of education is negatively correlated with faith that talent is the key to success. Among officials, 23.4 percent of those with university education strongly agree that the *gaige kaifang* policies allow anyone with ambition and skill to succeed, compared to 59.3 percent of those with a junior high school education. Among entrepreneurs, 33.3 of those with university education, 47.2 percent of those with junior high school education, and 53.1 percent of those with primary education strongly agree with this viewpoint. Within the group of entrepreneurs alone, however, education is not a statistically significant variable when other variables are held constant. On this question, only gender and length of experience in business are significant. Among entrepreneurs, 45.6 percent of men strongly agree with the statement, but only 30.8 percent of women. As most other reports have found, even under the *gaige kaifang* policies, there are limited, unequal opportunities available to women. Not surprisingly, the longer an entrepreneur has been in business, the more he or she is likely to attribute success to ambition and skill.[9]

The vast majority of both entrepreneurs and officials also do not agree *guanxi* is the most important thing in business. The difference between these two groups of elites is not significant when other factors are held constant. Party members, whether cadres or entrepreneurs, are more likely to deny the importance of *guanxi* than are non-members. This is particularly apparent among entrepreneurs, where red capitalists are significantly different from non-party members. The better educated are also more likely to deny the importance of *guanxi*. This is ironic, since the better educated were also less likely to agree with the importance of ambition and skill (at the end of this chapter, I will discuss the issue of inconsistency in political beliefs revealed in this survey). The two questions concerning skill and *guanxi* seem to be flip sides of the same question, but they elicited inconsistent answers. Private entrepreneurs and officials in the more developed counties are much more likely than their colleagues in less developed areas to reject the notion that *guanxi* is the key to enterprise success. Officials may be more inclined to respond this way, especially in the more developed areas, in order to not be tainted by the increased attention given to cadre corruption. Both entrepreneurs and officials also overwhelmingly agree that relying on the legal system is an effective way of solving business disputes. Both groups convey confidence in the legal system, regardless of age, education, party membership, level of development, or other variables.[10] This suggests that economic development, and privatization in particular, is changing one of the most fundamental aspects of traditional values and behavior in China: the primacy of *guanxi*. This would have important implications for both the commercial culture and potentially the political culture more generally. This is a controversial assertion, of course, but fits nicely with Guthrie's findings from Shanghai.

[9] On this question, the variable for members of the Private Entrepreneurs Association is significant at the .05 level, the only time on all the questions concerning political beliefs that it is so. Since this appears more of an aberration than part of a pattern, it does not warrant further explanation.

[10] The only exception to this statement is the variable for members of the Industrial and Commercial Federation. As in the previous note, this is the only question for which this variable is statistically significant at the .05 level, so it is not necessary to dwell on this exception.

While it is understandable that private entrepreneurs would believe their wealth is due to their hard work and talent, perhaps as a consequence of this they are more likely than officials to agree that rich people should have more influence over policy matters. Among entrepreneurs, those in the more developed areas are more likely to agree than those in poorer areas (55 percent versus 44.5 percent). The logic may be that people with ambition and skill should be influential, and if those same attributes are responsible for wealth then wealthy people should have more influence. This goes directly against the political rights of citizenship, however, by arguing the privileged should enjoy greater rights of representation than others.[11] This viewpoint is not unique to China, however. Many democratic countries began by first enfranchising property owners and other elites with socioeconomic privileges, only later expanding citizenship rights to a wider range of society. The belief that talents, not personal connections or birthright, deserve the reward of greater influence also leaves open the door to others who become successful through merit. Many of the Chinese entrepreneurs in my sample (and those interviewed by Pearson, Wank, and other scholars) have an elitist attitude on this question that is not conducive to democratization. They support their own increased participation on policy matters, but do not support broader political participation.

Furthermore, entrepreneurs are more likely than officials to agree with the "GM theory": What is good for business is also good for the local community. Education is also a strong influence on this question, but again negatively, with the better educated less likely to tie business interests with the collective interests of the community. For example, among all respondents with a university education, only 14.1 percent strongly agree with the statement, compared to 43.2 percent of those with junior high school and 51.2 percent of those with primary school education. Among entrepreneurs, *xiahai* entrepreneurs are surprisingly less supportive of this perspective. Only 31.0 percent of them strongly agree, compared to 45.5 percent of co-opted entrepreneurs and 41.6 percent of non-party members. The longer an entrepreneur has been in business, all else being equal, the more he or she is likely to agree with the GM theory.

On all of these questions concerning the causes and consequences of success, difference of means tests and multivariate regressions show that private entrepreneurs and officials are distinct groups, although the differences are ones of degree, not of kind. In other words, where private entrepreneurs may strongly

---

[11] For a general discussion of the concept of citizenship, see Martin Bulmer and Anthony M. Rees, eds., *Citizenship Today: The Contemporary Relevance of T. H. Marshall* (London: UCL Press, 1996); for its relevance to China, see Merle Goldman and Elizabeth J. Perry, eds., *Changing Meanings of Citizenship in Modern China* (Cambridge: Harvard University Press, 2002).

agree with a proposition, officials will simply agree. It is the intensity of views that distinguishes the two groups, not the nature of those views, but that difference of degree can be significant, substantively as well statistically, during public policy debates. And as the multivariate analyses show, other factors besides occupation help influence what basic political beliefs an individual holds.

### *Threats to Stability*

A second group of basic political belief questions concerns issues of maintaining stability, widely viewed as a core feature of Chinese political culture (see Table 5.7 and Appendix). One of the concerns expressed by those who oppose privatization is that market competition is a threat to stability. This viewpoint finds little support among the officials surveyed here, but entrepreneurs are divided based on the level of development of their counties. The vast majority of officials oppose the notion that "competition between firms and individuals is harmful to social stability." However, 44.7 percent of private entrepreneurs in the more developed counties and almost 88.4 percent – almost twice as many – in less developed counties believe that competition *is* harmful. Here is a good indication that increased experience with competition among firms reduces concern over potential risks of instability. For now, though, the concern is still quite strong, at least among private entrepreneurs in less developed areas.

The age and length of residence also influence entrepreneurs' thinking on this issue, but in opposite ways. All else being equal, the older a person is, the less likely he or she is to believe that economic competition harms stability; but the

Table 5.7 *Comparing Beliefs on the Causes of Instability* (percentages)

| | Strongly agree | Agree | Disagree | Strongly disagree |
|---|---|---|---|---|
| Competition between firms and individuals is harmful to social stability. | | | | |
| Private entrepreneurs | 27.9 | 40.8 | 21.3 | 10.0 |
| Officials | 3.1 | 8.8 | 54.6 | 33.5 |
| If everybody does not share the same thinking, society can be chaotic. | | | | |
| Private entrepreneurs | 15.5 | 22.8 | 42.8 | 19.6 |
| Officials | 6.2 | 15.9 | 51.5 | 26.4 |
| Locally, if there were many groups with different opinions, that can influence local stability. | | | | |
| Private entrepreneurs | 15.4 | 27.9 | 40.1 | 16.6 |
| Officials | 11.4 | 22.4 | 50.0 | 16.2 |

longer a person has lived in their current county, the more likely he or she is to fear the consequences of competition. Apparently, more recent arrivals are less concerned about the impact of economic competition, whereas long time residents are more concerned, and perhaps concerned about the destabilizing effects of recent arrivals. The concern about the link between economic competition and instability is particularly strong in the poorer counties.

Two related questions were also asked: whether diversity of individual thinking and groups with different opinions can lead to chaos. There is a subtle but important difference between these two questions: one concerns individuals, the other organized interests. And the results are also subtly, but significantly (at least in a statistical sense) different. Officials were more likely than entrepreneurs to oppose the question concerning individual differences of opinion, and the better educated among both officials and entrepreneurs were also less concerned with the threat posed by diversity of individual views. The differences between private entrepreneurs and officials were not statistically significant concerning threats to stability posed by organized interests. Here again, those with more education were less likely to be concerned with the potential threat from organized interests. Among entrepreneurs, those in more developed areas, all else being equal, were more likely to be concerned about groups with diverse viewpoints.

One inference from these data is that local officials feel the strongest threats to stability are, first, organized groups, second, diverse individual viewpoints, and least economic competition. This would also fit with observations of the type of threats local officials are quick to suppress. However, entrepreneurs see threats to stability quite differently. They tend to see economic competition between firms and individuals as the greatest threat, followed distantly by organized groups and finally diverse individual viewpoints. It may be the unfamiliarity of the marketplace that most concerns entrepreneurs, considering that the fear of economic competition is most concentrated in the less developed counties in this survey. Remarkably, level of development is never a factor in explaining differences among cadres on the threats to stability, even though it is for entrepreneurs.

### Policy And Political Preferences

Other questions on political beliefs concern more concrete policy and political issues (see Table 5.8 and Appendix). On the issue of the pace of economic reform, a clear majority of both groups believe the pace is about right, and a sizeable minority would prefer the pace to be even faster; the difference between the groups was not statistically significant. But on the issue of economic opportunity, there is again a large and statistically significant difference of

Table 5.8 *Comparing Policy Views of Private Entrepreneurs and Local Officials* (percentages)

| | Private entrepreneurs | Officials |
|---|---|---|
| Do you think the pace of economic reform is: | | |
| too fast | 9.7 | 8.9 |
| about right | 58.9 | 60.6 |
| too slow | 31.4 | 30.5 |
| *Gaige kaifang* policies have not given the vast majority of people the opportunity to get rich. | | |
| strongly agree | 11.6 | 3.6 |
| agree | 13.8 | 8.0 |
| disagree | 39.8 | 33.3 |
| strongly disagree | 34.8 | 55.1 |
| Currently, some people believe the government should slow down the pace of economic development in order to control inflation; others believe inflation is a regular phenomenon of economic development. What do you think the government's current top priority should be? | | |
| speed up the pace of economic development | 70.1 | 75.3 |
| control inflation | 29.9 | 24.7 |
| Some people are afraid that rapid economic development may be harmful to social stability; others believe the best way to preserve stability is to promote further economic development. What do you believe the government's top priority should be? | | |
| maintain social stability | 58.3 | 39.4 |
| promote economic development | 41.7 | 60.6 |
| Measures to improve the political structure should be initiated by the party and government, not by society (*laobaixing*). | | |
| strongly agree | 21.9 | 24.5 |
| agree | 28.2 | 23.6 |
| disagree | 34.5 | 40.6 |
| strongly disagree | 15.4 | 11.4 |

degree: the majority of officials (55.1 percent) strongly disagree with the notion that "*gaige kaifang* policies have not given the vast majority of people the opportunity to get rich," whereas a plurality of entrepreneurs (39.8 percent) simply disagree. No other variable was statistically significant on this issue. This of course is a politically explosive issue at a time when regional variations in levels of development and the gap between rich and poor have been growing.

Entrepreneurs and officials express different preferences when asked to make tradeoffs between economic growth and some of its consequences. Officials are willing to emphasize policies of growth even if they result in inflation or – surprisingly enough – instability. Private entrepreneurs, on the other hand, are willing to risk inflation in order to achieve growth, but they are not willing to sacrifice stability. This is one of the few issues where the differences between the officials and entrepreneurs are differences of *kind*, and where there are also sharp differences between officials and red capitalists. The majority of officials (60.6 percent) support growth as the top priority, but a similar majority of red capitalists (64.1 percent) prefer maintaining stability over growth. Entrepreneurs who are not party members fall in between, with 46.1 percent favoring growth and 53.9 favoring stability. This identifies one potential area for discord between entrepreneurs and local officials, who have been selected and promoted on the basis of support for growth-oriented policies, and at any cost it would seem from these data. But if those policies begin to undermine stability – as anecdotal evidence of recent years indicates they are – it may lead entrepreneurs to question their support for these policies, even though they have until now benefited so much from them. Earlier, we saw that officials were least concerned with economic competition as a threat to stability, whereas entrepreneurs were most concerned about this threat. Their views on this tradeoff between growth and stability squares nicely with the earlier differences over the risks of economic competition.

On the fundamental issue of political reform, however, the majority of private entrepreneurs surveyed for this project show the conservative view that other scholars have found[12]: nearly equal percentages of private entrepreneurs and officials agree that political reform should be initiated by the party and government, rather than by society. However, these survey data do not support the view that businessmen are universally, or even overwhelmingly, opposed to societal pressure on the state for political reform: in fact, they are evenly divided between those who feel society should have a role and those who feel the state alone should initiate political reform. The level of development is a significant factor on this issue: Private entrepreneurs in less developed areas are more supportive of a societal role than those in developed areas. This reinforces the point that economic development is not yet leading to demands for greater autonomy by entrepreneurs, as the literatures on citizenship and civil

---

[12] See for instance Wank, "Private Business, Bureaucracy, and Political Alliance in a Chinese City"; Baogang He, *The Democratic Implications of Civil Society in China* (New York: St. Martin's Press, 1997); and Margaret M. Pearson, "China's Emerging Business Class: Democracy's Harbinger," *Current History*, vol. 97, no. 620 (September 1998), pp. 268–272.

society would lead us to expect. There is another noticeable difference among private entrepreneurs: 58.6 percent of red capitalists agree that the state alone should initiate political reform, but only 44.9 percent of non-members agree. By belonging to the party, either before going into business or after, these red capitalists *are* part of the state. What types of political reform – if any – might be desired by them remains to be seen. Moreover, what part they will play in bringing about political change may be determined by how they view their role: as members of the state or as a societal force.

A related question regarding whether further economic reform should also be initiated by the state, rather than society, was only asked of entrepreneurs, which limits its analytical value.[13] An even larger percentage of private entrepreneurs – 96.6 percent – agree that "measures to further deepen economic reform should be initiated by party and government leaders, not by society," and 65.4 percent strongly agree. Those in poorer counties are particularly in favor of following the state's leadership in economic reform, in contrast to their lesser support for state leadership in political reform. There is also a linear and positive relationship between the level of education and support for state leadership: for instance, 51.3 percent of those with primary education strongly agree that the state alone should initiate economic reform, but 75.6 percent of those with university education strongly agree with state leadership in this area.

Questions of political beliefs expose discernible, and in most cases statistically significant, differences between private entrepreneurs and officials. It is worth emphasizing again that these differences are primarily of degree, however; only on the tradeoff between growth and stability are the two groups diametrically opposed. This is an important finding. But it is also important to find that such discernible differences exist between the two groups, on both core beliefs and policy specific issues.

One of the key findings from the above analysis is that the views of entrepreneurs, especially regarding their willingness to restrict political participation to elites and to follow the lead of the state in political and especially economic reform, suggest that they may have more in common with the neoconservative perspective prominent in some intellectual circles in China than a liberal faith in participatory democracy.[14]

---

[13] The wording on the questionnaire for officials was slightly, but fundamentally, different: it asked if party and government leaders *along with private entrepreneurs* should initiate further economic reform measures; 94 percent of officials agreed with this statement, and over 77 percent strongly agreed, but because the wording of the two questions is different it is impossible to compare the two groups on this important issue.

[14] The "neo-conservative" viewpoint advocates, among other things, a strong state to both promote economic development and limit demands for broader political participation. Its adherents tend

### IMPLICATIONS FOR POLITICAL CHANGE

The purpose of analyzing the behavior and political beliefs of entrepreneurs is to ascertain whether they are likely to be agents of change in China's political system, either by working from within the system or by engaging in collective action to pressure the state. To have much confidence in their potential for promoting political change, we should expect to find evidence in support of some basic hypotheses:

*The political views and aspirations of entrepreneurs will diverge from local officials; in particular, entrepreneurs will exhibit greater support for political change, regardless of whether entrepreneurs are party members or not, and will be able to press for change from within the party and from the outside. If entrepreneurs are to be agents of change, they should demonstrate more progressive, even liberal, values than local officials.*

While the survey data do show sharp differences between officials and entrepreneurs, it is not fair to conclude that entrepreneurs have clear preferences for political change, or hold progressive or liberal values. In fact, the survey data presented here suggest that most entrepreneurs have elitist views that support greater participation by people like themselves but not more widespread political participation. On the key question of who should initiate political reform efforts, officials and entrepreneurs were nearly equally divided on whether society should have a role, or whether the state alone should take the lead. And on the related question about initiating further economic reform, entrepreneurs were nearly unanimous in preferring state leadership without societal input. Entrepreneurs are much more concerned about the impact of economic competition on stability than are officials, and ironically red capitalists are the most willing to enforce stability at the expense of continued economic growth.

These views are most prominent among the most experienced entrepreneurs. The longer the entrepreneurs have been in business, the more likely they have been a candidate for village chief or village council; the more likely they believe that ambition and skill determine economic success, that rich people should have more influence in policy making, that what is good for business is good for the community, and that diversity of individual views and groups is a threat to stability. If people with these kinds of viewpoints were to gain positions of policy influence, they would be unlikely to champion wider

to be strongly nationalistic, but not necessarily pro-CCP. For assessments of this viewpoint and its political influence, see Suisheng Zhao, "Chinese Intellectuals' Quest for National Greatness and Nationalistic Writing in the 1990s," *China Quarterly*, no. 152 (December 1997), pp. 725–745.

political participation or increased pluralism. For those who hope that China's private entrepreneurs will be agents of change, the data here do not offer much support.

*Those who were co-opted into the party as a consequence of their economic success will have more support for political change and different political views than* xiahai *entrepreneurs who left their posts to go into business. While the former officials' recent business experience may modify their beliefs, their longer socialization in the party's traditions will still be influential. Entrepreneurs recently co-opted into the party will be less influenced by party traditions and ideology.*

Leftists ideologues in the party fear the inclusion of private entrepreneurs because their class nature may lead them to prefer policies contrary to the party's traditions. As noted in Chapter 4, this is a common observation of organization theory: the recruitment of new members into an organization will contribute to its adaptation, for better or worse. However, the expectation that co-opted entrepreneurs would hold different views than those who were already party members before going into business (*xiahai* entrepreneurs) is not borne out by the data. On the vast majority of questions regarding political beliefs, policy views, or the roles of business associations, there is no discernible difference between the two groups. In fact, co-opted entrepreneurs and *xiahai* entrepreneurs have virtually identical opinions on these matters. For that matter, there are few differences between entrepreneurs who are party members and those who are not. The main distinction is between social role, that is, whether a person is an official or an entrepreneur, and not whether he or she is a party member. In short, there is little evidence from these survey data to support the hypothesis that co-opted entrepreneurs have distinctly different political or policy views that will come to influence the party.

When differences do arise, they are often in unexpected places, for instance that *xiahai* entrepreneurs are much less likely than other entrepreneurs (but still much more likely than officials) to see a correspondence between business interests and community interests. What this suggests is that the party does not effectively socialize its members, new or old. While there are differences between entrepreneurs and officials, differences among entrepreneurs are rarely influenced by party membership when all else is held constant. For party traditionalists who are concerned that allowing the growing influence of red capitalists, both co-opted and *xiahai* entrepreneurs, will undermine the party's integrity, this finding will reinforce their fears. But this finding also makes clear that preventing entrepreneurs from joining the CCP will not alleviate the impact of economic reform on the party. Those who were party members first and entrepreneurs second exhibit attitudes similar to those of other entrepreneurs.

*Support for political change is positively correlated with individual prosperity and collective prosperity.*

One of the main corollaries of modernization theory is that economic development promotes political change. Similarly, many scholars have argued that personal prosperity leads to modern values and support for democratization.[15] In the survey data reported above, individual prosperity was not a significant factor in respondents' attitudes regarding the pace of political reform, state leadership in initiating political and economic reform, the influence of business associations in local policy implementation, or whether wealthy individuals should have particular influence in policy making, or in predicting which entrepreneurs have been candidates in local elections.[16] It is necessary to remember, however, that the nature of the sample used in this survey may distort the relationship between individual prosperity and political beliefs and behaviors. The entrepreneurs in the sample are not a random sample of the entire population, nor of entrepreneurs as a group. Instead, they are the economic elites of their communities, characterized by high levels of income. While a more representative sample might yield different results, among this select group of economic elites, there is no relationship between indicators of individual prosperity and support for political reform.

There was a closer relationship between the level of development of a given county and the support for various aspects of political reform, but the nature of that relationship was unexpected. Rather than having support for reform increase with the level of development, more often the impact was negative. In Chapter 3, we saw that the views of entrepreneurs toward business associations and their relationships with local party and government officials were less optimistic in the rich counties than in the poorer ones. Similarly, in this chapter we saw again that the effect of greater development was not in the predicted direction. Entrepreneurs in the more developed counties were more likely to

---

[15] See for example, Adam Przeworski and Fernando Limongi, "Modernization: Theories and Facts," *World Politics*, vol. 49, no. 2 (January 1997), pp. 155–183; Ronald Inglehart, *Modernization and Post-Modernization: Cultural, Economic, and Political Change in 43 Societies* (Princeton: Princeton University Press, 1997).

[16] The questionnaire also asked about the size of the entrepreneurs' firms, such as number of permanent and short-term workers, level of capitalization, and annual sales revenue. None of them were statistically significant on any of the attitudinal or behavioral questions in the survey, nor did they interact with the other independent variables. As a result, they were dropped from the multivariate models.

support state leadership in initiating political reform and more likely to have elitist attitudes regarding who should be able to participate in policy making. On questions concerning stability, however, the level of development had mixed effects: Those in more developed counties were less concerned that economic competition would threaten stability, but were slightly more concerned about the presence of groups with diverse viewpoints. On most questions, the level of development did not have a demonstrable effect; when it did have an effect, it did not support the expectation that support for reform would increase along with the level of development.

### THE COHERENCE OF POLITICAL BELIEFS

One of the interesting findings from this survey is the diversity of views on the full range of basic political beliefs and policy-specific views. Responses to most questions elicited a great variety of responses among officials and entrepreneurs. Ideally, we would hope that within this welcome variation we would find clear patterns, in particular, that similar questions were answered in similar ways by the respondents. For instance, if a person agreed that skill and ambition are primarily responsible for enterprise success, we would expect that person to disagree that *guanxi* is the most important asset. It is a common practice in survey research to ask several similar questions in slightly different ways, both to assess the coherence of beliefs but also to use those similar questions to compose an index of responses. This allows us to analyze an underlying value that links the questions together, rather than analyze each question separately.

Unfortunately, the responses to questions in this survey questionnaire designed to form an index of liberal values are not well correlated, so it makes little sense to build such an index. Some of the questions were adopted from surveys used in Taiwan over a period of years that were able to show the growing support for democratic values there.[17] But in my sample, answers to separate questions about whether individuals and groups with diverse opinions would be harmful to stability were not well correlated with one another. Other questions designed to measure liberal values, such as the obligation of entrepreneurs to help the poor and needy in their communities, the role of law, and the role of society in initiating political and economic reforms, are also weakly correlated.

Why are the answers to seemingly related questions so weakly correlated? This could be for several reasons. The nature of the sample itself may be

---

[17] See for example William L. Parish and Charles Chi-hsiang Chang, "Political Values in Taiwan: Sources of Change and Continuity," in Hung-mao Tien, ed., *Taiwan's Electoral Politics and Democratic Transition: Riding the Third Wave* (Armonk, NY: M. E. Sharpe, 1996), pp. 27–41.

responsible. This is not a random sample, nor is it very large. It includes only economic and political elites. A larger and more representative sample may find that the answers are in fact correlated in ways that would allow us to measure the prevalence of liberal beliefs in China. Or it may be that the questions themselves do not accurately reflect the underlying concepts they are designed to measure, even though many of them had been able to do so in previous survey work in another Chinese cultural setting.[18] Finally, it may be that the views of the respondents were simply not very consistent. They may hold liberal or modern beliefs on some questions but conservative or traditional beliefs on other seemingly similar questions. Or their political beliefs may not be fully developed or well articulated: Their responses to the survey questions may not reflect deeply held values but simply spur of the moment answers to things they had not given much thought to previously.

In a larger sense, this also points out the difficulty in doing empirical research related to the fuzzy concept of political culture. Ideally, we would like to demonstrate how political beliefs influence political behavior, but there is little consensus on how to accurately and reliably measure political beliefs. Moreover, cultural values are but one of many influences on behavior, and may not be the primary influence. Elkins and Simeon[19] caution us to eliminate structural and contextual determinants of behavior because it is easier to measure socioeconomic factors such as education, age, gender, race, religion, or the nature of the political system. Only once those more tangible factors are found to not satisfactorily explain variation on the dependent variable should the more subjective variables of shared beliefs and values enter in. This advice is too often ignored. In this chapter, we saw how certain basic socioeconomic variables influenced some basic political behaviors, but the responses to questions on political beliefs were not consistent enough to demonstrate the extent to which shared beliefs also influence behavior. That is indeed frustrating, but

---

[18] A question on whether a multi-party system would threaten stability is one example. This question was adopted from Taiwan surveys designed to measure support for democracy. Before the lifting of martial law in 1987, many Taiwanese feared that opposition parties would lead to political instability. The CCP refuses to allow new opposition parties to form because it is unwilling to tolerate political competition. Do China's local party and government officials and private entrepreneurs also fear such competition? Almost 60 percent of officials and almost 52 percent of entrepreneurs replied that a multi-party system would not lead to political chaos. Does this show latent support for a democratic system? Probably not. In follow-up interviews, many respondents claimed China already had a multi-party system, including not just the CCP but also the so-called eight democratic parties. This is of course true, but hardly what we had in mind when we constructed the survey. In this case, the wording of the question did not elicit the kinds of responses we had hoped for.

[19] David J. Elkins and Richard E. B. Simeon, "A Cause in Search of Its Effect, or What Does Political Culture Explain?" *Comparative Politics*, vol. 11, no. 2 (January 1979), pp. 125–145.

we always need to acknowledge the limitations of our data. Using my survey data, it is easier to demonstrate differences between entrepreneurs and officials on specific attitudinal questions than to demonstrate how political beliefs cohere around concepts such as liberal versus conservative or modern versus traditional.

It may also be true that the statist orientation of most entrepreneurs in this survey do not reflect their political preference, but merely their recognition of the political realities they face. They may be willing to follow the state's leadership in economic and political reform because they do not see a viable alternative to it.[20] This explanation is not inconsistent with the conclusion that they are not likely to be independent agents of political change. Whether their attitude toward the state is based on political beliefs, policy preferences, or a rational calculation of available options, their political behavior may end up being the same. The CCP's strategy has been to include private entrepreneurs into the political system through corporatist arrangements and co-optation into the party. If the consequence is that private entrepreneurs support the existing institutional arrangements and do not push for political change, the strategy will largely be successful.

## SUMMARY

In this chapter, we have examined a variety of behaviors and beliefs of China's entrepreneurs. Contrary to the expectations of many observers, but consistent with previous case studies, entrepreneurs in China do not exhibit the kinds of basic beliefs or political activism that would make them likely to be agents of political change. Instead, we may find that the CCP's strategy of creating institutional links and co-optation as means of bolstering its authority is likely to be successful. Political change would then be more likely to be initiated by political actors other than entrepreneurs. For those who are anticipating China's entrepreneurs to be proponents of democratization, especially of liberal democracy as it is understood and practiced in the West, they may be betting on the wrong horse.

It is premature to reject the hypotheses above, given the limitations of survey data used to test them. Suffice it to say that the data presented here, coupled with previous findings, give us no reason to accept them. But the political situation in China is dynamic, and the beliefs analyzed here are not terribly coherent and may not be deeply held. Even without a change of basic beliefs, a change in the political situation may tilt the orientation of entrepreneurs away from

---

[20] My thanks to Minxin Pei for this observation.

the state and toward the "critical realm" of civil society. This scenario, while speculative, is not unprecedented. Indeed, the CCP's strategy of co-optation and forging corporatist-style links with the private sector is designed to prevent such a development. How well and how long this strategy is successful may help determine the course of political change in China.

# *Appendix*

## *Multivariate Analyses of Political Beliefs of Officials and Entrepreneurs*

This appendix presents a series of tables upon which the analysis of the political beliefs of officials and entrepreneurs in Chapter 5 is based. For all tables, the data source is the survey of local party and government officials and private entrepreneurs. I used ordered probit regression analysis instead of the more familiar ordinary least squares regression because ordered probit assumes the dependent variable has only a small number of possible values and that these values are rank ordered. For most of the questions concerning political beliefs, there were four possible responses: strongly disagree, disagree, agree, and strongly agree. When a different set of responses was used, this is indicated in the wording of the question presented at the top of each table.

For each question, the results of two models are presented. The first includes all respondents in the survey, officials and entrepreneurs alike, and is intended to show where there are significant differences between the two groups when other factors, such as age and education, are held constant. The second model looks just at the entrepreneurs, and includes variables specific to their entrepreneurial pursuits. The descriptions of the variables used in the two models are as follows:

*Cadre*: coded 1 if the respondents were incumbent officials, 0 if they were entrepreneurs.

*CCP*: coded 1 if the respondents were party members, 0 if they were not.

*Age*: coded according to their age at the time of the survey.

*Gender*: coded 1 if male, 0 if female.

*Level of education*: coded 0 if no education, 1 if primary education, 2 if junior high, 3 if senior high, 4 if vocational secondary school, and 5 if university or college.

*Level of development*: coded 1 for the most developed counties (based on per capita gross domestic product), 0 for the less developed counties.

*Years in county*: coded according to the number of years the respondents had lived in their current county at the time of the survey.

*Co-opted entrepreneur*: coded 1 if entrepreneurs joined the party after going into business, 0 for all others.

*Xiahai entrepreneur*: coded 1 if entrepreneurs belonged to the party before going into business, 0 for all others.

*Family income*: respondents were asked to give their family incomes in broad categories: coded 1 if less than 5000 yuan, 2 if 5000–9999, 3 if 10,000–29,999, 4 if 30,000–49,999, 5 if 50,000–99,999, 6 if 100,000–249,999, 7 if 250,000–499,999, 8 if 500,000–999,999, and 9 if over 1,000,000 (the median response for entrepreneurs was 4, and the mean value was 3.88).

*Years in business*: coded as the number of years the entrepreneurs had been in business at the time of the survey.

*Enterprise revenue*: based on the entrepreneurs' estimates of the total revenue for the previous year (median was 1 million yuan, mean was 3.53 million yuan; the mean was skewed by the top 5 percent of the entrepreneurs who had reported revenues of over 15 million yuan).

*SELA*: coded 1 if the respondent belonged to the Self-Employed Laborers' Association, 0 for all others (when entrepreneurs reported belonging to more than one business association, they were asked which one they felt closest to and were coded accordingly).

*PEA*: coded 1 if the respondent belonged to the Private Entrepreneurs' Association, 0 for all others.

*ICF*: coded 1 if the respondent was a member of the Industrial and Commercial Federation, 0 for all others.

*Other business associations*: coded 1 if the respondent was a member of some other business association, 0 for all others.

*Getihu*: coded 1 if the respondent was currently or formerly registered as a *getihu* (literally an individual household, a designation created in the 1980s for those who ran small-scale enterprises not part of the state or collective sectors of the economy), 0 for all others.

Appendix Table 5.1 *Comparing Beliefs on the Causes and Consequences of Economic Success*

Q1: Because of the *gaige kaifang* policies, anyone with ambition and skill can succeed in business.

| Model I: Comparisons between local party and government officials and private entrepreneurs | | Model II: Comparisons among private entrepreneurs | |
|---|---|---|---|
| Cadre | −.342*** | Co-opted | .052 |
| | (.125) | entrepreneur | (.181) |
| CCP | .030 | *Xiahai* | .061 |
| | (.116) | entrepreneur | (.156) |
| Age | .002 | Age | .005 |
| | (.006) | | (.009) |
| Gender | .352** | Gender | .497** |
| | (.168) | | (.206) |
| Level of | −.086** | Level of | −.077 |
| education | (.041) | education | (.060) |
| Level of | −.052 | Level of | −.022 |
| development | (.087) | development | (.131) |
| Years in county | .007** | Years in county | .004 |
| | (.004) | | (.006) |
| | | Family income | −.032 |
| | | | (.036) |
| | | Years in business | .048*** |
| | | | (.016) |
| | | Enterprise | .000 |
| | | revenue | (.000) |
| | | SELA | −.243 |
| | | | (.162) |
| | | PEA | .393** |
| | | | (.169) |
| | | ICF | −.087 |
| | | | (.163) |
| | | Other business | −.136 |
| | | associations | (.286) |
| | | *Getihu* | .005 |
| | | | (.123) |

*Notes:* N = 666; $\chi^2 = 39.61$
p($\chi^2$) = .000; pseudo $R^2$ = .026
\* p < .1;  \*\* p < .05;  \*\*\* p < .01;
\*\*\*\* p < .001

*Notes:* N = 405; $\chi^2 = 29.55$
p($\chi^2$) = .014; pseudo $R^2$ = .033

Q2: Enterprise success depends mostly on relationships (*guanxi*)
and connections (*menhu*).

| Model I: Comparisons between local party and government officials and private entrepreneurs | | Model II: Comparisons among private entrepreneurs | |
|---|---|---|---|
| Cadre | −.026 | Co-opted | −.391** |
| | (.124) | entrepreneur | (.178) |
| CCP | −.196* | *Xiahai* | −.315** |
| | (.114) | entrepreneur | (.153) |
| Age | .002 | Age | .004 |
| | (.006) | | (.008) |
| Gender | −.084 | Gender | −.029 |
| | (.163) | | (.204) |
| Level of | −.107*** | Level of | −.095 |
| education | (.041) | education | (.059) |
| Level of | −.355**** | Level of | −.265** |
| development | (.087) | development | (.129) |
| Years in county | .004 | Years in county | −.002 |
| | (.004) | | (.006) |
| | | Family income | −.061* |
| | | | (.035) |
| | | Years in business | −.009 |
| | | | (.016) |
| | | Enterprise | −.000 |
| | | revenue | (.000) |
| | | SELA | −.286* |
| | | | (.158) |
| | | PEA | −.255 |
| | | | (.163) |
| | | ICF | .181 |
| | | | (.162) |
| | | Other business | −.302 |
| | | associations | (.296) |
| | | *Getihu* | −.038 |
| | | | (.120) |

*Notes:* N = 658; $\chi^2 = 39.19$
$p(\chi^2) = .000$; pseudo $R^2 = .024$
* $p < .1$;   ** $p < .05$;   *** $p < .01$;
**** $p < .001$

*Notes:* N = 395; $\chi^2 = 39.77$
$p(\chi^2) = .001$; pseudo $R^2 = .040$

Q3: The law is an effective means of solving economic disputes.

| Model I: Comparisons between local party and government officials and private entrepreneurs. | | Model II: Comparisons among private entrepreneurs. | |
|---|---|---|---|
| Cadre | −.120 | Co-opted | .289 |
| | (.139) | entrepreneur | (.212) |
| CCP | .154 | *Xiahai* | .101 |
| | (.127) | entrepreneur | (.171) |
| Age | .005 | Age | .001 |
| | (.007) | | (.010) |
| Gender | .152 | Gender | .020 |
| | (.182) | | (.230) |
| Level of | −.043 | Level of | .172 |
| education | (.046) | education | (.068) |
| Level of | −.037 | Level of | −.073) |
| development | (.097) | development | (.145) |
| Years in county | .002 | Years in county | .003 |
| | (.004) | | (.007) |
| | | Family income | .063 |
| | | | (.041) |
| | | Years in business | .021 |
| | | | (.018) |
| | | Enterprise | −.000 |
| | | revenue | (.000) |
| | | SELA | .198 |
| | | | (.176) |
| | | PEA | .181 |
| | | | (.179) |
| | | ICF | .511*** |
| | | | (.191) |
| | | Other business | .056 |
| | | associations | (.309) |
| | | *Getihu* | .065 |
| | | | (.136) |

*Notes:* N = 669; $\chi^2 = 4.619$
$p(\chi^2) = .708$; pseudo $R^2 = .004$
$^*p < .1$;    $^{**}p < .05$;    $^{***}p < .01$;
$^{****}p < .001$

*Notes:* N = 403; $\chi^2 = 19.52$
$p(\chi^2) = .191$; pseudo $R^2 = .029$

Q4: Rich people should have more influence in policy making than poor people.

| Model I: Comparisons between local party and government officials and private entrepreneurs | | Model II: Comparisons among private entrepreneurs | |
|---|---|---|---|
| Cadre | −.440**** | Co-opted | −.029 |
| | (.122) | entrepreneur | (.173) |
| CCP | .056 | *Xiahai* | −.022 |
| | (.111) | entrepreneur | (.150) |
| Age | .010* | Age | .011 |
| | (.006) | | (.008) |
| Gender | −.175 | Gender | −.093 |
| | (.170) | | (.211) |
| Level of | −.036 | Level of | −.043 |
| education | (.040) | education | (.058) |
| Level of | .065 | Level of | .287** |
| development | (.085) | development | (.128) |
| Years in county | −.006 | Years in county | −.007 |
| | (.004) | | (.006) |
| | | Family income | −.015 |
| | | | (.039) |
| | | Years in business | −.011 |
| | | | (.015) |
| | | Enterprise | −.000 |
| | | revenue | (.000) |
| | | SELA | −.020 |
| | | | (.158) |
| | | PEA | −.127 |
| | | | (.161) |
| | | ICF | .028 |
| | | | (.159) |
| | | Other business | .021 |
| | | associations | (.277) |
| | | *Getihu* | −.002 |
| | | | (.119) |

*Notes:* N = 652; $\chi^2$ = 25.41
$p(\chi^2) = .001$; pseudo $R^2 = .015$
$^*p < .1$;    $^{**}p < .05$;    $^{***}p < .01$;
$^{****}p < .001$

*Notes:* N = 393; $\chi^2$ = 10.08
$p(\chi^2) = .815$; pseudo $R^2 = .010$

*Appendix*

Q5: What is good for business is good for the local community.

| Model I: Comparisons between local party and government officials and private entrepreneurs | | Model II: Comparisons among private entrepreneurs | |
|---|---|---|---|
| Cadre | −.356*** | Co-opted | .045 |
| | (.123) | entrepreneur | (.182) |
| CCP | −.226 | *Xiahai* | −.414*** |
| | (.116) | entrepreneur | (.155) |
| Age | .011* | Age | .012 |
| | (.006) | | (.009) |
| Gender | −.017 | Gender | −.123 |
| | (.170) | | (.213) |
| Level of | −.166**** | Level of | −.158*** |
| education | (.042) | education | (.061) |
| Level of | −.045 | Level of | .055 |
| development | (.087) | development | (.130) |
| Years in county | .001 | Years in county | −.000 |
| | (.004) | | (.006) |
| | | Family income | −.032 |
| | | | (.035) |
| | | Years in business | .052*** |
| | | | (.016) |
| | | Enterprise | −.000 |
| | | revenue | (.000) |
| | | SELA | −.062 |
| | | | (.161) |
| | | PEA | .265 |
| | | | (.167) |
| | | ICF | .131 |
| | | | (.165) |
| | | Other business | −.085 |
| | | associations | (.294) |
| | | *Getihu* | .089 |
| | | | (.122) |

*Notes:* N = 658; $\chi^2 = 78.99$
$p(\chi^2) = .000$; pseudo $R^2 = .051$
* $p < .1$;   ** $p < .05$;   *** $p < .01$;
**** $p < .001$

*Notes:* N = 399; $\chi^2 = 45.12$
$p(\chi^2) = .000$; pseudo $R^2 = .050$

## Appendix Table 5.2 *Comparing Beliefs on the Causes of Instability*

Q1: Competition between firms and individuals is harmful to social stability.

| Model I: Comparisons between local party and government officials and private entrepreneurs | | Model II: Comparisons among private entrepreneurs | |
|---|---|---|---|
| Cadre | -1.118**** | Co-opted | -.152 |
| | (.128) | entrepreneur | (.176) |
| CCP | -.080 | *Xiahai* | -.196 |
| | (.114) | entrepreneur | (.155) |
| Age | -.009 | Age | -.018** |
| | (.006) | | (.008) |
| Gender | -.325* | Gender | -.498** |
| | (.169) | | (.209) |
| Level of | -.050 | Level of | -.005 |
| education | (.041) | education | (.060) |
| Level of | -.867**** | Level of | -1.053**** |
| development | (.090) | development | (.135) |
| Years in county | .009* | Years in county | .023**** |
| | (.004) | | (.006) |
| | | Family income | .014 |
| | | | (.035) |
| | | Years in business | -.021 |
| | | | (.016) |
| | | Enterprise | -.000 |
| | | revenue | (.000) |
| | | SELA | .040 |
| | | | (.159) |
| | | PEA | -.034 |
| | | | (.164) |
| | | ICF | .098 |
| | | | (.166) |
| | | Other business | -.322 |
| | | associations | (.295) |
| | | *Getihu* | .064 |
| | | | (.122) |

*Notes:* N = 656; $\chi^2 = 265.92$  
$p(\chi^2) = .000$; pseudo $R^2 = .150$  
* $p < .1$;  ** $p < .05$;  *** $p < .01$;  
**** $p < .001$

*Notes:* N = 394; $\chi^2 = 108.87$  
$p(\chi^2) = .000$; pseudo $R^2 = .107$

Q2: If everybody does not share the same thinking, society can be chaotic.

| Model I: Comparisons between local party and government officials and private entrepreneurs | | Model II: Comparisons among private entrepreneurs | |
|---|---|---|---|
| Cadre | −.320*** | Co-opted | .161 |
| | (.122) | entrepreneur | (.172) |
| CCP | .095 | Xiahai | .016 |
| | (.111) | entrepreneur | (.151) |
| Age | .007 | Age | .012 |
| | (.006) | | (.008) |
| Gender | −.320* | Gender | −.275 |
| | (.164) | | (.203) |
| Level of | −.139*** | Level of | −.170*** |
| education | (.041) | education | (.059) |
| Level of | .037 | Level of | .194 |
| development | (.086) | development | (.128) |
| Years in county | −.003 | Years in county | −.012** |
| | (.004) | | (.006) |
| | | Family income | −.079** |
| | | | (.034) |
| | | Years in business | .035** |
| | | | (.016) |
| | | Enterprise | −.000 |
| | | revenue | (.000) |
| | | SELA | −.275* |
| | | | (.156) |
| | | PEA | −.287* |
| | | | (.163) |
| | | ICF | .048 |
| | | | (.160) |
| | | Other business | −.370 |
| | | associations | (.286) |
| | | Getihu | .024 |
| | | | (.119) |

*Notes:* N = 659; $\chi^2 = 40.48$
$p(\chi^2) = .000$; pseudo $R^2 = .024$
* p < .1;   ** p < .05;   *** p < .01;
**** p < .001

*Notes:* N = 397; $\chi^2 = 33.38$
$p(\chi^2) = .004$; pseudo $R^2 = .032$

Q3: Locally, if there were many groups with different opinion,
that could influence local stability.

| Model I: Comparisons between local party and government officials and private entrepreneurs | | Model II: Comparisons among private entrepreneurs | |
|---|---|---|---|
| Cadre | −.087 | Co-opted | .222 |
| | (.122) | entrepreneur | (.173) |
| CCP | .056 | *Xiahai* | −.102 |
| | (.112) | entrepreneur | (.151) |
| Age | .008 | Age | .011 |
| | (.006) | | (.008) |
| Gender | −.234 | Gender | −.347* |
| | (.166) | | (.209) |
| Level of | −.106*** | Level of | −.106* |
| education | (.040) | education | (.058) |
| Level of | .046 | Level of | .271** |
| development | (.085) | development | (.127) |
| Years in county | −.004 | Years in county | −.006 |
| | (.004) | | (.006) |
| | | Family income | −.028 |
| | | | (.034) |
| | | Years in business | −.016 |
| | | | (.015) |
| | | Enterprise | .000 |
| | | revenue | (.000) |
| | | SELA | −.052 |
| | | | (.156) |
| | | PEA | −.214 |
| | | | (.163) |
| | | ICF | .015 |
| | | | (.160) |
| | | Other business | −.508* |
| | | associations | (.292) |
| | | *Getihu* | .273** |
| | | | (.119) |

*Notes:* N = 652; $\chi^2 = 15.30$
$p(\chi^2) = .032$; pseudo $R^2 = .009$
* $p < .1$;   ** $p < .05$;   *** $p < .01$;
**** $p < .001$

*Notes:* N = 392; $\chi^2 = 30.27$
$p(\chi^2) = .011$; pseudo $R^2 = .030$

Appendix Table 5.3 *Comparing Policy Views of Private Entrepreneurs and Local Officials*

Q1: Do you think the pace of economic reform is too fast, about right, or too slow?

| Model I: Comparisons between local party and government officials and private entrepreneurs | | Model II: Comparisons among private entrepreneurs | |
|---|---|---|---|
| Cadre | .029 | Co-opted | −.152 |
| | (.129) | entrepreneur | (.185) |
| CCP | .010 | *Xiahai* | .021 |
| | (.119) | entrepreneur | (.162) |
| Age | −.015** | Age | −.013 |
| | (.007) | | (.009) |
| Gender | −.331* | Gender | −.090 |
| | (.180) | | (.220) |
| Level of | .063 | Level of | −.025 |
| education | (.043) | education | (.063) |
| Level of | −.027 | Level of | −.235* |
| development | (.091) | development | (.136) |
| Years in county | .003 | Years in county | −.002 |
| | (.004) | | (.006) |
| | | Family income | −.040 |
| | | | (.037) |
| | | Years in business | .013 |
| | | | (.017) |
| | | Enterprise | .000 |
| | | revenue | (.000) |
| | | SELA | −.078 |
| | | | (.169) |
| | | PEA | .034 |
| | | | (174) |
| | | ICF | .006 |
| | | | (.172) |
| | | Other business | .261 |
| | | associations | (.310) |
| | | *Getihu* | .002 |
| | | | (.128) |

*Notes:* N = 658; $\chi^2$ = 12.91
$p(\chi^2)$ = .074; pseudo $R^2$ = .011
*p < .1; **p < .05; ***p < .01;
****p < .001

*Notes:* N = 398; $\chi^2$ = 10.83
$p(\chi^2)$ = .765; pseudo $R^2$ = .016

Q2: *Gaige kaifang* policies have not given the vast majority of the people the opportunity to get rich.

| Model I: Comparisons between local party and government officials and private entrepreneurs | | Model II: Comparisons among private entrepreneurs | |
|---|---|---|---|
| Cadre | −.448**** | Co-opted | −.143 |
| | (.128) | entrepreneur | (.175) |
| CCP | −.099 | *Xiahai* | −.206 |
| | (.114) | entrepreneur | (.153) |
| Age | −.005 | Age | −.009 |
| | (.006) | | (.009) |
| Gender | −.085 | Gender | −.101 |
| | (.169) | | (.205) |
| Level of | −.018 | Level of | .003 |
| education | (.042) | education | (.060) |
| Level of | −.103 | Level of | .016 |
| development | (.088) | development | (.128) |
| Years in county | .007* | Years in county | .013** |
| | (.004) | | (.035) |
| | | Family income | −.014 |
| | | | (.035) |
| | | Years in business | −.007 |
| | | | (.016) |
| | | Enterprise | −.000 |
| | | revenue | (.000) |
| | | SELA | .102 |
| | | | (.157) |
| | | PEA | −.043 |
| | | | (.163) |
| | | ICF | .049 |
| | | | (.163) |
| | | Other business | .141 |
| | | associations | (.304) |
| | | *Getihu* | .081 |
| | | | (.121) |

*Notes:* N = 660; $\chi^2$ = 40.53
$p(\chi^2)$ = .000; pseudo $R^2$ = .026
$^*p < .1;$ $^{**}p < .05;$ $^{***}p < .01;$
$^{****}p < .001$

*Notes:* N = 399; $\chi^2$ = 8.23
$p(\chi^2)$ = .914; pseudo $R^2$ = .040

*Appendix*

Q3: What do you think the government's current top priority should be: speed up the pace of economic development or control inflation?

| Model I: Comparisons between local party and government officials and private entrepreneurs | | Model II: Comparisons among private entrepreneurs | |
|---|---|---|---|
| Cadre | −.134 | Co-opted | .202 |
| | (.149) | entrepreneur | (.210) |
| CCP | −.041 | *Xiahai* | −.084 |
| | (.138) | entrepreneur | (.191) |
| Age | .000 | Age | −.008 |
| | (.008) | | (.253) |
| Gender | .024 | Gender | .009 |
| | (.203) | | (.253) |
| Level of | .007 | Level of | .086 |
| education | (.050) | education | (.073) |
| Level of | .122 | Level of | .221 |
| development | (.106) | development | (.160) |
| Years in county | −.002 | Years in county | .000 |
| | (.005) | | (.007) |
| | | Family income | −.060 |
| | | | (.043) |
| | | Years in business | .016 |
| | | | (.019) |
| | | Enterprise | .000 |
| | | revenue | (.000) |
| | | SELA | −.100 |
| | | | (.192) |
| | | PEA | −.153 |
| | | | (.204) |
| | | ICF | −.336* |
| | | | (.204) |
| | | Other business | −.180 |
| | | associations | (.337) |
| | | *Getihu* | .175 |
| | | | (.148) |

*Notes:* N = 658; $\chi^2$ = 3.20
$p(\chi^2)$ = .856; pseudo $R^2$ = .024
$^*p < .1$;   $^{**}p < .05$;   $^{***}p < .01$;
$^{****}p < .001$

*Notes:* N = 395; $\chi^2$ = 14.92
$p(\chi^2)$ = .457; pseudo $R^2$ = .031

154

*Appendix*

Q4: What do you believe the government's top priority should be:
maintain social stability or promote economic development?

| Model I: Comparisons between local party and government officials and private entrepreneurs | | Model II: Comparisons among private entrepreneurs | |
|---|---|---|---|
| Cadre | .428*** | Co-opted | −.381* |
|  | (.143) | entrepreneur | (.208) |
| CCP | −.350*** | *Xiahai* | −.372** |
|  | (.132) | entrepreneur | (.178) |
| Age | .011 | Age | .006 |
|  | (.007) |  | (.010) |
| Gender | −.244 | Gender | −.153 |
|  | (.198) |  | (.244) |
| Level of | .163*** | Level of | .084 |
| education | (.050) | education | (.069) |
| Level of | .148 | Level of | −.165 |
| development | (.101) | development | (.151) |
| Years in county | −.006 | Years in county | .005 |
|  | (.004) |  | (.007) |
|  |  | Family income | .092** |
|  |  |  | (.040) |
|  |  | Years in business | −.019 |
|  |  |  | (.018) |
|  |  | Enterprise | −.000 |
|  |  | revenue | (.000) |
|  |  | SELA | −.035 |
|  |  |  | (.186) |
|  |  | PEA | .306 |
|  |  |  | (.189) |
|  |  | ICF | .162 |
|  |  |  | (.189) |
|  |  | Other business | .452 |
|  |  | associations | (.331) |
|  |  | *Getihu* | −.149 |
|  |  |  | (.141) |

*Notes:* N = 666; $\chi^2$ = 45.40
p($\chi^2$) = .000; pseudo $R^2$ = .049
* p < .1;  ** p < .05;  *** p < .01;
**** p < .001

*Notes:* N = 403; $\chi^2$ = 18.32
p($\chi^2$) = .246; pseudo $R^2$ = .034

Q5: Political reform measures should be initiated by the party and government, not by society.

| Model I: Comparisons between local party and government officials and private entrepreneurs | | Model II: Comparisons among private entrepreneurs | |
|---|---|---|---|
| Cadre | −.138 | Co-opted | .175 |
|  | (.120) | entrepreneur | (.171) |
| CCP | .235** | *Xiahai* | .228 |
|  | (.110) | entrepreneur | (.149) |
| Age | .019*** | Age | .017** |
|  | (.006) |  | (.008) |
| Gender | −.157 | Gender | −.233 |
|  | (.166) |  | (.203) |
| Level of | −.055 | Level of | −.007 |
| education | (.040) | education | (.058) |
| Level of | .202*** | Level of | .312** |
| development | (.085) | development | (.127) |
| Years in county | −.003 | Years in county | −.001 |
|  | (.004) |  | (.006) |
|  |  | Family income | .002 |
|  |  |  | (.034) |
|  |  | Years in business | .012 |
|  |  |  | (.015) |
|  |  | Enterprise | −.000 |
|  |  | revenue | (.000) |
|  |  | SELA | −.160 |
|  |  |  | (.156) |
|  |  | PEA | −.176 |
|  |  |  | (.162) |
|  |  | ICF | .039 |
|  |  |  | (.159) |
|  |  | Other business | −.137 |
|  |  | associations | (.275) |
|  |  | *Getihu* | −.063 |
|  |  |  | (.118) |

*Notes:* N = 664; $\chi^2$ = 28.30
$p(\chi^2)$ = .000; pseudo $R^2$ = .016
*p < .1;  **p < .05;  ***p < .01;
****p < .001

*Notes:* N = 399; $\chi^2$ = 24.28
$p(\chi^2)$ = .060; pseudo $R^2$ = .023

# 6

# *Conclusion*

THE emergence of "red capitalists" in China is a perfect metaphor for the entire reform era. Red capitalists symbolize the competing and seemingly contradictory nature of contemporary China: the existence of a free-wheeling economy alongside Leninist political institutions. China's leaders have wrestled with how to allow the free flow of information, labor, capital, and goods and services necessary for economic development without losing their hold on political power. Red capitalists therefore represent the merger of economic and political power in China.

Red capitalists also represent the hopes and fears of those who expect economic reform to lead to political change in China. Some hope that red capitalists represent the cutting edge of an emerging civil society in China and will push the CCP to allow even greater political liberalization, which would bring the economic and political systems into greater harmony. Others fear that the admission of capitalists into the CCP blurs the class nature of the party and introduces interests that are inimical to party traditions. Where some see development, others see disintegration. Either way, there is widespread agreement that economic growth and privatization are undermining the communist institutions in China, which in turn will lead to political change and perhaps democratization.

## INCLUSION AND ITS CONSEQUENCES

What role will the beneficiaries of economic reform, especially the red capitalists, play in this process? What measures has the Chinese Communist Party (CCP) adopted to preserve its authority against the potential threat of new elites? Do entrepreneurs seek political change, and if so, what kind? These are the questions with which this study has been concerned. The answers to these questions also have implications for one of the most important issues facing scholars and

157

policy makers: will political change in China be gradual and incremental, or tumultuous and potentially destabilizing?

This chapter will review the main findings of previous chapters and discuss their implications for scholarly debates and popular understanding of trends in contemporary China.

### Adapting the Party to its New Task

At the historic Third Plenum of the 11th Central Committee in December 1978, the CCP announced the end of the period of class struggle and its commitment to economic modernization as the key task of the party. Gone were the extreme policy swings of transformation and consolidation of the Maoist era, when the party alternated between waging class struggle and pursuing economic recovery. China's post-Mao leaders not only set the country on the path of economic reform, they also changed the CCP's organization and recruitment policies to lead the effort. It retired the old and poorly educated veteran cadres and sought younger people with professional and technical skills to join the party and assume leadership positions. This was a concerted effort over a period of many years, and was basically successful in meeting its goals. The educational standards of the party, and especially leading cadres, improved dramatically, and leaders of the first and second generations symbolized by Mao and Deng, respectively, were replaced by those from the third and fourth generations.

The shift from waging class struggle to producing economic growth also had unintended consequences for the party. The opportunity to seek work in the private sector opened up new avenues of mobility that did not require party membership. This made it more difficult to recruit new members, especially in the countryside, and to monitor the whereabouts and activities of existing party members. Traditional party building efforts could not keep pace with the expansion of the private sector, leaving the CCP without a strong organizational foothold in the fastest growing sector of the economy. New social strata, including private entrepreneurs and traditional clans, moved into the spaces created by the reduced presence of the party.

To address these new challenges, the CCP is attempting to adapt itself to the requirements of economic reform. It has adopted policies of inclusion to better integrate itself with the changing economic and social environments. It has created corporatist links with non-party organizations and co-opted new elites with the technical and entrepreneurial skills needed for economic development. At the same time, some in the party lament the loss of its capacity to monitor and control economic and social trends. Some local party officials, and many scholars, argue that the solution to this dilemma is to de-emphasize these standard

Leninist goals for the sake of greater economic growth. From their perspective, party organs should not be present in the non-state sectors of the economy because they tend to retard growth and frighten off potential investors. From the perspective of orthodox party leaders, however, the CCP's organizational interests are being challenged by these policies of inclusion. As its capacity to monitor compliance with its policies, enforce norms of behavior, and mobilize society on behalf of regime goals deteriorates, the Leninist attributes of the CCP and its viability as the ruling party are also being undermined. As Samuel Huntington noted, the stability of an authoritarian regime depends largely on the strength of the ruling party; as the party weakens, so too does the regime it governs.[1] Corporatist links and co-opting new elites are expedient strategies of inclusion but they have other consequences that may be detrimental in the long run.

## Forging Corporatist Links

The CCP sanctioned the formation of numerous associations in recent years. This has allowed a variety of social and professional activities to become organized and to interact with the state. The most common question regarding these new associations is whether they are simply tools of the state or if they can represent the views of their members. In China, this dichotomy is a false choice. Although scholars looking for an emerging civil society typically look for evidence of autonomy for individuals and especially groups, most individuals and groups in China do not seek autonomy but rather closer embeddedness with the state. In the Chinese context, autonomy is akin to powerlessness. Those who want to best pursue their interests and maximize their leverage look for ways of being connected to the state.

Most organizations have a dual character: they ensure state leadership over the organized group but at the same time convey the views of their members to the state. This dualism seems acceptable to the members of business associations surveyed in this project. While the vast majority of these businessmen believe that their business associations represent the interests of their members, and even share their personal views, many also believe the associations represent the government's perspective. Instead of seeking an officially recognized and protected autonomy, they seek to be embedded in the state, and the state in turn has created the institutional means for linking itself with private business

---

[1] Samuel P. Huntington, "Social and Institutional Dynamics of One-Party Systems," in Samuel P. Huntington and Clement H. Moore, eds., *Authoritarian Politics in Modern Society: The Dynamics of Established One-Party Systems* (New York: Basic Books, 1970), p. 9.

interests. This fits the findings of other studies from China, and other developing countries, of a balance between autonomy and embeddedness in government-business relations.[2]

Entrepreneurs show an evolving concept of organized interests and are willing to use the business associations for collective and individual purposes to address business concerns. But can business associations influence the implementation of policy? This is the ultimate test of their role, and also their potential as an element of civil society. A clear majority – almost 70 percent – of private entrepreneurs believe business associations can influence policy. However, an even larger majority of officials – 75 percent – believe that business associations *cannot* influence policy. This difference of opinion shows the potential for future conflict. If the associations and their members grow more confident in their ability to influence policy, they will become more likely to try to do so on a wider range of issues, and eventually try to influence the actual making of policy.

If private entrepreneurs and their business associations are to be agents of political change, we would expect to find evidence of increased autonomy in the most prosperous areas. However, the evidence here suggests that the perceived harmony of interests between the state and business associations *rises* with economic development. Entrepreneurs in the most developed counties were much more likely to agree that their business associations represented the government's viewpoint than were those in the less developed counties. Ironically, the level of economic development did not affect the views of local officials. Entrepreneurs in the most prosperous counties were most likely to think that business associations represented the state, entrepreneurs in the poorer counties were least likely to agree, and officials fell in between. Economic development affects the views of private entrepreneurs toward the state, but not in ways that we would expect. In the areas where the economy as a whole and the private economy in particular is more prosperous, the government-business relationship in China may also be more developed and the belief in shared interests more pronounced. These findings again suggest increased embeddedness, not greater autonomy, for private entrepreneurs in China, making it less likely that entrepreneurs will serve as agents of political change in China and raising the possibility that the CCP's strategy of co-opting

[2] Jean C. Oi, "Fiscal Reforms and the Economic Foundations of Local State Corporatism," *World Politics*, vol. 45, no. 1 (October 1992), pp. 99–126; Andrew G. Walder, "Local Governments as Industrial Firms: An Organizational Analysis of China's Transitional Economy," *American Journal of Sociology*, vol. 101, no. 2 (September 1995), pp. 263–301; the concept of embedded autonomy was elaborated by Peter Evans, *Embedded Autonomy: States and Industrial Transformation* (Princeton: Princeton University Press, 1995).

entrepreneurs and creating corporatist links with business associations will be successful.

Taken together, these data suggest that businessmen see their associations as able to represent their views, solve their problems, and influence the local implementation of policy. Both businessmen and officials support the organization of business interests as legitimate, which in the future may lead business associations to more likely engage in collective action on behalf of the shared interests of their members. Although these business associations were created as part of the CCP's strategy of adaptation, the associations are not simply the means for party leadership over the private sector. They also are able to represent the interests of their members and at least in some cases provide useful services to them. If they can develop a reputation for delivering the goods to their members, and not just serve as agents of the state, business associations could strengthen the foundations of a civil society in China. That is a potential development to be watched for in the future, however. For the present, we should recognize that China's entrepreneurs believe that their associations represent both their interests and the viewpoint of the government.

## Co-opting New Elites

Despite the ban on recruiting entrepreneurs into the party that was imposed in August 1989, local officials found ways to circumvent the ban or simply ignored it. The co-optation of private entrepreneurs was a source of contention between the center and the localities. Throughout the 1990s, central officials repeatedly reiterated the ban and criticized local leaders who did not abide by it. Even the discussion of whether to keep or lift the ban was declared off limits, even though the debate continued. Local leaders, however, were caught in a bind between contradictory party policies: foster faster economic growth, but keep at arm's length the people responsible for providing that growth. Many felt that entrepreneurs provided the types of skills the party needed and represented a potential source of political opposition if they were excluded from the party. Co-opting entrepreneurs into the party would therefore bring immediate benefits and avoid a potential threat.

Jiang Zemin's July 1, 2001 speech marked a dramatic breakthrough in the party's relationship with the private sector. By recommending that private entrepreneurs be welcomed into the party in recognition of their contributions to the country's modernization, Jiang tacitly acknowledged that the ban had outlived its usefulness and sanctioned the prevailing local trend. His "three represents" slogan, the subject of a massive propaganda effort for the previous year, provided the ideological justification for his recommendation. Under this

161

formulation, the CCP not only represents China's workers and peasants but also the broad masses of people who are contributing to the economic and cultural development of the country. Even this inclusive rendering of the party's ideology seemed out of date in a rapidly changing China. The "three represents" theory was widely ridiculed by those felt it was simply anachronistic. Instead of trying to update the party's ideology, they suggested it would be better to simply abandon it.

To the few remaining leftists in the party, however, Jiang's "three represents" theory and his subsequent recommendation to lift the ban on entrepreneurs went too far in trying to adapt the party and its ideology to the needs of economic reform. They warned that the growing numbers of red capitalists, both party members who went into business (what I have termed *xiahai* entrepreneurs) and especially private entrepreneurs who were co-opted into the party, were undermining the party's cohesiveness and betraying its original class nature. They warned that if Jiang's recommendation were allowed to stand, and the ban on admitting entrepreneurs was lifted, the result might be the disintegration of the CCP.

Both the leftists and those observers who anticipate that China's red capitalists will promote political change make the same basic assumption: that the interests and policy preferences of private entrepreneurs in China are substantially different from those of party and government officials. If that is so, then as the influence of red capitalists grows, the pressure for political change will also grow. And because they have already been accepted into the political elite, they will be in an advantageous position to push for change from within. Does this assumption hold merit? The survey data presented throughout this book allow us to test this assumption by comparing the views of entrepreneurs and officials in China.

### Comparing Beliefs and Behaviors

The survey of Chinese private entrepreneurs and local officials reveals several trends in their beliefs and behaviors. First, there are clear differences between entrepreneurs and officials on many issues concerning policy preferences and basic political beliefs, but they are mostly differences of degree, not of kind. Only rarely do the two groups take opposing views, such as on the question of the policy influence of business associations or whether economic competition leads to instability. More surprising is that the beliefs of *xiahai* entrepreneurs have more in common with other entrepreneurs than they do with incumbent officials. On the key issue of political reform, entrepreneurs and officials have a similar range of views: both groups are roughly evenly divided between those who believe the party and government should initiate political reform and those who believe society should also be involved. The entrepreneurs, pronounced fear of instability may make them a conservative force, rather than a liberalizing one.

Second, while China's entrepreneurs do not exhibit a clear and explicit concept of citizenship, they are developing a sense of shared beliefs and shared interests which may open the door to collective action, and which therefore merits closer attention. Entrepreneurs clearly believe in their importance and efficacy. They have a greater corporate identity, facilitated by the state's corporatist strategy of creating business associations and co-opting successful businessmen into the CCP. They have a greater self-awareness and belief that their social status is rising. Moreover, they believe their interests are communal interests, that what is good for business is also good for the community as a whole. They share a belief that entrepreneurs and their associations can engage in collective action, and that the legal system is an effective means of solving problems. They have confidence in the ability of institutional mechanisms to deal with their concerns, and downplay the importance of personal relations as a factor in business success. As the legal status of private entrepreneurs becomes better institutionalized, and the laws protecting the private sector are implemented and enforced, their appreciation of the opportunities available to them may evolve into expectations of rights enjoyed by citizens. They already exhibit a strong belief in the efficacy of their business associations and their ability to influence policy that may one day lead them to play a more assertive role.

If entrepreneurs are to be agents of change, then those in the more economically developed areas should be more supportive of external pressures on the state. That is not what the survey data show, however. Private entrepreneurs in more developed areas are *less* supportive of a societal role in political reform than those in less developed areas. This not only fits previous studies that found private entrepreneurs in China are not enthusiastic supporters of democratization, it suggests economic development may lower support for democratization among entrepreneurs, at least in the short run.[3]

Red capitalists in China are generally assumed to be a primary catalyst for change. Their emergence as a distinct group, combined with their close ties

---

[3] David L. Wank, "Private Business, Bureaucracy, and Political Alliance in a Chinese City," *Australian Journal of Chinese Affairs*, no. 33 (January 1995), pp. 55–71; Margaret M. Pearson, *China's New Business Elite: The Political Consequences of Economic Reform* (Berkeley: University of California Press, 1997); Pearson, "China's Emerging Business Class: Democracy's Harbinger," *Current History*, vol. 97, no. 620 (September 1998), pp. 268–272; Baogang He, *The Democratic Implications of Civil Society in China* (New York: St. Martin's Press, 1997).

to the state, have led many to assume that they will add to the growing pluralism in China. But while there are notable differences in the basic political beliefs and policy preferences between private entrepreneurs and local party and government officials, they are primarily differences of degree. Their views may simply reinforce the trend of opening and reform, rather than push the state in a new direction. On issues of political participation, they exhibit an elitist perspective that is not conducive to full democratization. The available evidence – based upon the data presented here and in previous research by other scholars – does not support the contention that red capitalists and other entrepreneurs will necessarily be proponents of political change. They represent the "non-critical realm" of civil society, created by the market dynamic of the post-Mao reforms. They seek to be partners with the state, not challengers to it. As noted in Chapter 4, *who* is co-opted has important implication for *how* the party will adapt. Because the CCP has chosen to co-opt only members of the non-critical realm, but continues to exclude those from the critical realm, its strategy of inclusion may not produce demands for democratization felt by other Leninist parties that co-opted advocates of political reform from the critical realm.

Nevertheless, the same processes that led to the growth of red capitalists are also creating other pressures for political reform. It may be more appropriate to see red capitalists as a symptom of changes underway in China, rather than their cause. They may serve to reinforce those changes, even if they are not leading them. Therefore, the rise of red capitalists has implications for China's political future and the fate of the CCP.

### PROSPECTS FOR POLITICAL CHANGE

One of the principle themes of this book has been the adaptability of Leninist parties. The track record in this regard has not been very impressive. Communist parties in Eastern and Central Europe and the former Soviet Union fell out of power in quick succession beginning in 1989. They were ultimately unable to adapt to the rising demands for political change emanating from society and in some cases even from within the ruling party. The CCP has so far managed to avoid the fate of other ruling Leninist parties. Has it discovered the secret of adaptation through its policies of inclusion? Although corporatist links and the co-optation of new elites are having positive impacts on China's economy and the CCP, neither is likely to lead to the transformation of China's political system. The evolutionary forces now at work are likely to be incompatible with the Leninist political system in China and will serve to undermine the foundations of that system, rather than prop it up.

## Conclusion

### Implications for the CCP

As the CCP embarked on its policies of reform and opening, it also changed its organizational and personnel policies and relations with society. These changes supported the reform effort, but also undermined the Leninist pillars of the political system that were the foundations of the CCP's political power. Corporatist links with business associations partially substituted for traditional party building practices, but left the party without a prominent presence in the private sector. The co-optation of new economic and social elites supported the reform effort and brought much needed expertise into key party and government positions, but came at the expense of workers and farmers, the party's traditional base. These policies of inclusion were expedient and beneficial to the party's key task of economic modernization, but they also reduced the party's ability to monitor and control what was taking place throughout society. Co-optation and organizational links with non-party organizations are key elements of adaptation, but they both come with risks attached. While they are necessary for the party's adaptation, they are not guarantors of the party's survival and may in fact contribute to its demise.

As the reform logic took hold within the party, its Leninist features began to wane, even though they have not yet been replaced. Can the CCP survive without a Leninist foundation? Probably not. That is why it tries so hard to square its adaptation and policies of inclusion with ideological rhetoric. Few inside the party, and even fewer outside the party, give much credence to the party's traditional ideology or the strenuous efforts it is now making to justify its reform policies. But these efforts are necessary to maintain the myth that underlies the party's continued right to rule.

James March once wrote that hypocrisy had a potential virtue: it might be evidence of norms changing.[4] So too may non-Leninist behavior have virtues for the CCP, despite its continued Leninist ideology. The CCP still makes rhetorical references to party traditions, but its behavior is more in keeping with the priorities of economic reform. This hypocrisy irritates orthodox party members but at the same time it allows the party to remain relevant and even essential at lower levels. It is unlikely the party could survive a challenge were it to end this hypocrisy – if it completely shed its orthodox ideology which is not in keeping with its policies and practices. Remaining hypocritical may sustain the CCP, at least in the short run.

---

[4] James G. March, *Decisions and Organizations* (Oxford, UK and Cambridge, MA: Basil Blackwell, 1988), pp. 262–263.

165

The leftists who criticize the party's endorsement of the market and the recruitment of entrepreneurs into the party are unsatisfied with this hypocrisy. In the end, they may lose the battle but win the war. Their objections are being ignored by party leaders intent on promoting further reform, but their prognosis for the party's future may prove accurate. Ironically, their complaint is not so different from what makes other observers excited about the potential for change in China. They agree that economic reforms are giving rise to new social strata, that they are becoming increasingly politically active, that the interests of these new strata may not be consistent with the party's traditions, and that as the party becomes increasingly integrated with them the party itself will inevitably change. Whereas outside observers are in favor of these trends because they promise political change, the leftists in the party oppose them and for the same reason. Both offer the same prognosis, but vehemently disagree about the desirability of their shared vision of the future.

The lament of the leftists is being ignored, and to some degree suppressed, because it is inconsistent with the overall policy scheme of reform and opening, even though it is largely on the mark.[5] Their appeal to party traditions and use of ideological terminology seems quaint in an age of globalization. These artifacts of the party's past are also less salient with the rising generation of leaders, who are noted for their disdain of ideology and their pragmatic ap-proach to policy questions.[6] Rather than directly refuting the allegations of the party's ideological watchdogs, supporters of inclusion point to the contribu-tions private entrepreneurs have made to the party's task of economic growth. They also warn obliquely that co-optation is necessary to prevent private en-trepreneurs from organizing themselves to oppose the party. The CCP's policies of inclusion are therefore designed in part to create "red capitalists" and pre-vent the emergence of a political opposition with economic resources and social support. These policies, however, are undeniably inconsistent with the party's traditionally Leninist orientation.

The CCP is not in imminent danger of collapse or replacement. It still enjoys a variety of advantages that may allow it to muddle through indefinitely. Its policies have produced tremendous economic growth, rising living standards, and increased mobility. These have produced a measure of support, even though rampant corruption and malfeasance have undermined its legitimacy and the

---

[5] In the wake of Jiang Zemin's speech on July 1, 2001, and the firestorm of protest from the party's orthodox leaders, leftist journals were either shut down or put under the editorial control of mainstream newspapers and magazines more sympathetic to the party's policies of inclusion, and Jiang's proposal in particular. For example, the party ordered *Zhenli de zhuiqiu* and *Zhongliu* to cease publication.

[6] Cheng Li, *China's Leaders: The New Generation* (Lanham, MD: Rowman and Littlefield, 2001).

growing economic inequality within society and among regions has damaged the popularity of its policies. Membership in the party is still advantageous for many careers, including in business, and is highly sought after. Most importantly, it enjoys and protects at all costs its monopoly on political power. It has repeatedly shown the lengths it is willing to go to defend that monopoly, not just in 1989 but also the more recent crackdown on the Chinese Democracy Party and the Falungong spiritual movement. Most people in China recognize the high cost of challenging the party's political authority. Without a viable alternative and a good probability of success, most people make the rational decision to tolerate the status quo, even if they are not fully satisfied with it.[7] This is not a ringing endorsement of the CCP's right to rule, but it may be sufficient to remain in power indefinitely.

Predicting that the CCP will somehow muddle through for the foreseeable future is not a very controversial claim, but it may be the best case scenario for the CCP. The CCP is unlikely to initiate democratization, and is unlikely to be successful if it tries. Many of the intellectuals who previously had faith in the party's ability to reform itself, and were committed to helping it do so, grew disenchanted with it after the violent end to the 1989 demonstrations and gave up hope of "transforming the untransformable."[8] As I argued in my previous book, the CCP has developed such a backlog of grievances against it, including corruption and the suppression of voices for liberalization, it would have a hard time coping with demands for democratization once it lifted the lid on them. Moreover, political events in China have an episodic quality to them, quickly snowballing out of control, which would compound the CCP's difficulties if it tried to initiate and manage the democratization process. Instead, the party tries to prevent the airing of those demands, rather than to cope with them.[9]

Not all people share this view. Many observers hope that political change can be incremental, just as economic reform has been, thereby avoiding the instability that would otherwise ensue. The argument that the CCP can ultimately be

---

[7] Adam Przeworski, "Some Problems in the Transition to Democracy," in Guillermo O'Donnell, Philippe C. Schmitter, and Laurence Whitehead, eds., *Transitions from Authoritarian Rule, vol. 3: Comparative Perspectives* (Baltimore: Johns Hopkins University Press, 1986); Timur Kuran, "Now Out of Never: The Element of Surprise in the East European Revolution of 1989," *World Politics*, vol. 44, no. 1 (October 1991), pp. 7–48.

[8] Liu Junning, "Classical Liberalism Catches On In China," *Journal of Democracy*, vol. 11, no. 3 (July 2000), pp. 48–57. Although Liu may exaggerate the popularity of liberalism, he describes how "the 1989 Tiananmen Square Incident shocked and awakened [China's] intellectuals. They gave up hope of 'transforming the untransformable'" (p. 51).

[9] Bruce J. Dickson, *Democratization in China and Taiwan: The Adaptability of Leninist Parties* (Oxford and New York: Oxford University Press, 1997).

the agent for gradual and peaceful political change in China (in other words that democratization in China will follow the transformation path[10]) is not based on any tangible evidence in this regard. Indeed, the lesson of the CCP's tenure as the ruling party in China suggests that it forcibly represses all efforts by non-state actors to expand the parameters of political participation. The prospects for an alternative mode of democratization – the replacement of the CCP by a spontaneous social rebellion – are discounted because of the costly turmoil that may result. The conclusion is based on what people hope will happen, as opposed to what is most likely to happen, given China's recent political history and the examples of political change in other countries. The expectation of incremental change, while reassuring in its depiction of political change without turmoil and instability, may therefore be misplaced. A third alternative, a pacted transition resulting from negotiations between the state and societal groups requires more autonomy than China's organizations currently enjoy and is therefore unlikely.[11] China today has no equivalent of Solidarity or the Roman Catholic church, which proved instrumental in negotiating political transitions in other countries. However, if the growing number of civic organizations, including business associations, can develop greater autonomy, political influence, and popular support, a pacted transition would be the most likely means of achieving democratization with a minimum of instability. This is where the corporatist perspective could prove most insightful: not as a way of explaining the changes occurring within China's still Leninist political system, but for laying the foundation for a transition away from the remaining Leninist institutions.

## The Impact of Red Capitalists

In considering the prospects for political change, it may seem odd to focus on private entrepreneurs. After all, China's entrepreneurs had previously been labeled class enemies and nearly persecuted into extinction. Their re-emergence as a significant and increasingly coherent economic and political force has generated much interest among policy makers and scholars inside and outside China. Some see entrepreneurs as the vanguard of an emerging (or re-emerging) civil society, which is seen by many as a necessary prerequisite for political development and democratization in particular. Barrington Moore's succinct prediction "no bourgeoisie, no democracy" conveys their important historical role. In China,

---

[10] Samuel P. Huntington, *The Third Wave: Democratization in the Late Twentieth Century* (Norman: University of Oklahoma Press, 1991).

[11] Baohui Zhang, "Corporatism, Totalitarianism, and Transitions to Democracy," *Comparative Political Studies*, vol. 27, no. 1 (April 1994), pp. 108–136.

the business associations are among the rare organizations available for collective action, and recent research suggests that these associations occasionally act on behalf of their members against the interests of the state, at least on business related issues.[12] Others go even further, predicting that the same people who are promoting and benefiting from economic liberalization will also advocate political democratization. However, previous research suggests that private entrepreneurs in China have been reluctant to promote democratization, and the evidence presented here supports those earlier findings.

China's private entrepreneurs are therefore receiving increased attention – by outside observers and China's leaders alike – because they are potential "king makers" between the state and the "critical realm" of civil society. Although their political views are essentially compatible with local officials, what could make that change? What could turn their allegiance with the state into collaboration with the critical realm in pursuit of political change? To avoid having to answer those kinds of questions, the party has adopted the two-pronged strategy of creating corporatist links between the state and the business sector and co-opting individual entrepreneurs into the CCP. This strategy has been successful so far in pre-empting demands for increased autonomy or citizenship rights. Whether it will continue to be successful in the future may determine whether private entrepreneurs remain in the "non-critical realm" of civil society or use their organizations to promote collective action on behalf of overtly political issues. The fact that private entrepreneurs are not engaging in collective action for political reform does not negate their importance or collective identity. As in other countries, China's entrepreneurs are focused primarily on business interests, rather than overtly political ones. They believe local officials are as much a part of the solution as they are part of the problem. This fits nicely with the idea that a market dynamic is leading to the formation of a non-critical sphere of civil society that is not necessarily a threat to the state, but is largely beneficial to it.

---

[12] See for example Gordon White, Jude Howell, and Shang Xiaoyuan, *In Search of Civil Society: Market Reform and Social Change in Contemporary China* (Oxford: Oxford University Press, 1996) and Jonathan Unger, "'Bridges': Private Business, the Chinese Government and the Rise of New Associations," *China Quarterly*, no. 147 (September 1996), pp. 795–819. Business associations in developing countries typically concentrate their activities on business and economic matters of immediate interest to their members. See for example Leroy Jones and Il Sakong, *Government, Business, and Entrepreneurship in Economic Development* (Cambridge: Harvard University Press, 1980); Sylvia Maxwell and Ben Ross Schneider, eds., *Business and the State in Developing Countries* (Ithaca: Cornell University Press, 1997); Gregory B. Noble, *Collective Action in East Asia: How Ruling Parties Shape Industrial Policy* (Ithaca: Cornell University Press, 1998); Samantha F. Ravich, *Marketization and Democracy: East Asian Experiences* (Cambridge: Cambridge University Press, 2000).

Red capitalists have attracted special attention. In part, there is interest in red capitalists because of the novelty of their label. What could be more incompatible than the joinder of communism and capitalism in one person? And yet a growing number of communist party members are going into private business and successful businessmen are joining the CCP. More importantly, red capitalists merit special attention because they have the combination of political and economic resources that few others enjoy. That is what makes them worth watching, and also what makes the party's orthodox leaders so concerned. They may have the capacity to affect political change, but previous scholarship and the results of this study suggest they are more likely to support the status quo than to challenge it. They will support and reinforce the policies of reform and opening, but seem to have little interest in more ambitious democratization.

Jiang Zemin's recommendation to admit entrepreneurs into the party will boost the number of red capitalists even higher. As has been the case throughout the reform era, official policy is simply catching up with local practice. To varying degrees, local officials were already circumventing the ban despite the publicity given to it. But by lifting the ban, the local practice of co-opting entrepreneurs will expand. More entrepreneurs are likely to seek party membership. As this study found, there is a large number of entrepreneurs who would like to be in the CCP but for various reasons have not yet joined. Local party officials who were reluctant to violate the ban will now be free to recruit local entrepreneurs. Those who felt constrained by the ban and limited the number of entrepreneurs they co-opted will now be emboldened to expand this practice. In fact, local officials may have no choice but to co-opt entrepreneurs into the party if the central organization department sets guidelines for doing so. While Jiang's proposal represents a significant departure for party policy, it sanctions and reinforces behavior that has already been underway for years.

Red capitalists are neither the cause of nor the solution to the party's problems. They will most likely reinforce the party's commitment to the policies of reform and opening, and as a consequence contribute to the disintegration of the Leninist foundations of the party. But red capitalists are the product of the party's reform policies and ironically proof of their success: the prosperity they enjoy was made possible because of the post-Mao reforms. Similarly, although red capitalists contribute to the party's goal of economic development, growth alone will not save the CCP. Other social and political problems – inequality, unemployment, corruption, environmental degradation – challenge the party, and most of them are exacerbated if not created by its commitment to growth. Lasting solutions to those problems will likely require the kinds of political reforms that the CCP has so far been unwilling to accept: open policy debates, competition between organized interests, an impartial legal system, in short democratization. The party is unwilling to accept these kinds of reforms because they would constrain its authority. The goal of the reform era has been to enjoy the rewards of economic development without having to accommodate their political consequences. Most observers expect that a thriving market economy and a Leninist political system will inevitably prove to be incompatible, but the CCP's strategy has been to try to make them coexist. Red capitalists embody the contradictory elements of the party's reform policies.

# Bibliography

Almond, Gabriel and Sidney Verba. *Civic Culture: Political Attitudes and Democracy in Five Nations* (Princeton: Princeton University Press, 1963).

Baum, Richard. *Burying Mao: Chinese Politics in the Age of Deng Xiaoping* (Princeton: Princeton University Press, 1994).

Baum, Richard and Alexei Shevchenko. "The 'State of the State,'" in Merle Goldman and Roderick MacFarquhar, eds., *The Paradox of China's Post-Mao Reforms* (Cambridge: Harvard University Press, 1999).

Becker, Jasper. "Capitalists Infiltrating Party, Article Warns," *South China Morning Post*, July 14, 2000.

Beiner, Ronald. ed., *Theorizing Citizenship* (Albany: SUNY Press, 1995).

Bernstein, Thomas. "Farmer Discontent and Regime Responses," in Merle Goldman and Roderick MacFarquhar, eds., *The Paradox of China's Post-Mao Reforms* (Cambridge: Harvard University Press, 1999), pp. 197–219.

Bernstein, Richard and Ross H. Munro. *The Coming Conflict with China* (New York: Knopf, 1997).

*"Bixu jiaqiang geti laodongzhe zhong dang de zuzhi jianshe"* (Must Strengthen the Party's Organization Building among Private Workers), *Dangzheng luntan* (Shanghai) (October 1988), pp. 28–31.

Blecher Marc. "Development State, Entrepreneurial State: The Political Economy of Socialist Reform in Xinju Municipality and Guanghan County," in Gordon White, ed., *The Chinese State in the Era of Economic Reform: The Road to Crisis* (Armonk, NY: M. E. Sharpe, 1991).

Brook, Timothy and B. Michael Frolic. eds., *Civil Society in China* (Armonk, NY: M. E. Sharpe, 1997).

Bulmer, Martin and Anthony M. Rees. eds., *Citizenship Today: The Contemporary Relevance of T. H. Marshall* (London: UCL Press, 1996).

Burkhart, Ross E. and Michael A. Lewis-Beck. "Comparative Democracy: The Economic Development Thesis," *American Political Science Review*, vol. 88, no. 4 (December 1994), pp. 903–910.

Chalmers, Douglas A. "Corporatism and Comparative Politics," in Howard J. Wiarda, ed., *New Directions in Comparative Politics* (Boulder: Westview Press, 1985).

173

Chamberlain, Heath B. "On the Search for Civil Society in China," *Modern China*, vol. 19, no. 2 (April 1993), pp. 199–215.

Chan, Anita. "Revolution or Corporatism? Workers and Trade Unions in Post-Mao China," in David S. G. Goodman and Beverly Hooper, eds., *China's Quiet Revolution: New Interactions between State and Society* (New York: St. Martin's Press, 1994).

Chang, Gordon G. *The Coming Collapse of China* (New York: Random House, 2001).

Cheek, Timothy. "From Priests to Professionals: Intellectuals and the State under the CCP," in Jeffrey Wassertrom and Elizabeth J. Perry, eds. *Popular Protest and Political Culture in Modern China* (Boulder: Westview Press, 1992).

Chen, Baoheng and Qian Yushen. "*Nongcun gaige yu xingzheng cun dang de jianshe*" (Rural Reform and Party Building in Administrative Villages), *Nantong xuekan* (April 1991), pp. 9–15.

Chen, Chih-jou Jay. "Local Institutions and Property Rights Transformations in Southern Fujian," in Jean C. Oi and Andrew G. Walder, eds., *Property Rights and China's Economic Reforms* (Stanford: Stanford University Press, 1999).

Chen, Shaoyi. "*Dui guoyou gongsizhi qiye jianchi dang guan ganbu yuanze de sikao*" (Thoughts on the 'Party Controlling Cadres' Principle in State Owned Enterprises), *Lilun tantao* (Harbin) (February 1999), pp. 88–90.

Ch'i, Hsi-sheng. *Politics of Disillusionment: The Chinese Communist Party under Deng Xiaoping, 1978–1989* (Armonk, NY: M. E. Sharpe, 1991).

Coble, Parks M., Jr. *The Shanghai Capitalists and the Nationalist Government 1927–1937* (Cambridge: Harvard University Press, 1980).

Coleman, James S. "Social Capital in the Creation of Human Capital," *American Journal of Sociology*, vol. 94, *Supplement: Organizations and Institutions: Sociological and Economic Approaches to the Analysis of Social Structure* (1988), pp. S95–S120.

Dahl, Robert A. *Polyarchy: Participation and Opposition* (New Haven: Yale University Press, 1971).

Dickson, Bruce J. *Democratization in China and Taiwan: The Adaptability of Leninist Parties* (Oxford and New York: Oxford University Press, 1997).

Dickson, Bruce J. and Maria Rost Rublee. "Membership Has Its Privileges: The Socio-economic Characteristics of Communist Party Members in Urban China," *Comparative Political Studies*, vol. 33, no. 1 (February 2000), pp. 87–112.

Ding, Yijiang. "Corporatism and Civil Society in China: An Overview of the Debate in Recent Years," *China Information*, vol. 12, no. 4 (Spring 1998), pp. 44–67.

Dong, Lianxiang and Zu Qiang. "*Guanyu waishang touzi qiye dang de jianshe*" (Regarding Party Building in Enterprises with Foreign Investment), *Tansuo: Zhe-she ban* (Chongqing) (June 1995), pp. 11–13.

Dong, Wanmin. "*Yange anzhao biaozhun fazhan dangyuan*" (Recruit Party Members Strictly According to Standards), *Henan ribao*, January 7, 1991.

Eckholm, Erik. "At China's Colleges, a Rush To Party, as in Communist," *New York Times* (January 31, 1998).

Elkins, David J. and Richard E. B. Simeon. "A Cause in Search of Its Effect, or What Does Political Culture Explain?" *Comparative Politics*, vol. 11, no. 2 (January 1979), pp. 125–145.

# Bibliography

Evans, Peter. *Embedded Autonomy: States and Industrial Transformation* (Princeton: Princeton University Press, 1995).

Fewsmith, Joseph. *Party, State, and Local Elites in Republican China: Merchant Organizations and Politics in Shanghai, 1890–1930* (Honolulu: University of Hawaii Press, 1985).

Fields, Karl J. *Enterprise and the State in Korea and Taiwan* (Ithaca: Cornell University Press, 1995).

Frolic, B. Michael. "State-led Civil Society," in Timothy Brook and B. Michael Frolic, eds., *Civil Society in China* (Armonk, NY: M. E. Sharp, 1997).

Garton Ash, Timothy. *The Uses of Adversity: Essays on the Fate of Central Europe* (New York: Vintage, 1990).

Gold, Thomas B. "The Resurgence of Civil Society in China," *Journal of Democracy*, vol. 1, no. 1 (Winter 1990), pp. 18–31.

Goldman, Merle. *China's Intellectuals: Advise and Dissent* (Cambridge: Harvard University Press, 1981).

*Sowing the Seeds of Democracy in China: Political Reform in the Deng Xiaoping Era* (Cambridge: Harvard University Press, 1994).

Goldman, Merle and Elizabeth J. Perry. eds. *Changing Meanings of Citizenship in Modern China* (Cambridge: Harvard University Press, 2002).

Goldstein, Steven M. "China in Transition: The Political Foundations of Incremental Reform," *China Quarterly*, no. 144 (December 1995), pp. 1105–1131.

Goldstone, Jack A. "The Coming Chinese Collapse," *Foreign Policy*, no. 99 (Summer 1995), pp. 35–52.

Gong, Kaijin. "*Qiye lingdao tizhi yu dang zuzhi zai qiye zhong de diwei*," (The Enterprise Leadership System and the Role of Party Organizations within Enterprises,) *Qiye wenming* (Chongqing) (March 1995), pp. 25–28.

Goodman, David S. G. "The New Middle Class," in Merle Goldman and Roderick MacFarquhar, eds., *The Paradox of China's Post-Mao Reforms* (Cambridge: Harvard University Press, 1999).

"The Interdependence of State and Society: The Political Sociology of Local Leadership," in Chien-min Chao and Bruce J. Dickson, eds., *Remaking the Chinese State: Strategies, Society, and Security* (London and New York: Routledge, 2001).

"*Guanyu Shanghai shi Chuanshe xian nongcun jiceng dang zuzhi jianshe zhuangkuang de diaocha*" (An Investigation of Basic Level Party Organization Building in the Rural Areas of Shanghai's Chuanshe County), *Dangzheng luntan* (Shanghai) (November 1988), pp. 38–42.

Guthrie, Doug. *Dragon in a Three-Piece Suit: The Emergence of Capitalism in China* (Princeton: Princeton University Press, 1999).

Habermas, Jurgen. *The Structural Transformation of the Public Sphere* (Cambridge: MIT Press, 1989).

Hamrin, Carol Lee and Timothy Cheek. eds., *China's Establishment Intellectuals* (Armonk, NY: M. E. Sharpe, 1986).

Hannan, Michael T. and John Freeman. *Organizational Ecology* (Cambridge: Harvard University Press, 1991).

He, Baogang. *Democratic Implications of Civil Society in China* (New York: St. Martin's Press, 1997).

175

He, Qinglian. *Xiandaihua de xianjing: Dang dai Zhongguo de jingji shehui wenti* (*The Trap of Modernization: Economic and Social Problems in Contemporary China*) (Beijing: Jinri Zhongguo chubanshe, 1998).

Hendrischke, Hans. "Expertocracy and Professionalism," in David S. G. Goodman and Beverly Hooper, eds., *China's Quiet Revolution: New Interactions Between State and Society* (New York: St. Martin's Press, 1994).

Hu, Shaohua. *Explaining Chinese Democratization* (Westport, CT: Praeger, 2000).

Huang, Jun. "*Kaichuang nongcun dangjian gongzuo xin jumian*" (Initiate a New Phase in Rural Party Building Work), *Lilun yu dangdai* (Guiyang) (July 1994), pp. 20–21.

Huang, Yasheng. "Why China Will Not Collapse," *Foreign Policy*, no. 99 (Summer 1995), pp. 54–68.

*Inflation and Investment Controls in China: The Political Economy of Central-Local Relations during the Reform Era* (New York: Cambridge University Press, 1996).

Huang, Youtai and Zhou Yuping. "*Nongcun dang de jianshe yu shehui wending*" (Party Building and Social Stability in the Countryside), *Huxiang luntan* (Changsha) (June 1999), pp. 48–49.

Huntington, Samuel P. *Political Order in Changing Societies* (New Haven: Yale University Press, 1970).

"Social and Institutional Dynamics of One-Party Systems," in Samuel P. Huntington and Clement H. Moore, eds., *Authoritarian Politics in Modern Society: The Dynamics of Established One-Party Systems* (New York: Basic Books, 1970), pp. 3–47.

*The Third Wave: Democratization in the Late Twentieth Century* (Norman: University of Oklahoma Press, 1991).

Inglehart, Ronald. *Modernization and Post-Modernization: Cultural, Economic, and Political Change in 43 Societies* (Princeton: Princeton University Press, 1997).

Ishiyama, John. "Communist Parties in Transition: Structures, Leaders, and Processes of Democratization in Eastern Europe," *Comparative Politics*, vol. 27, no. 3 (January 1995), pp. 147–166.

Jia, Hao and Lin Zhimin. eds., *Changing Central-Local Relations in China* (Boulder: Westview, 1994).

"*Jiji tansuo shehui zhuyi shichang jingji tiaojian xia dang de lingdao shixian xingshi*" (Exploring the Realization of the Party's Leadership under the Conditions of the Socialist Market Economy), *Tequ lilun yu shixian* (Shenzhen) (August 1999), pp. 13–17.

Jones, Leroy and Il Sakong. *Government, Business, and Entrepreneurship in Economic Development* (Cambridge: Harvard University Press, 1980).

Jowitt, Ken. *New World Disorder: The Leninist Extinction* (Berkeley: University of California Press, 1992).

Kelliher, Daniel. "The Chinese Debate over Village Self-Government," *China Journal*, no. 37 (January 1997), pp. 63–86.

Kennedy, Scott. "The Stone Group: State Client or Market Pathbreaker?" *China Quarterly*, no. 152 (December 1997), pp. 746–777.

*In the Company of Markets: The Transformation of China's Political Economy*, Ph.D. dissertation (George Washington University, 2001).

Kuran, Timur. "Now Out of Never: The Element of Surprise in the East European Revolution of 1989," *World Politics*, vol. 44, no. 1 (October 1991), pp. 7–48.

Lawrence, Susan V. "Three Cheers for the Party," *Far Eastern Economic Review* (October 26, 2000).

Lee, Hong Yung. *From Revolutionary Cadres to Party Technocrats in Socialist China* (Berkeley: University of California Press, 1991).

"China's New Bureaucracy," in Arthur Lewis Rosenbaum, ed., *State and Society in China: The Consequences of Reform* (Boulder: Westview Press, 1992).

Li, Cheng. *Rediscovering China: Dynamics and Dilemmas of Reform* (Lanham, MD: Rowman and Littlefield, 1997).

*China's Leaders: The New Generation* (Lanham, MD: Rowman and Littlefield, 2001).

Li, Cheng and Lynn White. "Elite Transformation and Modern Change in Mainland China and Taiwan: Empirical Data and the Theory of Technocracy," *China Quarterly*, no. 121 (March 1990), pp. 1–35.

Li, Lianjiang. "The Two-Ballot System in Shanxi Province: Subjecting Village Party Secretaries to a Popular Vote," *China Journal*, no. 42 (July 1999), pp, 103–118.

Li, Lianjiang and Kevin J. O'Brien. "Villagers and Popular Resistance in Contemporary China," *Modern China*, vol. 22, no. 1 (January 1996), pp. 28–61.

Li, Lieman. "*Gongchandang 70 nian dangyuan fazhan gailue yi qishi*" (Outline and Revelation of 70 Years of CCP Recruitment), *Lilun xuexi yuekan* (Fuzhou), August 30, 1991, pp. 30–33.

Li, Yanxi. "*Shelun dangyuan duiwu de shuliang kongzhi*" (Limit the Number of CCP Members), *Xuexi yu shixian* (Wuchang) (January 1989), pp. 49–51.

Liang, Yanhui and Yuan Yidao. "*Xiangzhen qiye zhuanzhi hou dang de jianshe xin bianhua*" (New Changes in Party Building in Township and Village Enterprises That Have Changed Their Ownership Modes), *Zhongguo dangzheng ganbu luntan* (Beijing) (February 1999), pp. 32–33.

Liang, Yanjia and Li Kaisheng. "*Jiguan qishiye danwei dangyuan liudong de diaocha he sikao*" (Investigation and Reflection on Mobile Party Members in Administrative and Enterprise Units), *Lingnan xuekan* (Guangzhou) (January 1994), pp. 53–56.

Lieberthal, Kenneth. "U.S. Policy Toward China," *Brookings Policy Review*, no. 72 (March 2001).

Lin, Nan. "Local Market Socialism: Local Corporatism in Action in Rural China," *Theory and Society*, vol. 24, no. 3 (June 1995), pp. 301–354.

Lin, Yanzhi. "How the Communist Party Should 'Lead' the Capitalist Class," *Shehui kexue zhanxian* (Jilin), June 20, 2001, translated in FBIS, July 14, 2001.

Lipset, Seymour Martin. "Some Social Requisites of Democracy: Economic Development and Political Legitimacy," *American Political Science Review*, vol. 53, no. 1 (March 1959), pp. 69–105.

"*Liudong dangyuan shequ guanli wenti tansuo*" (Exploring District Management of Mobile Party Members), *Tequ lilun yu shixian* (Shenzhen) (July 1999), pp. 13–16.

Liu, Junning. "Classical Liberalism Catches On In China," *Journal of Democracy*, vol. 11, no. 3 (July 2000), pp. 48–57.

Liu, Kaishou. "*Nongcun jiceng dang zuzhi jianshe mianlia de xin qingkuang he xin wenti*" (New Conditions and New Problems for Building Rural Grass Roots Party Organizations), *Tansuo: Zhe-she ban* (Chongqing) (March 1999), pp. 21–23, 27.

Liu, Yia-ling. "Reform from Below: The Private Economy and Local Politics in the Rural Industrialization of Wenzhou," *China Quarterly*, no. 130 (June 1992), pp. 293–316.

Lou, Ximing and Wu Jian. "*Dang guan ganbu yuanze yu jingyingzhe jingzheng shang-gang*" (The 'Party Controlling Cadres' Principle and the Advantages of Competitive Recruitment of Enterprise Managers), *Xingzheng yu renshi* (Shanghai) (January 1999), pp. 26–27.

Lowenthal, Richard. "Development versus Utopia in Communist Policy," in Chalmers Johnson, ed., *Change in Communist Systems* (Stanford: Stanford University Press, 1970).

Lu, Ruifeng, Zhong Yinteng, Xu Libin, et al. "*Shenzhen shi siying qiye dangde jianshe wenti yu duice*" (Problems and Countermeasures in Party Building in Shenzhen's Private Enterprises), *Tequ lilun yu shixian* (Shenzhen) (December 1995), pp. 37–39.

Lü, Xiaobo and Elizabeth J. Perry. eds., *Danwei: The Changing Chinese Workplace in Historical and Comparative Perspective* (Armonk, NY: M. E. Sharpe, 1997).

Manion, Melanie. *Retirement of Revolutionaries in China: Public Policies, Social Norms, Private Interests* (Princeton: Princeton University Press, 1993).

March, James G. *Decisions and Organizations* (Oxford, UK and Cambridge, MA: Basil Blackwell, 1988).

March, James G. and Johan P. Olsen. *Rediscovering Institutions: The Organizational Basis for Politics* (New York: The Free Press, 1989).

Maxwell, Sylvia and Ben Ross Schneider. eds. *Business and the State in Developing Countries* (Ithaca: Cornell University Press, 1997).

"*Nantong shi yi liuzhong moshi guanli liudong dangyuan*," (Nantong City Uses Six Methods to Manage Mobile Party Members), *Dangjian wenhui* (Luoyang) (November 1997), p. 21.

Nathan, Andrew. *Chinese Democracy* (Berkeley: University of California Press, 1985).

Nevitt, Christopher Earle. "Private Business Associations in China: Evidence of Civil Society or Local State Power," *China Journal*, no. 36 (July 1996), pp. 25–45.

Noble, Gregory B. *Collective Action in East Asia: How Ruling Parties Shape Industrial Policy* (Ithaca: Cornell University Press, 1998).

"*Nongcun jiceng dang zuzhi shezhi de tansuo yu wanshan*" (Exploration and Perfection of Building Grass Roots Party Organizations in the Countryside), *Zuzhi renshixue yanjiu* (Lanzhou) (January 1999), pp 45–48.

"*Nongmin rudang yaoqiu danhua xianxiang toushi*" (Examination of the Phenomenon of the Peasants' Weakened Demand to Enter the Party), *Renmin ribao*, March 31, 1989, p. 5.

O'Brien, Kevin J. *Reform without Liberalization: China's National People's Congress and the Politics of Institutional Change* (New York: Cambridge University Press, 1990).

"Chinese People's Congresses and Legislative Embeddedness: Understanding Early Organizational Development," *Comparative Political Studies*, vol. 27, no. 1 (April 1994), pp. 80–107.

"Implementing Political Reform in China's Villages," *Australian Journal of Chinese Affairs*, no. 32 (July 1994), pp. 33–59.

Odom, William E. "Soviet Politics and After: Old and New Concepts," *World Politics*, vol. 45, no. 1 (October 1992), pp. 66–98.

O'Donnell, Guillermo and Philippe C. Schmitter. *Transitions from Authoritarian Rule: Tentative Conclusions about Uncertain Democracies* (Baltimore: Johns Hopkins University Press, 1986).

Oi, Jean C. "Fiscal Reforms and the Economic Foundations of Local State Corporatism,"*World Politics*, vol. 45, no. 1 (October 1992), pp. 99–126.

O'Neil, Patrick H. "Revolution from Within: Institutional Analysis, Transitions from Authoritarianism, and the Case of Hungary," *World Politics*, vol. 48, no. 4 (July 1996), pp. 579–603.

Organization Department of the Sichuan Provincial Party Committee, "*Shilun 'sankua' qiye jituan dang zuzhi zhengzhi hexin zuoyong de shixian xingshi he jiben tujing*" (On the Practical Form and Basic Means of the Party's Organizational and Political Core Role in 'Three Trans' Enterprises), *Zuzhi renshixue yanjiu* (Lanzhou) (June 1998), pp. 35–39.

Parish, William L. and Charles Chi-hsiang Chang. "Political Values in Taiwan: Sources of Change and Continuity," in Hung-mao Tien, ed., *Taiwan's Electoral Politics and Democratic Transition: Riding the Third Wave* (Armonk, NY: M. E. Sharpe, 1996).

Parris, Kristen. "Local Initiative and National Reform: The Wenzhou Model of Development," *China Quarterly*, no. 134 (June 1993), pp. 242–263.

"Private Entrepreneurs as Citizens: From Leninism to Corporatism," *China Information*, vol. 10, nos. 3/4 (Winter 1995/Spring 1996).

"The Rise of Private Business Interests," in Merle Goldman and Roderick MacFarquhar, eds., *The Paradox of China's Post-Mao Reforms* (Cambridge: Harvard University Press, 1999).

Pearson, Margaret M., "The Janus Face of Business Associations in China," *Australian Journal of Chinese Affairs*, no. 31 (January 1994), pp. 25–46.

*China's New Business Elite: The Political Consequences of Economic Reform* (Berkeley: University of California Press, 1997).

"China's Emerging Business Class: Democracy's Harbinger," *Current History*, vol. 97, no. 620 (September 1998), pp. 268–272.

Pei, Minxin. "'Creeping Democratization' in China," *Journal of Democracy*, vol. 6, no. 4 (October 1995), pp. 65–79.

"Is China Democratizing?" *Foreign Affairs*, vol. 77, no. 1 (1998), pp. 68–82.

"Chinese Civic Associations: An Empirical Analysis," *Modern China*, vol. 24, no. 3 (July 1998), pp. 285–318.

Pfeffer, Jeffrey and Gerald R. Salancik. *The External Control of Organizations: A Resource Dependence Perspective* (New York: Harper and Row, 1978).

Pomfret, John. "China Allows Its Capitalists To Join Party: Communists Recognize Rise of Private Business," *Washington Post*, July 2, 2001.

Przeworski, Adam. "Some Problems in the Transition to Democracy," in Guillermo O'Donnell, Philippe C. Schmitter, and Laurence Whitehead, eds., *Transitions from Authoritarian Rule, vol. 3: Comparative Perspectives* (Baltimore: Johns Hopkins University Press, 1986).

Przeworski, Adam and Fernando Limongi. "Modernization: Theories and Facts," *World Politics*, vol. 49, no. 2 (January 1997), pp. 155–183.

Putnam, Robert D. *Making Democracy Work: Civic Traditions in Modern Italy* (Princeton: Princeton University Press, 1993).

*Bowling Alone: The Collapse and Revival of American Community* (NY: Simon and Schuster, 2000).

Rankin, Mary Backus. *Elite Activism and Political Transformation in China: Zhejiang Province, 1865–1911* (Stanford: Stanford University Press, 1986).

Ravich, Samantha F. *Marketization and Democracy: East Asian Experiences* (Cambridge: Cambridge University Press, 2000).

Rosen, Stanley. "The Chinese Communist Party and Chinese Society: Popular Attitudes toward Party Membership and the Party's Image," *Australian Journal of Chinese Affairs*, no. 24 (July 1990), pp. 51–92.

"Chinese Youth in the Year 2000: Internationalization, Nationalism, and Pragmatism," paper prepared for the China Times Conference on the Chinese Media, University of Minnesota, May 19–20, 2001.

Rowe, William T. *Hankow. Commerce and Society in a Chinese City, 1796–1889* (Stanford: Stanford University Press, 1984).

"The Problem of 'Civil Society' in Late Imperial China," *Modern China*, vol. 19, no. 2 (April 1993), pp. 139–157.

Rowen, Henry S. "The Short March: China's Road to Democracy," *The National Interest*, no. 45 (Fall 1996), pp. 61–70.

Saich, Tony. "Negotiating the State: The Development of Social Organizations in China," *China Quarterly*, no. 161 (March 2000), pp. 124–141.

Schmitter, Philippe C. "Still the Century of Corporatism?" in Schmitter and Gerhard Lehmbruch, eds., *Trends towards Corporatist Intermediation* (Beverly Hills: Sage, 1979).

Scott, W. Richard. *Organizations: Rational, Natural and Open Systems*, 4th ed. (Englewood Cliffs, NJ: Prentice-Hall, 1998).

Selznick, Philip P. *TVA and the Grass Roots* (Berkeley: University of California Press, 1949).

"'*Shuangxiang jinru jiaocha renshi' shi yizhong youxiao de jizhi*" ('Two-way Entry and Overlapping Personnel' Is an Effective Mechanism), *Dangjian yanjiu* (September 1999), pp. 15–17.

Shue, Vivienne. "State Power and Social Organization in China," in Joel S. Migdal, Atul Kohli, and Vivienne Shue, eds., *State Power and Social Forces: Domination and Transformation in the Third World* (Cambridge: Cambridge University Press, 1994).

Skinner, G. William and Edwin A. Winckler. "Compliance Succession in Rural China: A Cyclical Theory," in Amitai Etzioni, ed., *A Sociological Reader on Complex Organizations* (New York: Holt, Rinehart, and Winston, 1969).

Smith, Craig S. "China's Leader Urges Opening Communist Party to Capitalists," *New York Times*, July 2, 2001.

Solinger, Dorothy. *Chinese Business under Socialism: The Politics of Domestic Commerce in Contemporary China* (Berkeley: University of California Press, 1984).

"Urban Entrepeneurs and the State: The Merger of State and Society," in Arthur Lewis Rosenbaum, ed., *State and Society in China: The Consequences of Reform* (Boulder: Westview Press, 1992).

"China's Urban Transients in the Transition from Socialism and the Collapse of the Communist 'Urban Public Goods Regime'," *Comparative Politics*, vol. 27, no. 2 (January 1995), pp. 127–146.

Stepan, Alfred C. *The State and Society: Peru in Comparative Perspective* (Princeton: Princeton University Press, 1978).

Strand, David. *Rickshaw Beijing: City People and Politics in the 1920s* (Berkeley: University of California Press, 1989).

Tanner, Murray Scot. "The Erosion of Central Party Control over Lawmaking," *China Quarterly*, no. 138 (June 1994), pp. 381–403.

Teiwes, Frederick C. "Establishment and Consolidation of the New Regime," in Roderick MacFarquhar, ed., *The Politics of China: The Eras of Mao and Deng*, 2nd ed. (New York: Cambridge University Press, 1997).

Tismaneanu, Vladimir. *Reinventing Politics: Eastern Europe from Stalin to Havel* (New York: The Free Press, 1992).

Tong, Yanqi. "State, Society, and Political Change in China and Hungary," *Comparative Politics*, vol. 26, no. 3 (April 1994), pp. 333–353.

Unger, Jonathan. "'Bridges': Private Business, the Chinese Government and the Rise of New Associations," *China Quarterly*, no. 147 (September 1996), pp. 795–819.

Unger, Jonathan and Anita Chan. "Corporatism in China: A Developmental State in an East Asian Context," in Barrett L. McCormick and Jonathan Unger, eds., *China after Socialism: In the Footsteps of Eastern Europe or East Asia* (Armonk, NY: M. E. Sharpe, 1996),

Wakeman, Frederic. "The Civil Society and Public Sphere Debate: Western Reflections on Chinese Political Culture," *Modern China*, vol. 19, no. 2 (April 1993), pp. 108–138.

Walder, Andrew G. "Industrial Workers: Some Observations on the 1980s," in Arthur Lewis Rosenbaum, ed., *State and Society in China: The Consequences of Reform* (Boulder: Westview Press, 1992).

"The Decline of Communist Power: Elements of a Theory of Institutional Change," *Theory and Society*, vol. 23, no. 2 (April 1994), pp. 297–323.

"Career Mobility and the Communist Political Order," *American Sociological Review*, vol. 60, no. 3 (June 1995), pp. 309–328.

"The Quiet Revolution from Within: Economic Reform as a Source of Political Decline," in Walder, ed., *The Waning of the Communist State: Economic Origins of Political Decline in China and Hungary* (Berkeley: University of California Press, 1995).

Wang, Changjiang and Jin Peixing. *"Dui feigong youzhi jingji zhong 'youxiu fenzi' de zhengce xuyao diaocha"* (An Examination of the Policy Requirements towards 'Outstanding Elements' in the Non-State Owned Enterprises), *Lilun qianyan* (Beijing), no. 21 (1998), pp. 20–22.

Wang, Shaoguang. "The Rise of the Regions: Fiscal Reform and the Decline of Central State Capacity in China," in Andrew G. Walder, ed., *The Waning of the Communist State: Economic Origins of Political Decline in China and Hungary* (Berkeley: University of California Press, 1995).

Wank, David L. "Private Business, Bureaucracy, and Political Alliance in a Chinese City," *Australian Journal of Chinese Affairs*, no. 33 (January 1995), pp. 55–71.

Wasserstrom, Jeffrey N. and Elizabeth J. Perry. eds. 1994. *Popular Protest and Political Culture in Modern China* (Boulder: Westview Press, 1994).

Weston, Timothy B. "China's Labor Woes: Will Workers Crash the Party?" in Timothy B. Weston and Lionel M. Jensen, eds., *China beyond the Headlines* (Lanham: MD: Rowman and Littlefield, 2000), pp. 245–272.

White, Gordon. "Prospects for Civil Society in China: A Case-Study of Xiaoshan City," *Australian Journal of Chinese Affairs*, no. 29 (January 1993), pp. 63–87.

White, Gordon, Jude Howell, and Shang Xiaoyuan. *In Search of Civil Society: Market Reform and Social Change in Contemporary China* (Oxford: Oxford University Press, 1996).

White, Tyrene. "Village Elections: Democracy from the Bottom Up?" *Current History*, vol. 97, no. 1 (September 1998), pp. 263–267.

Whyte, Martin King. "Urban China: A Civil Society in the Making?" in Arthur Lewis Rosenbaum, ed., *State and Society in China: The Consequences of Reform* (Boulder: Westview Press, 1992).

Wiegle, Marcia A. and Jim Butterfield. "Civil Society in Reforming Communist Regimes: The Logic of Emergence," *Comparative Politics*, vol. 25, no. 1 (October 1992), pp. 1–24.

Wong, R. Bin. *China Transformed: Historical Change and the Limits of European Experience* (Ithaca: Cornell University Press, 1997).

Xiang, San and Yang Junfa. "*Guanyu zai shehui zhuyi chuji jieduan baochi dang de xianjinxing de sikao*" (Thoughts on Preserving the Advanced Nature of the Party during the Primary Stage of Socialism), *Shehui kexue zhanxian* (Changchun) (February 1999), pp. 222–226.

Xu, Genyi and Cheng Huiqiang. "*Qieshi jiaqiang waishang touzi qiye de dangjian gongzuo*" (Strengthen the Work of Party Building in Enterprises with Foreign Investment), *Lilun xuekan* (Jinan) (February 1995), pp. 31–34.

Yang, Dali. "Reform and Restructuring of Central-Local Relations," in David S. G. Goodman and Gerald Segal, eds., *China Deconstructs: Politics, Trade, and Regionalism* (London: Routledge, 1994).

Yang, Yongmin. "*Ba nongcun dangjian gongzuo tigao dao xin de shuiping*" (Raise Rural Party Building Work to New Levels), *Dangjian yanjiu* (Beijing) (July 1994), pp. 13–16.

You, Longbo. "*Xin shiqi Fujian yanhai nongcun xianjin dang zhibu jianshe de chenggong jingyan*" (The Successful Experiences of Building Party Branches in the Coastal Villages of Fujian), *Zhonggong Fujian shengwei dangxiao xuebao* (July 1999), pp. 53–56.

Young, Susan. "Private Entrepreneurs and Evolutionary Change," in David S. G. Goodman and Beverly Hooper, eds., *China's Quiet Revolution: New Interactions between State and Society* (New York: St. Martin's Press, 1994).

Young, Susan. *Private Business and Economic Reform in China* (Armonk, NY: M. E. Sharpe, 1995).

"*Zhagen hezi qiye fahui dang de zhengzhi youshi*" (Establish Joint Ventures, Promote the Party's Political Superiority), *Dangzheng luntan* (Shanghai) (October 1999), pp. 21–23.

Zhang, Baohui. "Corporatism, Totalitarianism, and Transitions to Democracy," *Comparative Political Studies*, vol. 27, no. 1 (April 1994), pp. 108–136.

Zhang, Dejiang. "*Jiaqiang feigong youzhi qiye dang jianshe gongzuo xu yanjiu jiejue de jige wenti*" (Several Questions about Party Construction in Non-State Owned Enterprises that Require Study and Solution), *Dangjian yanjiu* (Beijing) (April 2000), pp. 13–16.

# Bibliography

Zhang, Mingchu. "*Xiandaihua yu nongcun dang zhibu shezhi de xin bianhua*" (Modernization and New Changes in Party Branches in the Countryside," *Shanghai dangshi yanjiu* (Supplement) (1999), pp. 143–146.

Zhang, Mingchu. "*Xin qingkuang, xin bianhua, xin qushi: Shanghai diqu nongcun dang zhibu zuzhi shezhi de diaocha*" (New Conditions, New Changes, and New Trends: A Survey of Grass Roots Party Branches in Shanghai's Countryside), *Dangzheng luntan* (Shanghai) (February 1999).

Zhang, Yunqiu. "From State Corporatism to Social Representation: Local Trade Unions in the Reform Years," in Timothy Brook and B. Michael Frolic, eds., *Civil Society in China* (Armonk, NY: M. E. Sharpe, 1997).

Zhao, Dingguo, Wang Yonghuo, and Xu Di. "*Jiji wentuo di tuijin feigong youzhi qiye dangjian gongzuo*" (Actively Promote Party Building in Non-State Owned Enterprises), *Shaoxing wenli xueyuan xuebao: Zhe-she ban* (April 1999), pp. 66–73.

Zhao, Shenghui. *Zhongguo gongchandang zuzhi shi gangyao* (Outline of the CCP's Organizational History) (Anhui: Anhui renmin chubanshe, 1988).

Zhao, Suisheng. "Chinese Intellectuals' Quest for National Greatness and Nationalistic Writing in the 1990s," *China Quarterly*, no. 152 (December 1997), pp. 725–745.

Zheng, Yusheng. "*Dui shichang jingji tiaojian xia cunji dang zuzhi jianshe de wudian*" (Five Suggestions for Village Level Party Organization Work under Market Economy Conditions), *Qiuzhi* (Tianjin) (September 1994), pp. 27–28.

*Zhongguo siying jingji nianjian, 1996* (China's Private Economy Yearbook, 1996) (Beijing: Zhongguo gongshang lianhe chubanshe, 1996).

*Zhongguo siying qiye fazhan baogao (1978-1998)* (Report on the Development of China's Private Enterprises, 1978-1998) (Beijing: Shehui kexue wenxian chubanshe, 1999).

Zhong, Zhushang. "*Nongcun jiceng dang zuzhi xianzhuang tanxi*" (Examination of Current Conditions in Rural Basic Level Party Organizations), *Liaowang yuekan*, January 1990, pp. 12–14.

Zhou, Heling. "*Dangqian jiceng dang zuzhi he dangyuan duiwu jianshe de jige wenti*" (Several Problems Regarding Grass Roots Party Organizations and Party Members), *Dangzheng luntan* (Shanghai) (April 2000), pp. 4–7.

Zhou, Linghua and Zheng Hefu. "*Siying qiye: Dangjian luohou de yuanyin ji duice*" (Private Enterprises: The Causes and Policies toward Sluggish Party Building), *Dangzheng luntan* (Shanghai) (January 1995), pp. 29–30.

Zhou, Peng. "*Shinian lai fazhan dangyuan gongzuo de huigu*" (Review of the Past Ten Years of Party Recruitment), *Dangzheng wenhui* (Luoyang) (January 1989), p. 12.

Zweig, David. "Undemocratic Capitalism: China and the Limits of Economism," *The National Interest*, no. 56 (Summer 1999), pp. 63–72.

# Index

185

# Index

corporatism: 23–26, 59–60
  application to China: 60–69, 168
  compatibility with Leninism: 62, 64–69, 84

democratization: 2, 11–14, 95–98, 137,
  167–171
Deng Liqun: 99–100
Deng Xiaoping: 6, 22, 101, 107
Ding, Yijiang: 63, 66–67
disintegration: 4, 55, 66, 69, 170
  "disintegration thesis": 14–16

Eastern Europe: 4, 58, 67

*gaige kaifang* (reform and opening) policies:
  2, 22, 32, 41, 69, 101–103, 127–128,
  131–132, 164–166, 170
*getihu*: 51, 74, 109–110, 125
government-business relations: 77–78, 83–85,
  106–107, 160–161
*guanxi*: 126–128, 138
Guthrie, Doug: 126, 128

Howell, Jude: 19–21, 61–63
Hungary: 4, 93–97
Huntington, Samuel P.: 8–9, 13–15, 55, 91, 159

inclusion: 8–10, 57–59, 65, 84, 107, 158–159
Industrial and Commercial Federation: 74–82,
  118; *see also* business associations
inconsistency of political beliefs: 138–140

Jiang Zemin: 1, 35, 102–104, 116
  proposal to lift CCP ban on entrepreneurs:
  1, 54, 103, 161–162, 170
Jowitt, Ken: 8–9, 57–59, 107

Kuomintang: 94–97

leftist critiques: 1, 99–101, 103–105, 166
Lee, Hong Yung: 33, 92, 96
Leninism:
  and market economy: 10, 171
  institutional pillars: 14–15, 20, 65 n. 28,
  91–92, 165
  transformation of: 7–10, 57–59, 164,
  170–171
Li, Cheng: 33, 96
Li Tieying: 36
liberalization: 12, 58–59, 68–70, 83, 93

Limongi, Fernando: 12
Lin Yanzhi: 89, 104
Liu Junning: 20, 167 n. 8
Lowenthal, Richard: 7

March, James: 58, 165
modernization theory: 2, 11–12, 137
Moore, Barrington: 13, 168

neo-conservatives: 134
Nevitt, Christopher: 63, 75, 78

O'Brien, Kevin: 49, 59
Odom, William: 63–64
Olsen, Johan P.: 58
organizational change: 9, 57–60, 90–92, 136

Parris, Kristen: 13, 92
Pearson, Margaret: 23, 62–63, 96, 129
Peru: 13, 64
Poland: 4, 19, 64, 68
political consequences of economic reform:
  10–16
political stability: 2–3, 21, 71, 168
Private Enterprises Association (PEA): 51,
  74–82; *see also* business associations
Przeworski, Adam: 12, 21
private entrepreneurs:
  as agents of change: 6, 12–13, 78, 81–85,
  95–98, 135–138, 160–164, 169
  community contributions: 117
  desire to join CCP: 106–107, 110–111
  elitist views of: 129, 134, 164
  in CCP: 107–114
  in early 1950s: 72
  in political posts: 100, 122
  in village elections: 123–126
  political impact of: 4–5, 114–115, 135–138,
  140–141
  political views of: 73, 96–97, 127–134,
  162–164
  pre-1949: 70–72
  social status of: 120–122
  views toward political stability: 96,
  130–131, 133–135, 138
  prospects for political change: 3, 164–171

Ravich, Samantha: 11
red capitalists: 4–6, 82, 111–114, 157,
  162–164, 166, 168–171